Democracy and Development

Bernard Berendsen (ed.)

Democracy and Development

Bernard Berendsen (ed.)

KIT Publishers – Amsterdam

Democracy and Development.
Bernard Berendsen (ed.)

KIT Publishers
Mauritskade 63
P.O.Box 95001
1090 HA Amsterdam
The Netherlands
E-mail: publishers@kit.nl
www.kit.nl/publishers
www.landenreeks.nl

The lecture series on *Democracy and Development* was supported by the Society for International Development (SID), Netherlands Institute for Multiparty Democracy (NIMD), The Ministry of Foreign Affairs, International Institute for Democracy and Electoral Assistance (IDEA), Socires and the Dutch National Committee for International Cooperation and Sustainable Development (NCDO).

Text editing: Deul and Spanjaard, Groningen, the Netherlands
Design: Henny Scholten, Amsterdam, the Netherlands
Lay-out: Nadamo Bos, Driebergen, the Netherlands
Production: Meester en de Jonge, Lochem, the Netherlands

ISBN 978 90 6832 611 6
NUR 754

Contents

Preface

Democracy faces daunting challenges everywhere it is being pursued but especially in the approximately 100 countries that make up democracy's "Third Wave". Development has been a live topic of resolutions by the international donor community for many years, culminating in the Millennium Development Goals (MDGs). The relationship between the two notions is a popular research topic and is heavily debated. The academic discourse swings from "Economy first, democracy later" to "No prosperity without democracy" and back.

In a path breaking lecture series organized by the Netherlands chapter of the Society for International Development (SID) in cooperation with the Netherlands Institute for Multiparty Democracy (NIMD), various high-level practitioners and academics shed light on the relationship between democracy and development. This book paints a nuanced but clear portrait of this complex relationship. The various chapters reflect key factors underlying the common shortcomings of development strategies in autocracies and new democracies and how the best intentions of aid providers are often frustrated in the face of hard-to-change structural conditions.

This compilation of the lecture series *Democracy and Development* is a vital contribution to the debates on development aid. The lectures provoke policy actors to ask basic questions about what they do and prompt further questions from the many leads they have opened up.

In short, this compilation will do precisely what a first-rate lecture series should do. It represents the essence of what both SID and the NIMD seek to offer the international policy community through its work in the Netherlands and around the world.

Jos van Gennip, President of the Society of International Development, Netherlands Chapter (SID)
&
Bernard Bot, President of the Board of the Netherlands Institute for Multiparty Democracy (NIMD)

Introduction

Bernard Berendsen

The decision to publish the lectures of the lecture series on democracy and development that was organised by the Society for International Development and the Netherlands Institute for Multiparty Democracy in the 2006/07 season was not a minor matter. SID and NIMD are to be recommended for this initiative as it enables a much larger audience to take cognizance of and benefit from the depth and scope of the lecture series in its entirety.

The series includes contributions from politicians and activists, scientists and international civil servants, engaging in a discussion that proved to be highly relevant in a continuously changing international environment. They deal with such diverse subjects as the relationship between democracy and development, the phenomenon of fragile states in Africa, the risky introduction of democracy in Eastern Europe and the former Soviet Union after 1989, the effects of the rising trend of populism in Latin America, the seeming incompatibility between democracy and Islam and the role of the state as a focal point of public decision making and a centre for the application of democratic principles in a national context. The history and merits of democracy promotion were discussed extensively as well as the contribution of development cooperation to democracy promotion, assuming that democracy is required for sustainable development, and *vice versa*.

The lecture series consisted of nine lectures given at the Vrije Universiteit of Amsterdam and one at the University of Nijmegen. Added to those in this volume are a background paper to the series by Berendsen and van Beuningen that highlights the relationship between democracy and nation building, and a substantive contribution by Vincent Cornell on democracy and Islam, in conjunction with Anwar Ibrahim's lecture on the same subject.

Finally, this volume contains lectures and contributions delivered at the final conference that was held on September 13, 2007, at the Netherlands Ministry of Foreign Affairs in The Hague. They include a comprehensive survey of the views on the subject by the present Minister for Development Cooperation, Bert Koenders, and a thought provoking contribution by William Easterly, linking liberalism as a precondition for economic growth to democracy as a precondition for development. Worth mentioning are the contributions by Vidar Helgesen, Secretary General of the Sweden based International Institute for Democracy and Electoral Assistance (IDEA) and Lena Hjelm-Wallén, Chairman of the Board of the same institution. They form a tribute to the outstanding intellectual role of this institution in the promotion of democracy.

Although there are more ways the lectures could have been grouped together, this book has been composed in five parts. Part I deals with the relationship between democracy and development, starting with a contribution by the former Netherlands Minister for Development Cooperation, Agnes van Ardenne, for whom democracy is a right not to be denied to poor people. Like Daniel Kaufmann in the second lecture, she links democracy to good governance and the fight against corruption. Kaufmann convincingly argues that there is a two-way street between improving civil liberties and political competition on the one hand and improving corruption control on the other and both contributing to economic development.

William Easterly, the third to contribute to this part, prefers to take freedom instead of democracy as a focal point of his lecture. Starting from the presumption that we do not really know how to achieve development, the best we can do is to let people free to choose for themselves. As he says: that makes a lot of sense theoretically, and empirically he finds that democracy is associated with prosperity as well as achieving economic development at the same time.

The second part deals with the relationship between democracy, nation building and development. In a background article on the lecture series Bernard Berendsen and Cor van Beuningen point out that the connection of democracy and state with nation is becoming more troublesome while democratic procedures are being used to promote and capitalise on religious and ethnic conflict undermining the stability of nation states.

Fragile states are also at the centre of attention of Paul Colliers contribution pointing out that political instability is very much a characteristic of poor nations which is even exacerbated by the presence of an abundance of natural resources in such nations. At the political level, the present Minister for Development Cooperation, Bert Koenders, makes fragile states one of the four pillars of his new policy, recognising that in a instable environment governments are unable to perform their core duties such as to protect their citizens, to maintain public order and security, to provide basic services and maintain stabile economic conditions.

The third part of this volume deals with the subject of democracy promotion. Thomas Carothers presents a short history of democracy promotion, concluding that, by the turn of the century, democracy promotion has become discredited and the overall democracy trend has stagnated. A major factor has been the reattachment of the geo-strategic agenda with the war on terrorism taking up a prominent position.

Kim Campbell in her contribution on democracy promotion directs our attention to Eastern Europe and the former Soviet Union, building on experiences from the Club de Madrid, of which she was a founder and Secretary General. On their turn, Vidar Helgesen and Lena Hjelm-Wallén take a global look at the present state of democracy promotion from the viewpoint of the International Institute of Democracy and Electoral Assistance. They very much take the view that democracy must grow from within and cannot be imposed from outside. They emphasise that external interventions tend to limit the internal democratic debate on development and take precedence over it. They also would like to see a more active European stance on democracy in development cooperation and give more explicit support to the role of regional organisations such as the African Union.

The fourth part of the volume deals with the relationship between culture and democracy and starts with a contribution by David Beetham on the structural and cultural preconditions for democracy. While being sceptical on such a precondition, he instead argues that low levels of public trust in democratic institutions are not the result of some pre-political cultural pattern but predominantly a response to their (dismal) performance.

Anwar Ibrahim on his turn deals with one particular instance of the relationship between culture and democracy which is the seeming (in)compatibility between democracy and Islam. He points at numerous examples in history and at present of democracy in Muslim societies and nations and demonstrates that there is not something inherent in Muslim societies that is not compatible with democracy. His viewpoint is supported by Vincent Cornell of Emory University in Atlanta, Georgia, on the basis of a thorough analysis of sociological, theological and political texts.

Finally, the volume turns on the role of important actors in the debate on and practise of democracy and development: the state, civil society and international organisations. Starting with international organisations, Nico Schrijver makes it clear that "they do not always practise what they preach", undermining the credibility of Western initiatives of democracy promotion. Likewise, Michael Edwards and Kumi Naidoo focus on the role of the civil society organisations. Michael Edwards attempts to broaden the concept of civil society to include a kind of society that was identified with certain ideals of the "good society". Kumi Naidoo places the international NGOs at the heart of the debate on the social effects of globalisation. He argues that globalisation results in democratic deficits both at the national and international level. NGOs can play a role to counter such developments. Furthermore he pleads for closer links between rights and development and for NGOs to rise up to the challenge of legitimacy and the related issues of transparency and accountability.

I started to say that the Society for International Development and the Netherlands Institute for Multiparty Democracy are to be commended for the initiative to publish this book on democracy and development containing the lectures of the lecture series. But they were not the only institutions involved in the initiative. From the start the International Institute for Democracy and Electoral Assistance (IDEA) has supported the initiative. Its staff provided an intellectual input at the time that the series was conceived, suggesting subjects to be discussed as well as speakers to be invited. Likewise it contributed to the closing conference both ways: materially as well as in the form of lectures by its Chairman of the Board and its Director General.

Likewise the Netherlands Ministry of Foreign Affairs contributed in many different ways. It hosted workshops of speakers invited by SID for its lecture series with staff at the ministry itself, and it hosted the final conference. The ministry participated in meetings with SID and other partners to determine the subjects to be included in the lecture series and the speakers to be invited. It supported the publication of the lecture series and last but not least it contributed to the lecture series by lectures of the two Ministers for Development Cooperation of two different consecutive governments, one at the beginning of the series and one at the final conference.

The Institute of Social Studies in The Hague was one of the partners closely involved in the conception of the lecture series and during the series it remained an active partner. Several speakers were invited to speak for staff members and students of the Institute in The Hague and its staff and management were regular guests and participants at the Vrije Universiteit in Amsterdam where the lectures were held.

Other institutions involved in the conception of the lecture series and rendering their support throughout its implementation were The Netherlands Centre for Sustainable Development (NCDO) and the Netherlands Institute for International Relations Clingendael.

Three Universities were closely associated with the lecture series: the Vrije Universiteit in Amsterdam, the Radboud University in Nijmegen and Maastricht University where lectures were hosted throughout the year. They were closely involved in setting the agenda, choosing subjects and speakers and hosting meetings at their institutions. It is SID's intention to extend this cooperation into the future reaching out to staff and students of these renowned institutions.

The success of such an undertaking depends not only on institutions: after all these institutions are only structures that allow and encourage people to do their job and realise their objectives. It is these people who in the end individually and together made their contributions to and brought in their support for the realisation of the lecture series. Let me mention Ruud Treffers, Aart Jacobi, Louise Anten and Ruth Emmerink of the Netherlands Ministry of Foreign Affairs; Roel von Meijenfelt and Marieke van Doorn of the Netherlands Institute of Multiparty Democracy; Louk de la Rive Box, Kees Biekart and Inge van Verschuer of the Institute of Social Studies; Jan Donner and Rolf Wijnstra of the Royal Tropical Institute; Malcolm Turner-Key, Andrew Ellis and Keboitse Machanga of the Institute for Democracy and Electoral Assistance as well as their Chairman Lena Hjelm-Wallén, Secretary-General Vidar Helgesen and Ingrid Wetterquist; Ulrich Mans of the Netherlands Institute for International Affairs, Henny Helmich of the Netherlands Centre for Sustainable Development; Ruerd Ruben, Paul Hoebink and Lau Schulpen of Radboud University Nijmegen, Kees van Dongen of the Vrije Universiteit Amsterdam and Chris Leonards and Huub Mudde of Maastricht University. Last but not least I would like to mention the staff of the Society for International Development and its Chairman and driving force Jos van Gennip, my co-author Cor van Beuningen, ever present support staff Wilma Bakker, Gordana Stankovic, Veronica Rivera Santander and Annette de Raadt. Without their enthusiasm and continuous effort there would have been no lecture series and without that no publication to speak of. My special thanks are for Lianne Damen who very confidently offered the services of KIT Publishers to realise the publication and succeeded throughout the process to keep up her and my good spirits.

One final word on the way the lectures were edited. In some instances the lecturers provided a written version of their lectures, including notes and references. Editing could remain limited to putting them in the right context. In other instances the lecturers were provided with a transcript of the lectures and invited to prepare a final text for publication. In some cases as editor I was given complete liberty to finalise the text. In the end I aimed for a certain conformity in format but at the same time preserving some of the flavour of the spoken word.

What has come out as a result can be seen as a varied but rather complete sample of present day thinking about the topic of democracy and development coming from different parts of the world and professionals of different background that will hopefully stimulate further thinking and debate on this subject.

PART I

Democracy and development

Development Starts at the Ballot Box

Agnes van Ardenne-van der Hoeven

L et me begin with a brief quote. "Everyone who wanted to speak did so. It was democracy in its purest form. There may have been a hierarchy of importance among the speakers, but everyone was heard. . . People spoke without interruption and the meetings lasted for many hours. The foundation of self-government was that all men were free to voice their opinions and were equal in their value as citizens."

Many speakers in this lecture series will probably start with some reference to ancient Greece, beginning their speech where democracy supposedly began. Perhaps they will describe the Pnyx – the meeting ground of the Assembly of Athens, where all the great political struggles of the "Golden Age" took place. Where close to the Acropolis, Athenian statesmen such as Pericles and Aristides delivered their stirring speeches – and so did countless humbler citizens. However, I decided to open this series with a quote not from an Athenian statesman but from an African one: Nelson Mandela. In his autobiography "Long Walk to Freedom", Mandela describes the tribal meetings at the "Great Place", in the village where he grew up. The chief, who had probably never heard of Pericles, simply listened to what all the citizens had to say and only spoke at the end of the meeting – in search of a consensus. This is the type of leadership that inspired Nelson Mandela to become the first president of a democratic South Africa – after the dismantling of Apartheid. A triumph of homegrown democracy.

In a few weeks time, here in the Netherlands we will have the chance to participate in the main event of our own democracy: the parliamentary elections. Our votes will influence the future of the nation. Our voices will be heard. There is a lot to be said about these particular elections, but that is not why I am here today. Today I wish to speak not about our own votes, our own voices, but about the voices of the poorest people on the planet. About whether their voices should be heard. In my opinion, it is high time we abandoned the misguided view that only the rich can afford or cope with democracy and that the poor are best governed with an iron fist. In fact, democracy is their best hope for peace and prosperity. The voices of the poor must be heard.

A world of democracy

The daily television images coming out of Iraq seem to hammer home the point that democracy only works in Western cultures. But it would be very unfair to put all the blame for Iraq's ordeal on the very concept of non-Western democracy. Democratisation is impossible without a tradition of democracy, it is often said. But as Nobel Laureate Amartya Sen emphasised in a recent book, the essence of democracy is "government by discussion", and traditions of public deliberation can be found in nearly all countries. For example, for several centuries, the Iranian city of Susa had an elected council, a popular assembly and magistrates who were proposed by the council and elected by the assembly. And there is no reason to assert that Arab culture or Islam is inherently incompatible with democracy. According to surveys, most Arabs and Muslims think democratic leadership is important, and according to demographic figures, half of the world's Muslims live in democratic states. And a country like India had a long and distinguished tradition of Buddhist councils, where people got together to work out their differences. The seventh-century Japanese constitution says, and I quote: "Decisions on important matters should not be made by one person alone. They should be discussed with many." Remember, this was six hundred years before the Magna Carta was signed in medieval England – an event often seen as the founding of Western democracy.

The roots of democracy can be found in a great many places around the world. Obviously, Western thinkers and politicians made a monumental contribution to the development of democracy, especially during the Enlightenment. Even so, the West cannot claim exclusive title to democratic concepts – the chief of Mandela's village could uphold basic principles of democracy without being indebted to John Stuart Mill. Democracy is not dependent on certain cultural conditions – it is part of the human condition. While the practice of democracy differs across countries and cultures, the principles are universal.

Democracy works

Saint Augustine once prayed, "Give me chastity and continence, but not yet." Likewise, many political scientists and economic experts say of poor countries, "Give them democracy, but not yet." Rather than identifying culture as a permanent obstacle, prominent figures like Robert Barro and Fareed Zakaria point to underdevelopment as a temporary one. This school of thought says: development first, democracy later. In the early stages of development, the iron fist of an autocratic regime is better able to mobilise the nation's limited financial and human resources. Democracy, they say, is a luxury that a poor country cannot afford. Big-spending politicians, special interests and the compromises of coalition governments stand in the way of firm steps towards sustainable development.

Now let's look at the facts. First off, we must conclude that the world has seen a genuine wave of democratisation. Today, nearly seven out of ten countries are on the democratic path. This includes countries in every region of the world. In Africa, for example, practically every country is now formally a democracy and the number of countries that meet World Bank standards of good governance has tripled in the past few years. People always marvel about emerging economies, but emerging democracies are just as remarkable. For the first time in history, democracy has reached a majority of the human race. But has democracy brought freedom at the cost of empty stomachs?

Let's look at how poor autocracies and poor democracies have fared in the past. Recent research by Daniel Kaufman has shown that the causal link runs from better governance, including political and civil liberties, to economic development and not the other way around. And according to research published by the Council on Foreign Relations, democracies have outperformed their authoritarian counterparts on the full range of development indicators. There is no evidence of an authoritarian advantage when it comes to economic growth. Democracies have a thirty per cent edge. Taking only low-income countries into account, we see that democracies are still slightly ahead. Of course, it is not just the rate of growth that matters, but also its stability, especially for the poor. When sudden, sharp dips occur, the poor have no choice but to sell what few assets they have to stay alive. Poor democracies have been much better at avoiding economic disasters. Twice as often, poor autocracies have experienced drops of ten per cent or more in annual national income. The Pinochet regime in Chile is often cited as a dictatorship that brought economic success. What most people fail to see is that under Pinochet Chile suffered two economic crises that wiped away much of the growth that had been achieved. His iron fist led the country from boom to bust.

It has long been recognised that, though growth is indispensable, there is more to development. That is why in the year 2000 world leaders agreed on a development agenda that includes a wide range of social targets in the Millennium Development Goals. Of all the countries below the poverty line, it is the democracies that are most likely to cross the finishing line by 2015. Their citizens live a decade longer. Fifty per cent fewer of their children die before their fifth birthday. Twice as many children attend secondary school. And agricultural productivity is a third higher in poor democracies.

Of course, peace is another important condition for a successful society. Countries in conflict do not prosper. Often, dictatorships are said to maintain stability by repressing tribal, ethnic or political dissent. This is incorrect. Of the forty-nine poor countries embroiled in civil conflict in the 1990s, forty-one were dictatorships. Democracies appear to be especially good at managing ethnic diversity – they use ballots instead of bullets. In dictatorships, ethnic diversity reduces growth by up to three percentage points, while it has no adverse effects on economic growth in democracies. A democratic deficit contributed to many cases of state failure in the second half of the twentieth century. And there is a powerful pattern of "democratic peace" – democracies rarely go to war with each other.

Exceptions to the rule

Critics of this democratic peace theory, first put forward by Kant, often refer to exceptional cases where democracies did wage war on one another. One example is the 1999 Kargil War between India and Pakistan, which was then democratic, over the Kashmir issue – the first ground war between the two countries after they developed nuclear weapons. Or last summer's war between Israel and Lebanon. Whatever we conclude about these specific cases, most proponents of the democratic peace theory don't claim that democratic states are always at peace with one another. They merely say that the probability of war is very low, a prediction which is definitely borne out by the facts.

And this makes perfectly good sense. In democracies, a moderate majority will normally stop overzealous politicians from wasting money and lives on war. The majority generally prefers peaceful resolution of international conflicts – the same method used to settle conflicts at home. Democracies, both rich and poor, maintain stability by allowing people and countries to work out their differences with words instead of weapons.

Democracy's superior track record in the field of development also makes good sense. In functioning democracies, politicians are more likely to pursue the national interest instead of their own interests, because they know they will be held accountable at the next election. The free flow of information and the openness of public debate improve the quality of policy analysis, lay the groundwork for innovation and reduce the risk of corruption. Still, critics contest democracy's development success by coming up with counterexamples. Such as China, a one-party state with double digit growth. Similarly, Singapore, South Korea, Taiwan and Vietnam have all achieved high growth rates without the blessings of democracy. But just as with the democratic peace theory, what matters for policy is the rule, not the exception. And these are exceptions: over the last two decades, seven times as many dictatorships had poor growth rather than good growth, with several autocratic failures even in East Asia. The economic success of some East Asian countries, caused not by an iron fist but by the invisible hand of market forces, merely shows that democracy is not always a necessary condition for development. But the theory that democracy is more likely to promote development than autocracy still stands.

Democracy is right

The case for democracy is not just built on its superior track record of promoting peace and prosperity. It is also built on a foundation of moral values. The freedom to have a say in hiring and firing your government is a human right. That makes democracy not just a means to an end, but also an end in itself. This point is often missed in today's lengthy discussions on whether spreading democracy is a sensible strategy for fighting terrorism. Democracy is really much more than a strategy, it is a goal. The UN Charter does not mention the word democracy, but the democratic tradition does inform its opening words: "We the peoples of the United Nations". This expresses the view that both the sovereignty of the member states and the legitimacy of the world body are rooted in the popular will. The Universal Declaration of Human Rights is more explicit, and I quote: "The will of the people shall be the basis of the authority of government." The declaration also outlines the other rights that are necessary to guarantee, in the words of Abraham Lincoln, "a government of the people, by the people and for the people."

Encouraging homegrown democracy

So encouraging democracy in poor countries is not just a sound development policy, it is also the right thing to do. That is why I have led the way from a technocratic approach to development cooperation to a development policy that embraces the political dimension. A development policy that embraces democracy. Public debate centres on whether it is feasible to impose democracy from the outside. But as Amartya Sen has noted, this is the wrong question. The roots of democracy can be found everywhere: in the North, South, East and West. The real question is therefore how to support homegrown democracy effectively. How to make sure every country's Nelson Mandela gets a chance.

The most straightforward approach is to make sure that elections are held in the first place and that they are free and fair. And that is what we are working on. For example, we supported elections last year in Burundi and this year in Congo. We financed both the hardware and the software of Congolese democracy. That is, we paid for the ballot boxes for the presidential elections, which culminated yesterday in the second-round run-off between Joseph Kabila and Jean-Pierre Bemba. But we also educated personnel at voting stations and trained the police to provide crucial election-day security – backed up by an EU military force in which we also participated. With our support, a coalition of religious organisations close to the people told voters how to vote – but not what to vote! And we helped a human rights NGO in East Congo monitor whether independent and minority candidates got a fair chance. So that the people of the Democratic Republic of Congo can help their country live up to its name.

Building a stable and sustainable democracy is a tremendous task, going far beyond holding elections. Upholding freedom of speech and expression is especially vital – before people can govern themselves, they must be able to express themselves. That is why in several poor countries I am encouraging the emergence of a strong and independent press, willing and able to confront the government with a high level of scrutiny. In Yemen, we are training independent journalists. And in Kenya, where newspapers have done much to expose corruption, we support legislative reforms that enhance transparency, like the Freedom of Information Act. But freedom of speech and expression is not just about laws and institutions – in equal measure, it is about culture. A culture of tolerance is the breathing space needed for public debate, for "government by discussion", which is the essence of democracy. A society where minorities of any kind are not free, or do not feel free, to voice their opinions is not a democracy – it is oppression by the elite. A true democracy understands that uniformity is weakness and diversity is power. It is a learning organisation, where dissenting opinions and diverse views are recognised as essential for engendering human dignity and indispensable for improving policy.

Freedom of expression is an especially problematic issue in the Middle East – in the one region still relatively untouched by the democratisation. The Arab Human Development Reports speak of a freedom deficit. These are homegrown studies, written by Arab scholars who wonder what went wrong. Obviously, all is not well with freedom of expression in the Arab world: for example, there are almost no worthwhile think-tanks in the region. Some authors assert that religion is to blame, with its emphasis on finding the truth in scripture, rather than reflection and experience. Through the Knowledge Forum on Religion and Development Policy, I am analysing the role of religion in promoting or discouraging diversity and dissent, both inside and outside the Arab world. While some forms of Islamic teaching might hold back independent thought, it never stopped the great Arab astronomers and mathematicians of the Middle Ages. There are no straightforward answers here, but the Knowledge Forum offers an opportunity for careful analysis and tailored measures, for example by our embassies. One high priority is to energise public debate in closed societies, on both religious diversity and diversity in general. The Forum was established last year when the SID held its lecture series on religion and development. It takes the form of a partnership between the Dutch government and Dutch civil society.

A democratic society without a vital civil society is an empty shell, as I am sure everyone here would agree. Strengthening civil society is crucial since it represents the demand side of the political equation. Civil society organisations such as voluntary associations, educational institutions, clubs, unions, charities and churches can amplify the voices and voice the demands of the most silent, invisible and impoverished citizens. They also foster many elements essential to democracy, such as participation and accountability. Obviously, the job of helping to build civil society is best left to civil society, not governments. For this purpose, I have just pledged a total of over two billion euros to Dutch civil-society organisations for the next four years. Our new grant system puts a premium on quality, cooperation, complementarity and a results-based approach. It also puts the "civil" back into civil society organisations – they are now required to get at least twenty-five per cent of their funds from other sources. They will work side by side with intermediate institutions in the South, which have been the "missing middle" in many developing countries.

As our civil society works on the demand side of the political equation, I am also working on the supply side. This means engaging in honest and open political dialogue with poor-country governments on the state of their democracies. It also means working with them to make sure the state can live up to the expectations and demands of the governed. Many citizens judge their government by its ability to provide basic services such as security, health and education. If democratic governments in poor countries fail to do so, that could in time destroy public backing for democracy. But like democracy itself, state capacity for delivering public services must be homegrown – it's no use sending in our own people or imposing our own organisational models. Fortunately, last year the donor community rallied around the Paris Declaration, which states that the only way to improve a country's systems is by working with them. The Netherlands not only played a major role in forging this consensus, but also started implementing its principles years ago by channelling our funding through the national budgets of the recipient countries. And we run public finance management programmes that teach civil servants in those countries how to manage those national budgets properly. Of course, it takes not just good civil servants but responsive and responsible politicians as well. I also promote that cause through the Netherlands Institute for Multiparty Democracy – a joint initiative of political parties for political parties. According to recent research by the OECD, our early application of the Paris Principles has led to progress – in the form of an expansion of basic services in health and education.

International organisations such as the OECD measure aid effectiveness. At the national level, developing countries need their own public institutions to measure development results and monitor whether the government is playing by the rules. A democracy needs all the watchdogs it can get. That is why the Netherlands has supported independent audit offices in 22 countries in Africa. And through a wide array of projects we promote the rule of law. This ranges from improving legal education in Mali to providing legal aid to employees in China; and from educating journalists in Egypt about their legal rights to assisting in the reform of criminal law in Georgia. Without the rule of law there can be no rule by the people, of the people or for the people. Alongside the judiciary, parliamentarians are important watchdogs – I speak from experience, having served as a member of parliament for eight years. As a minister I strengthen parliaments all around the world, for instance with courses on lawmaking in Benin and on economic governance in Georgia. Any government with enough power to protect its citizens must be counterbalanced by a powerful parliament and a vibrant civil society.

Conclusion. Long walk to freedom

Throughout my lecture, I have emphasised that working on democracy means working with civil society. I have always enjoyed working with you and hope our good relationship will continue. The SID is not just a Society for International Development, but also a Society for International Democracy. For instance, we support your efforts in East Africa to foster dialogue between politicians, policymakers, researchers and NGOs.

Your new lecture series is another excellent initiative, and I was pleased to start it off with the words of a great African statesman. Nelson Mandela managed to breathe life into democratic principles rooted in his own culture – to realise his African dream. But, as the title of his autobiography says, it's a long walk to freedom. And in terms of political freedom, the African continent still has a long way to go. We do have every reason to be optimistic – look at NEPAD, where African countries assess each other's performance in the area of governance. I don't see that happening in the European Union! Democracy is on the march and that is good news for the poor. Along with free markets, democracy is one of human society's greatest inventions, and why should the poor be denied its fruits? Democracy has provided the best answer to the central question of politics, as expressed in the old Latin saying: "Who will watch the watchers?" Democracy's answer is simple: each and every one of us.

References

Halperlin, Morton H., Joseph T. Siegle, Michael M. Weinstein, 2004. "Why Democracies Excel". In: *Foreign Affairs*, vol. 83, no. 5.

Halperlin, Morton H., Joseph T. Siegle, Michael M. Weinstein, 2005. *The Democracy Advantage. Why democracies promote prosperity and peace*. New York: Routledge.

IDD and Associates, 2006. *Evaluation of General Budget Support: Synthesis Report. A Joint Evaluation of General Budget Support 1994-2004*. London: DFID.

Kaufman, Daniel, Aart Kraay, Massimo Mastruzzi, 2006. *A Decade of Measuring the Quality of Governance. Governance Matters 2006. Worldwide Governance Indicators*. Washington D.C.: World Bank.

Mandela, Nelson, 1995. *Long Walk to Freedom. The Autobiography of Nelson Mandela.* London: Little Brown & Co.

Sen, Amartya, 2006. *Identity and Violence. The Illusion of Destiny.* New York: W.W. Norton & Company.

UNDP, 2005. *Arab Human Development Report 2005: Towards the Rise of Women in the Arab World.* New York: Oxford University Press.

UNDP, 2004. *Arab Human Development Report 2004: Towards Freedom in the Arab World.* New York: Oxford University Press.

UNDP, 2003. *Arab Human Development Report 2003: Building a Knowledge Society.* New York: Oxford University Press.

UNDP, 2002. *Arab Human Development Report 2002: Creating Opportunities for Future Generations.* New York: Oxford University Press.

Governance, Corruption, Democracy and Development in Latin America: Empirics in an International Comparative Perspective

Daniel Kaufmann

It is good to talk about democracy, good governance, fighting corruption, etc., but the example starts at home. We at the World Bank are painfully aware that we have a major internal challenge within our own institution at present. First and foremost we who have been working in the World Bank for a long time on this issue of governance and anti-corruption, wanting to resolve this crisis, have been very clear. We have sent an explicit letter to the President and to the Board of Executive Directors, making it very clear that if this crisis of leadership and integrity is not resolved speedily, our work with our countries and outside, cannot continue. I therefore give this lecture with a bit of humility and suggest what we have said all along, even before the crisis, that first and foremost one has to start with a good example at home (May 2007).

The first point I want to talk about is the power of data, the power of empirical work. Contrary to some conventional views, the notions of governance can be measured and analysed rigorously and empirically. We and other colleagues and academics outside the bank, find that governance, including anti-corruption, democratic processes, are fundamental for growth and development. These institutional governance issues were a crucial gap in the so-called Washington Consensus of about 15 years ago, coined by the key institutions in Washington, the U.S. Treasury and the World Bank.

Second, we will address the issue of the recent spurt in growth of Latin America with its potential failings of what we call elevator economics, focusing sometimes too much on the short term at the expense of medium – or longer-term issues. Once we focus on the medium- and longer-term issues, the issues of institutions, capture of the state by elites and governance and corruption, cannot be swept under the carpet.

I think it is very important, knowing you are interested in the link between democracy and development and concerned about the recent electoral developments in Latin America, to talk about them and the question of whether democracy is endangered. We will suggest that this is not the case. Yes, there is fragility but the trend goes towards democratic consolidation, with some related hiccups.

Has there been a political tsunami recently towards a particular ideological spectrum, given the 11 elections that have taken place in the past year, half or so of which were in Latin America? We suggest this is not the case at all. In some sense, to be provocative, I am going to address and challenge myths in this context. However, we will suggest that there is disappointment with the free-market model and with privatisation in some quarters, which is not unrelated to the issues of poor governance, corruption and the very big challenge of inequality being part of this disenchantment.

Lastly, we will also suggest a constructive move forward on one of the issues we have been working on, which is the exciting area of transparency-related reforms. We have noticed there is enormous potential for progress here in very concrete terms.

The power of data

Let us start with the issue of data, data which will also be available on the website[1]. We have been working for almost a decade now on the world-wide aggregate governance indicators running until the end of 2005. Very soon, we will have them until the end of 2006. We are also moving to a multi-annual frequency in those indicators.

I will suggest a few things on how we are going to use these aggregate governance indicators. To build these indicators we relied on 250 variables from 30 or so sources. We also used these very disaggregated data for many other purposes as well in a major governance data base, which is all available on the web.

We started by defining governance rather broadly, basically the synthesis of a literature invented from scratch, that sees governance as a set of traditions and institutions by which authority in a country is exercised. This includes essentially three key clusters of governance:

1. the political dimension of governance, which is the process by which governments are selected, monitored and replaced;
2. the economic dimension of governance, which refers to the capacity of any government to effectively formulate and implement sound policies as well as provide public services for its citizens;
3. the institutional dimension of governance, which refers basically to the respect of citizens and the state for the institutions that govern social and economic interactions among them.

We then approximated each one of those clusters with two measurable indicators each. That makes a set of 6 indicators:

The political dimension:
- voice and democratic accountability;
- political stability and the absence of violence and terror.

The economic arena:
- the effectiveness of the government and bureaucracy;
- the quality of the regulatory framework.

The institutional arena:
- the rule of law;
- control of corruption.

By now, we cover 213 countries over the past decade and so, effectively, the world.

This puts the issue of corruption into perspective. Corruption and governance are not one and the same. Corruption is a subset of a much broader spectrum of governance within which the democratic process is also included. It is important to put this issue of corruption in a broader framework, however simplistically constructed, because one does not fight corruption by being an anti-corruption expert or creating another anti-corruption commission. Instead, one has to look at the whole system of governance because, at the end of the day, corruption is a symptom of poor institutional quality and governance, in terms of many of the other issues being sub par.

The construction of indicators

As I mentioned previously, we collected data from different institutions throughout the world. I will give some examples. There are 31 data sources from 25 organisations, capturing the views of thousands of informed stakeholders. I am not going to bother you by going through each one, we rely on cross-country services of firms as well as individuals and expert assessment by commercial risk rating agencies and government and multilateral institutions. The institutions are headquartered throughout the world, so there is no one region or country particularly biased or overrepresented.

We used a particular methodology to aggregate these data. It is a complicated statistical method with very advanced statistical techniques to minimise the margin of error, although it is still significant at the end of the day. This technique is an example of what is called the unobserved component model, which is a more advanced variant of the principle of component factor analysis. The benefits of aggregation, by the way, are that aggregate indicators are more informative about broad concepts of governance, are less likely to generate extreme outliers and generate explicit margins of error for country scores.

Ultimately, we come up with something like what we see in the next figure.

In figure 1 we see only 31 selected countries instead of the whole 250, but it is important to note here – and that is one of the advantages with this methodology – that it not only gives an estimate of

Figure 1   Control of Corruption, selected countries, 2005

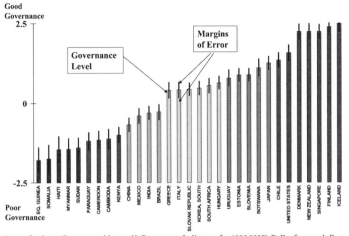

Source for data: 'Governance Matters V: Governance Indicators for 1996-2005', D. Kaufmann, A. Kraay and M. Mastruzzi, September 2006.
Note: Colors are assigned according to the following criteria (dark to light): below 10th percentile rank among all countries in the world; between 10th and 25th; between 25th and 50th; between 50th and 75th; between 75th and 90th; above 90th.

their rating for each one of the 6 indicators for each country – in this case, for illustration, of control of corruption – but it also gives a transparent and relatively precise sense of the degree of imprecision of that estimate, the margin of error, which is the thin line at the top of each of the cones.

The bad news is that any of these data, not only these, but any data on governance, investment climate and any of this type of issues, has to be used with caution because it always has a margin of error. We happen to be transparent and precise in trying to measure it, however – this is usually not done – but that means it is fallacious, it is misleading to try to run precise horse races and, say, Holland telling Sweden: "I beat you by a nose". It is meaningless when the differences in rating are very small. The good news however, is that, as we see here, on average the margin of error is not fatally large, for making comparisons.

One can group the world into 4 or 5 meaningful categories in a statistical sense. The dark countries at the right are examples of excellent governance, including the Nordic countries and the Netherlands. I am biased, I come from Chile, so I am going to show you a lot about Chile. Chile is among the dark countries as well, which shows that one does not have to be a highly-industrialised, rich country to reach a high level of governance.

Conversely, there are countries here – and you can see some in the light area, where we have Italy in the middle – that are quite wealthy but do not achieve the same level of governance. The dark countries at the right are statistically significantly different from the light ones and the light ones are very different from the dark countries at the left, which are undergoing a governance crisis.

Here is another way of looking at the same data.

Figure 2   World Map: Government Effectiveness, 2005

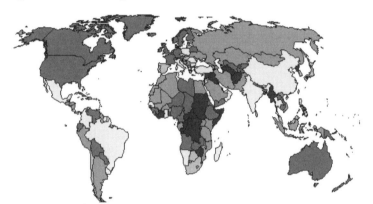

Source for data: 'Governance Matters V: Governance Indicators for 1996-2005', D. Kaufmann, A. Kraay and M. Mastruzzi, September 2006. www.govindicators.org.
Colors are assigned according to the following criteria (dark to light): country is in the bottom 10th percentile rank ('governance crisis'); between 10th and 25th percentile rank; between 25th and 50th; between 50th and 75th; between 75th and 90th; between 90th and 100th percentile (exemplary governance). Estimates subject to margins of error.

One thing that is immediately obvious when you look at the data carefully, is that they begin to challenge conventional or popular notions. The whole idea that every country that is more industrialised is necessarily in the dark category of good governance countries is challenged immediately, as there are also some countries like Botswana in Africa in the grey zone indicating reasonably good governance.

Similarly, there is enormous variation within each continent. We tend to generalise for the whole continent, whether Africa or Latin America, when in reality it is very dangerous to make these generalisations due to the variation. We have the whole spectrum of corruption within the same continent. It is therefore already clear that it is similar with regard to voice and accountability. On government effectiveness, South Africa attains very good levels, including Botswana and Mozambique.

In the next figure, the same data are generated for just one country.

Figure 3 Aggregate Governance Indicators for Chile (2005 vs. 1998)

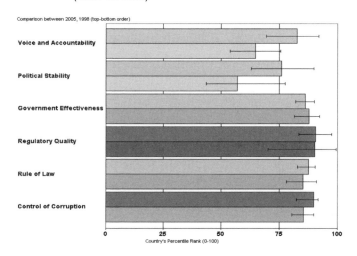

The lower bar in this case is 1998; the most recent year, 2005, is the higher bar. We can thus see how voice and accountability and democracy and civil liberties have been consolidated in my country, Chile; similarly with political stability. We also see how the control of corruption is among the best in general and certainly in the emerging world.

Do these data also help to challenge Afro-pessimism, however? There is a set of countries in Africa which is showing a possible improvement in governance, even in the short term. We see it in the case of Mozambique, which has a long way to go but is going in the right direction.

Figure 4   Governance Indicators for Mozambique, 1998–2005

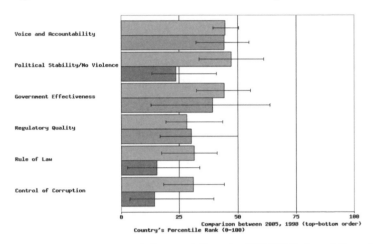

Source for data: 'Governance Matters V: Governance Indicators for 1996-2005', D. Kaufmann, A. Kraay and M. Mastruzzi, September 2006. www.govindicators.org.
Colors are assigned according to the following criteria (dark to light): country is in the bottom 10th percentile rank ('governance crisis'); between 10th and 25th percentile rank; between 25th and 50th; between 50th and 75th; between 75th and 90th; between 90th and 100th percentile (exemplary governance). Estimates subject to margins of error.

There is good news coming from the data but there is another way of looking at changes over time, using these data for Mozambique. Again, use the margin of error very carefully and do not fall into elevator economics, which says that any change is important or meaningful. There are a lot of positive changes in the grey area, even though, because of the margin of error, one cannot say that they are significant changes.

There are tales of about 20 countries. Each tale, and I have not listed them all, shows that within less than a decade there has been a significant change.

The good news is that some have significantly improved (this is on voice and accountability) like Mexico, Ghana, Nigeria, Indonesia, El Salvador, Tanzania, Bulgaria, Senegal, Liberia and so on. The bad

38

Figure 5 Changes in Voice and Accountability, 1996–2005

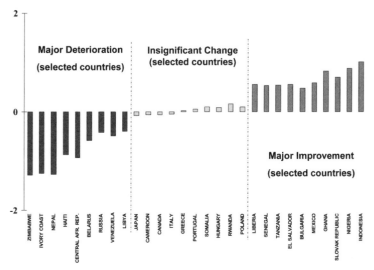

Changes were calculated on the basis of the differences in country estimates from 1996 and 2005. classification for major deteriorations and improvementswere based on 75% confidence interval.
Source for data: 'Governance Matters V: Governance Indicators for 1996-2005', D. Kaufmann, A. Kraay and M. Mastruzzi, September 2006. www.govindicators.org.

news again is that for every country that has on average improved, there has been one that has deteriorated. This is not a static situation. There are also Zimbabwe and Ivory Coast, Belarus, Russia, Venezuela, Libya, etc.

On average, we have found that there has been no significant improvement in governance around the world over the past 10 to 15 years, and that covers issues of voice and accountability, rule of law and control of corruption.

Elevator economics

This, in essence, is the picture of the empirical effort and the approach that we take and some of the lessons that emerge. Let us focus more on Latin America and the interface between politics, governance and growth. In the past few years, there has been quite rapid growth in many countries in the region. This has caused some excitement but let us take some perspective. Let me make a few points on this.

39

One may risk being too short-term in analysis. It is not that difficult to grow rapidly for 2 or 3 years, particularly in a region that is known to have volatile growth rates. There have been growth spurts in the past. The question is whether it can be sustained or will be followed by going down. By just focusing on a short term of two to three years, one risks falling into the trap of what we call elevator economics, which goes up and down. Let us keep in mind that a lot of the recent growth is driven by external factors. This does not apply to all of it, however. Some countries had much better policies than others. That should be commended. Overall, however, external factors like the high growth rates of China and the US, the global economy and its implications for the prices of raw materials, were driving a lot of these factors, including many remittances, which played a significant role.

This growth has not also been converted into a major spurt in job creation, which is a major challenge and very important for Latin America. Similarly, inequality appears to have stayed stagnant. Of course, it is hard to obtain very accurate up-to-date measures of inequality but there is no evidence to suggest that there has been a major improvement. There is total consensus that whatever the trend may have been over the past few years for inequality, the region remains extremely unequal in income distribution, including my own country. Chile is a major pending challenge.

If we take this more sobering perspective, while welcoming the growth of course, and begin to focus more on the medium term, one may ask the question, what is pending? Where improvements have not taken place it is hard to escape this implication with regard to the importance of improving institutions and governance and addressing the issues of equality.

Are we doing well enough?

Let us look very quickly from the data perspective at some of the above points.

Figure 6   5-Year Growth Rates in GDP per capita, 1990–2005

Best

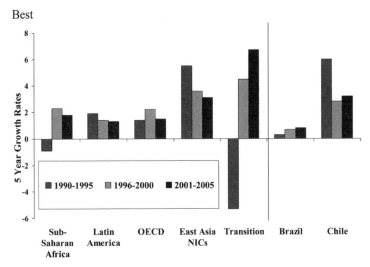

■ 1990-1995   ■ 1996-2000   ■ 2001-2005

Source: WDI 2006.

First, let us view the growth rate issue from a little more medium-term perspective. We take the last 15 years and bundle them into 5-year terms, and then we say: "Look, at the end of the day we live in a globalised world, so it is not good enough to say that Latin America is now growing faster than before. Instead, we have to ask ourselves if we are doing as well as some of the big winners in the rest of the world, because we nevertheless live in a globalised, competitive world.

For Latin America again, quite sobering, the 5 years between 2001 and 2005 show unsteady rates of per capita growth: less than 2% and below the previous two 5-year periods in fact, none of which were very impressive. Compare this with the Tigers of East Asia, which we know have grown very quickly. Even compared to much richer countries in the OECD, which by definition do not have the catch-up advantage, since they are already so rich. One would expect a country in an emerging economy group to grow more quickly. This is not the case, however. Even in Sub-Sahara Africa in the past 10 years, countries have grown faster than in Latin America, not to speak about the post-socialist economies in transition, following the depression right after the break up of the Soviet Union. They have made a major recovery in this direction.

Of course, as I said before, Latin America is an average and we should be very mindful of the enormous variations across countries. Again, I cannot resist being biased and show Chile. Everybody agrees that Chile is a country that demonstrates that it is possible and how it is possible, to grow much more quickly and not only during times when copper prices are high. Chile's growth has been rapid for some time, with less volatility than others, while Brazil, for instance, which is not among the worse performers, being in the middle, could have done better. We see here this type of variation.

Institutions in Latin America

Let us take a look at what has happened with institutions in Latin America. What about the quality of institutions? Let us take 2 of the 6 indicators that we already presented in an aggregate fashion.

In Figure 7 we see control of corruption in the left column and voice and democratic accountability in the right column. Higher is better in this case – it is a public good – bad being low. Once again, we see the extent of the challenge for Latin America here in being rated low on average and even lower, if you take out the three countries that show that it is at least possible to do better, which are Chile, Uruguay and Costa Rica.

Compare this with the countries of Eastern Europe that have just joined the European Union and even with the East Asian Tigers. We know that East Asia and even the Tigers of East Asia, which includes Singapore, were not very strong on voice and accountability and civil liberties and so on. It is no surprise that there is still a gap between control of corruption, where they reach a high level on the one hand, and voice and accountability on the other. Even there, Latin America reaches a very low level in comparison. We therefore have a major challenge on our continent on our hands and I am showing just two of the six dimensions in that aggregate context.

Figure 7 Control of Corruption and Voice and Accountability, Selected Regions

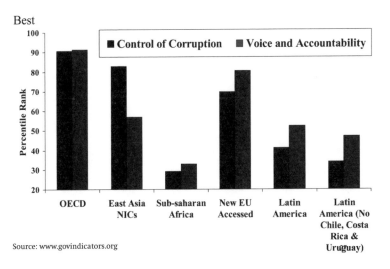

Source: www.govindicators.org

If we unravel it a bit more and look at the more disaggregated data, the picture of political corruption quickly emerges, termed undue political influence, on the one hand and capture by the elite of the key institutions of the state on the other. We have done quite a bit of empirical research on these issues.

The columns on the left in this case measure the extent to which bribes are paid by powerful firms in order to unduly influence and affect the rules, regulations and policies of the state. We are not talking about small administrative, petty bureaucratic bribes to get a license and so on. This is more grand-scale political corruption through this capture of state institutions.

The columns on the right are the extent of undue political influence by very powerful firms without necessarily a bribe taking place. They may not necessarily be totally corrupt in the legal sense of the word, but they still have enormous political influence.

Figure 9 is an inverse scale to illustrate poor governance. The rich OECD countries as well as the East Asia Tigers do relatively well. Latin America, Sub-Saharan Africa and the former Soviet Union have significant challenges in this regard.

Figure 8 Elite Capture, Political Corruption and Inequality of Influence in Latin America

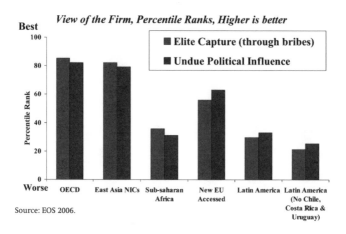

View of the Firm, Percentile Ranks, Higher is better

Source: EOS 2006.

Governance matters

Where these issues of capture by elites in those countries are prevalent, we find that the dynamic, small- and medium-scale enterprises in the private sector grow at only half the rate of countries that are more competitive and where these monopolistic captures do not take place (see figure 9).

Not surprisingly, as economists we also find that more competition, better liberalisation and better macro economic policies mitigate the risk of state capture, as is illustrated in figure 10.

At least as important, and this is even more interesting for economists, is the role of the degree of political openness, political stability and civil liberties and voice and freedom of the press in all of this. The freedom of the press is extremely important for mitigating state capture, illustrated in figures 11 and 12.

Press freedom is very important also for the control of corruption more generally as we see in figure 13, and for economic development and incomes (figure 14).

44

Figure 9   Development Dividend from Good Governance

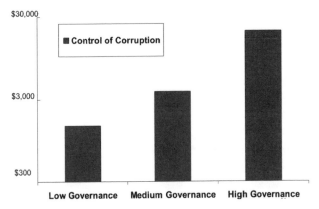

Data Source for calculations: KK 2204. Y-axis measures predicted GDP per capita on the basis of instrumental Variable (IV) results for each of the 3 categories. Estimations based on various authors' studies, including Kaufmann and Kraay.

Figure 10   Capture by Corporates Impairs Competitive Growth

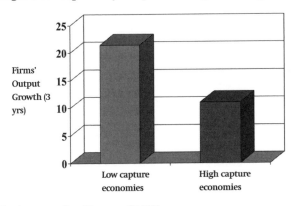

Based on survey of transition economies, 2000.

Figure 11 Fighting Capture: Economic Reform, Political Competition and Civil Liberties Matter

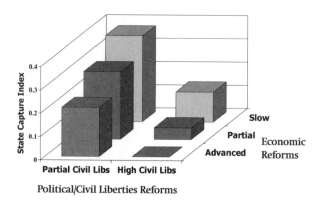

Figure 12 State Capture vs. Freedom of the Press, 2005

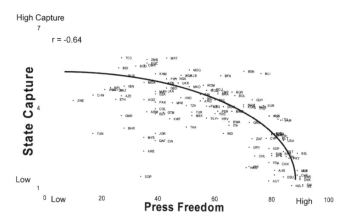

Source for state capture: EOS firm survey, WEF 2006. Source for Press Freedom: Freedom House, 2006.

Figure 13 Freedom of the Press is associated with better Control of Corruption (and civil liberties more generally is associated with better performance of World Bank-funded projects – see WBER article 1997)

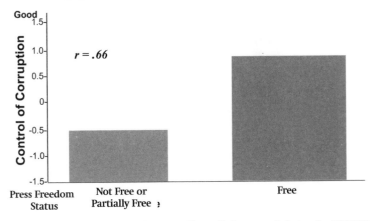

Source for control of corruption: 'Governance Matters V: Governance Indicators for 1996-2005', D. Kaufmann, A. Kraay and M. Mastruzzi, September 2006 (www.govindicators.org). Source for Press Freedom: 2006 Freedom House's Press Freedom Report. Terciles divided according to Press Freedom ratings (190 countries total). Free: 0-30 (69); Partly Free: 31-60 (54); Not Free: 61-100 (67).

Figure 14 Income per Capita vs. Freedom of the Press, 2005

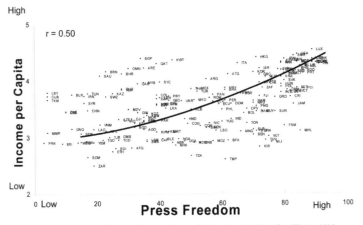

Source for income per capita: Heston-Summers. Source for Press Freedom: Freedom House, 2006.

Voice and accountability not only link very well with growth and incomes as one economic development outcome, but also with other socio-economic outcomes like infant mortality, as we see in figure 15.

Figure 15 Voice and Accountability Matters for Development

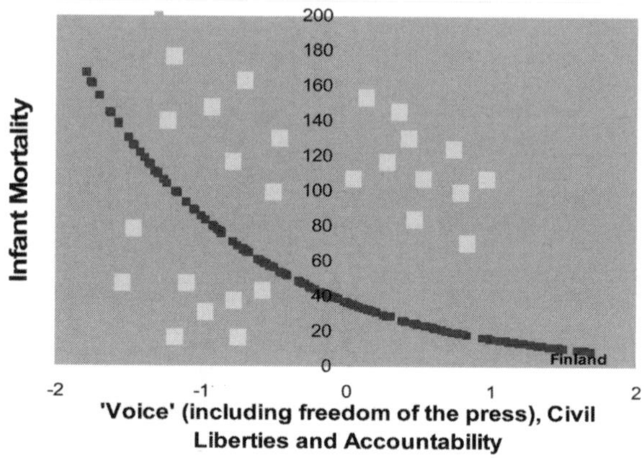

Source: KKZ 1999.

We find that voice as well as internal transparency matter enormously, concerning the budget, hiring mechanisms, etc. There are also lessons not only for institutions in developing countries, but for our own institutions as well. In general, we find that this whole notion of more transparency matters very significantly for the control of corruption.

Parliament is also a key institution in this context and it is, let us be frank among ourselves, a key challenge in many Latin American countries, where the institution of parliament is one of the reasons for poor governance. It is thus part of the problem and not always part of the solution. In many places it can be an agent for much better governance. This requires much more focus and a scenario of potential collaboration between European countries and others.

48

It takes two to tango

We would leave one very important stone unturned if we did not refer to a key aspect of misgovernance and that is that with corruption it takes two to tango. There are two sides at least for every bribe given: the giver and the receiver. It is very important to look at the role of the private sector, including the multinational private sector, where the richer OECD countries also have a responsibility. Again the data speak for themselves.

Figure 16 Responsibility of the Private Sector and Multinationals on Anti-Corruption (% of Firms Reporting Procurement Bribery, 2006)

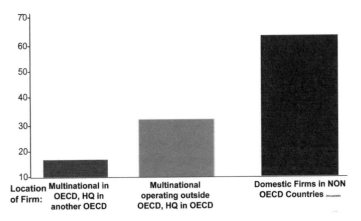

Source: EOS 2006. Questions: When firms like yours do business with the government, how much of the contract value must they offer in additional payments to secure the contract? Y-axis shows percentage of firms who admitted paying bribes. Last bar excludes small enterprises with less than 50 employees.

If a multinational has its headquarters in a rich OECD country and is operating in another rich OECD country, the extent to which multinationals pay bribes for procurement is relatively low. If they, with the same headquarters, go outside OECD countries, they begin to adapt very quickly to the environment in the recipient country, despite the fact that it is totally illegal according to the OECD convention on international bribery, which was adopted more than 5 years ago or, in the case of the US, the CPA, which goes back to the mid-70s.

They do not go all the way, as domestic firms do, so the OECD convention has had a firm impact. The column in the middle is higher than the one on the left, which is quite telling in itself. This is the responsibility of the multinational sector in this context. There is a responsibility in general from the corporate sector, even if they do not operate across borders.

We have attempted to measure the degree of corporate corruption, the extent to which they tend to offer bribes. The responsibility lies not always with the public sector.

Figure 17 Corporate Corruption, unbundled, 2004

% Firms report corruption type (1-4)

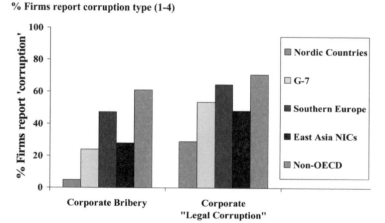

Source: Author's calculations based on EOS 2004.

This summarises a whole paper, which basically suggests that issues like corporate bribery can be unpackaged and measured in much more detail than in the past. One of the telling findings is that the picture is much more complex than just saying that the rich world is doing very well, thank you very much and the poor world is totally engaged in corruption. Not so. We have already seen with emerging economies that it is much more varied than that.

Interestingly enough, here we see that in the countries of southern Europe the extent of corporate bribery is extremely high, whether it is outright bribery or more legal forms of corruption, like undue influence or political funding. The real exemptions are the Nordic countries. The Netherlands does rather well, as well as New Zealand and so on, but many others face a very significant challenge. In fact, the Tigers in East Asia come out far better than southern Europe.

It is therefore somewhat sobering to begin looking at these issues and realising that there is a significant challenge a) for many in the rich world and b) for the corporate side too.

The political linkages between governance, democracy and development, issues for debate

Before going to the last part of the discourse, I want to focus a bit more on the political linkages between governance, democracy and development. These issues are rapidly evolving, lots of research is still being done and we find out with some frequency that we are not right.

Nothing is settled.

The first point for discussion and debate, based on the empirical work as we see it, is that there is a two-way street between improving civil liberties and political competition through voice and democratic accountability on the one hand and improving on corruption control on the other. As you can see, it goes in both directions: better corruption control can also give more legitimacy to political competition but we also find a clear link between civil liberties and better corruption control.

We also observed a very significant link, particularly in one direction, more so than in the other, between corruption control and other ways of improving governance, and improving socio-economic development. We also saw a fair amount of data based on which we find a clear link between corruption control and more legitimacy and credibility in the democratic process.

Economic growth has some impact in furthering democratic consolidation. We find a link between robust economic growth, particularly when there is less inequality and less corruption and increased satisfaction with the role of market forces and the private sector.

Unfortunately, some of these trends are not moving in the right direction, as we have seen in Latin America. This leads to some of the following issues for debate. The first is that in more mature democracies the link between economic cycles, whether they are going up or down, and satisfaction with democracy has weakened. In essence, it is no longer fatal for democracy to undergo some recession in Latin American countries. We find that corruption and inequality impact negatively on the satisfaction of citizens with democracy. However, neither economic recession nor corruption and inequality has resulted in citizens preferring non-democratic governance.

In general, there is no voice among the citizens of Latin America, contrary to some of the alarmist writings, saying: "Why don't we go back to non-democratic government?". There are complaints about democracy. It is still fragile but just because there may be a recession – and that was the case in 2002, the earlier part of the decade – this did not mean that the majority would have preferred non-democratic forms of government.

There is a warning sign, however. High levels of corruption and inequality result in questioning, not so much the democratic model – because it may be very imperfect, but nowadays they believe in the Churchillian expression that democracy is very bad, except for any other system – but they do question the market model, the model of continuously moving markets with less intervention from the government and with privatisation and which can also lead to further support for populism. Again, this results from the writings of others and does not come from our research, but let me put it up for debate.

Was there a political tsunami?

There has been a lot of quite alarmist talk and writing about the new trend and the political tsunami that has been occurring in Latin America because of recent elections. It is true, there has been an enormous amount of elections in Latin America, 11 out of 18 countries in the past year and a half or so. The first point to make in this analysis is that instead of looking in the typical conventional typology of two ideologies, left and right, I suggest it would be important to unbundle these into three. This comes also from the research of Rosendo Fraga.

There is a populist left as we have seen in recent elections in Ecuador, Nicaragua and Bolivia, in addition to the existent populist left in Cuba. This is a very distinct approach to policy making from that of the social-democratic left-of-centre of Brazil, Chile and Uruguay and to some extent, also Argentina. There is the right-of-centre like Mexico, Colombia and Peru in recent elections, plus many others that existed before.

A much more balanced picture emerges rather than the loud, dominant picture of a few leaders that one happens to see much more in the press. Thus, has there been a political tsunami in regime change? No. In fact, officialdom has won out in all these electoral processes. Basically, there has been a vote for continuity, not a political tsunami: 3 presidents have been re-elected out of these 11, 3 re-instated, 2 parties that were in power have stayed in power, such as Chile. Thus 8 out of 11 elections have shown continuity. That is far from a revolution. This interesting research at the country level shows that the electorate generally has had moderate tendencies. They do not want the extreme left-of-centre or the extreme right-of-centre any longer.

Summing up

We believe that the whole issue of anti-corruption needs to increasingly be seen through the broader lens of good governance. We have to look at the respective roles of governments, of civil society, of us donors taking our own responsibility, including having the legitimacy, transparency and integrity at home first, thus being able to help more effectively. The private sector has a key role to play in this context as well.

Voice, civil liberties and free press are extremely important for anti-corruption. It is very important to focus on areas that have been under-emphasised in the past. Political funding reform is a major area. We have tended to focus too much on traditional and administrative corruption issues but political finance is a major source of misgovernment. It is also a challenge in many industrial OECD countries.

Financial sector reform is also a crucial issue. Financial sector governance is crucial for macro-economic stability. It prevails over every other sector. We have tended to neglect the financial sector in this context.

Also on the positive side, there is this effective dynamic development of equity marks in a country that plays a very important disciplining role in having better governance because the market instantaneously reacts to poor governance. So any country that is interested in having stability in equity markets and good development and wants to attract foreign investors, would watch governance issues much more carefully.

The whole issue of transparency, which I will discuss later, is extremely important, as well as media reform. I will also focus much more on the private sector side of corruption and raising the cost to the bribers, including publicly blacklisting and disclosing firms that are implicated in bribery. We do this in the World Bank. You can go to the website and find 350 plus corporations and individuals that have been de-listed.

For the sake of time, I am not going to list all the very concrete measures that a country can take to improve transparency. It is like a score card, including on the political side the disclosure of assets and incomes of politicians, candidates and public officials and their dependents; political campaign contributions; disclosure of parliamentary votes, but also in the economic and financial arena, the budget, the extractive industry transparency initiative, E-procurement and so on.

I will show you one example to demonstrate the importance of transparency as well as the importance of collaboration between the industrialised world and emerging economies.

equiv. US$ per student

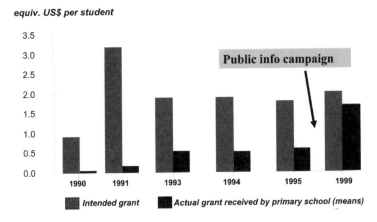

Source: Uganda Public Expenditure Tracking Surveys

This is a particular project – in this case in Uganda, but it must have been replicated in other countries – where the funds have been tracked for education spending. The left and lighter column is the extent to which the central budget allocated and sent funds to the schools at the village level in Uganda every year. The black (right) is the independent survey of how much of it was arriving at the school. Only between 5 and 15% was arriving. Thus, after '95, a major public information campaign was organised, with a lot of transparency, town-hall meetings, with the villages, community and others involved. What happened? Enormous savings and reductions in leakages and disappearances were immediately achieved.

Let me end with a more global trend, illustrating that it is possible to make significant improvements in governance and related areas in a short period of time and there is no need to wait three generations.

The light line in figure 19 are the countries in transition, post-socialists that in the mid- '90s where told by the European Union:

55

Figure 19 Governance has improved in Some Groups: e.g. "Pull Effect" of EU Accession

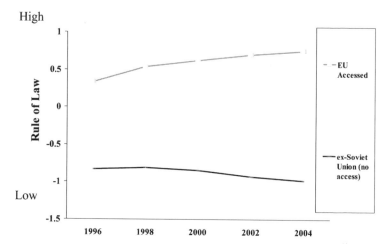

Source for data: www.worldbank.org/wbi/governance/govdata/EU EE Accessed Countries: Czech Republic, Estonia, Hungary, Latvia, Lithuania, Slovak Republic, and Slovenia.

"You have a fighting chance of being part of Europe some day if you do the internal homework on improving institutions, governance, fighting corruption and having the right policies". The black line (below) is the rest of the post-socialist world. I was living in one of them when I was the Chief of Mission in Ukraine and I told them: "Sorry but you do not stand a chance at this point. Let us wait, you may or not may be a part of the second phase".

The pool effect of belonging to a global elite, a political and economic club, is very clear. It is how they won this significantly improvement in governance. This is a very powerful example of how much can be contributed by the serious carrot of belonging to an important global club like the EU.

Note

1   The PowerPoint presentation that was used for Mr Kaufmann's lecture, including graphs, etc., can be found on: www.worldbank.org/wbi/gover-nance

Freedom and Development

William Easterly

W hy is the subject of freedom and democracy so very timely at the stages we are now at in development economics? I think it is because there is a new consensus among development economists. At last, after all these years of research, all these years of disagreements that we had on how to achieve development, we have finally reached consensus. The consensus is that there is no consensus. The consensus is that we do not really know how to achieve development.

To give you some particular examples of some of the lack of knowledge: Brazil and Côte d'Ivoire were success stories in the 1960s and '70s and everyone said: "Just be like Brazil and Côte d'Ivoire!". China and India were definitively not success stories during this period. Now, in the last 25 to 27 years, the situation has been reversed: China and India have been the success stories while Brazil and Côte d'Ivoire have definitively not been so. Côte d'Ivoire in particular is now mired in civil war, conflict and poverty.

When particular solutions that have been advocated as answers to development were tried, they mostly turned out to be insufficient for development. Investment, especially aid-financed investment, was tried and did not achieve development. Then there was education, which was expanded dramatically everywhere and still did not bring development. There was health. There was great progress in the field of health and yet that too did not bring development. And then more recently, there has been more emphasis on privatisation and structural adjustment and the Washington Consensus on how to achieve development. However, that also turned out to be disappointing.

And I could go on. I could talk about population control or about foreign aid. The World Bank makes ever longer and longer lists of the things you need to achieve development. I saw one list that even included something called "wind-up radios without batteries" as a previously overlooked key that was needed to achieve economic development.

Well, after all this disappointment and the great to-and-fro of what are the success stories, development economists now seem to agree that we do not know how to achieve development. The World Bank, in a report in 2005 called "The Lessons of the 1990s" says that there seem to be no lessons. They said: "Different policies can yield different results and the same policies can yield different results depending on country, institutional contexts and underlying growth strategies." What can we thus possibly know if different policies can yield the same results and the same policy different results? We obviously know nothing about which policies to recommend.

Then there was something called the Barcelona development agenda, with which some of you may be familiar and which included a "Who's Who" of the leading academic economists around the world, many of them Nobel laureates. They also concluded that there is no single set of policies that can be guaranteed to ignite sustained growth. Nations that have succeeded have faced different obstacles and have adopted widely varying policies regarding things like regulation, export and industrial promotion, technological innovation and knowledge acquisition.

There was an article by two development economists that I really respect, David Lindauer and Lance Pritchett, who said most honestly that it seems harder then ever to identify the keys to economic growth. For every example there is a counter-example. They said honestly that the current nostrum that one size does not fit all is not such a big idea. This is just a way of expressing the absence of any big ideas on how to achieve development.

What does this have to do with today's topic of democracy and development? Well, what do you do when you do not know what to do? What is the answer if you do not know what the answer is? I think the answer is then: you have freedom and democracy. Because under freedom, individuals are free to figure it out for themselves.

Since the experts do not know how to achieve development, the answer is obviously not to have the experts to come up with a new answer. It is simply to allow the individuals to figure it out for themselves. And what is the system that gives individuals the most freedom to figure it out for themselves? It is the system of democracy.

Here I give you a long quote from someone who predicted this state of affairs a long time ago, the Nobel laureate Friedrich von Hayek, who gave the following very impressive statement on the importance of freedom and development. He called it individualism but I think he meant individual freedom and democracy, which recognises the rights of individuals to express their views freely. Let me read the quote in its entirety, even if it is quite long, I think it is so important because if everyone understood the ideas that were contained in this quote we would be a lot further along in economic development and we would have had a lot happier era than the 20th century turned out to be.

He said: "The interaction of individuals possessing different knowledge and different views is what constitutes the life of thought. The growth of reason is a social process based on the existence of such differences". And here is the critical point where he is saying why it is that we do not know how to achieve development: "It is of essence that the results of this freedom cannot be predicted, that we can not know which views will assist the growth and which will not. In short, that this growth cannot be governed by any views which we now possess, without at the same time limiting it".

This is the idea that all development is innovation. Development is always innovation. If we knew how to achieve development we would already be developed, but we have to invent new answers as we go along. It is freedom and democracy that make possible this process of inventing new answers.

The quote continues: "To plan or organise the growth of mind or for that matter, progress in general, is a contradiction in terms". "Individualism," which again I am taking as a synonym for individual freedom, and democracy, "is thus an attitude of humility before this social process and of tolerance to other opinions and is the exact opposite of that intellectual hubris which is at the root of the demand for comprehensive direction of the social process."

Development economists have too often been guilty of wanting to be put in charge of comprehensive direction of the social process. The IMF and the World Bank bureaucrats wanted to be in charge through structural adjustment and comprehensive direction of the social process. The fashion of today for grand plans to achieve the Millennium Development Goals come from people who want to be put in charge of comprehensive direction of the social process.

But no, that is not what we need. What we need is individual freedom and democracy that has a humility before the social process and a tolerance to many different opinions and is the exact opposite of intellectual hubris that would put people in charge of the social process, according to von Hayek.

What do we mean by freedom? Well, we all know what we mean by freedom. The classical definition of individual freedom is when an individual can do whatever he wants as long as he doesn't hurt anyone else. This is the essence of democracy. Of course, democracy has a more narrow definition: it is the freedom to choose rulers, to dissent in politics and knowledge: innovation happens because there are dissenters who dissent from the prevailing conventional wisdom. Freedom also includes freedom to trade, invest and innovate and implies what we call free markets.

It includes freedom of speech, press, assembly and religion. It includes freedom from foreign control, the self determination of the society. If there is one thing that is a universal, human value around the world that everybody can agree on, it is that people do not like being told what to do by outsiders, by foreigners who do not understand their society.

Violations of democracy, including imperialism, invasion, colonialism, structural adjustment, are things that are the opposite of democracy, these do not mean freedom. All of these different shades of freedom are really one and indivisible. They all reinforce each other. We cannot say: "Well, let us have democracy but no free markets", or: "Let us have free markets but no democracy". Actually, the correlation of political with economic freedom is 0.74, which is very high.

The other thing we can say is that freedom is not in itself something that can be implemented by experts who fly in and say: "This is how to achieve freedom". To say that would even be a contradiction. Freedom has to be home grown. It depends on many social norms and values. It cannot be implemented mechanically, overnight, by just holding elections or decontrolling prices and then you will have a free market and democracy. No, that is not how to achieve freedom. Freedom is something that gradually evolves through many social norms and values.

I am talking about the big picture here, about the forest not the trees. We have had a lot of debates on development for the trees, the individual trees, about the transition paths from the lack of freedom towards democracy. We thus have lot of images, which we spend a great deal of time arguing about. We ask: "Is democracy appropriate for very poor countries? Is democracy appropriate for poor countries that are nevertheless abundant in natural resources? When do you hold elections after you have had a civil war and when you are recovering from a failed state?"

There are people that make very confident recommendations about these matters. What I want to argue is that we have almost no evidence that we can reliably trust. The results that we have seen in the literature on democracy and economic growth, or democracy and recovery from civil war and recovery from state failure, are extremely fragile results.

It is extraordinary that so much confidence is put in them when they are so fragile, because they depend so much on what else is controlled for. There are hundreds of other possible controls that make up these correlations, these regressions that some advice is confidently based on.

I therefore have a great discomfort with statements like the following. These are, and I am picking on one particular author to whom I apologise, my old friend and colleague Paul Collier, who has recently come up with a book called The Bottom Billion, in which he makes some very confident statements about democracy. He said: "Whether democracy contributes to stability depends on the per capita income in a country. A rich society makes democracy a lot safer. In poor countries it has the opposite effect". So democracy is good for the rich but cannot be entrusted to the poor.

He also said: "At income levels below $2500 per capita, democracy appears to increase the risk of civil war." In other words: do not trust those poor people with democracy, they might start fighting each other. If the poor country is rich in natural resources, then it is even worse: then poor people can be trusted even less with democracy. Democracy will actually make matters worse in poor countries that are resource rich.

What is this based on? Well, it is based on these statistical regressions, these cross-country regressions in which you have democracy and holding elections on one side and some civil war variable or some recovery from state failure variable on the other, and then there are about a dozen other possible controls and results that you get, you can get any results you want, depending on the controls you put in. There is also the huge problem of knowing what causes what.

In my view, civil war and democracy are endogenous outcomes of very complex social processes. They might have some statistical association but this does not mean that democracy has some kind of causal or negative effect on the likelihood of civil war or any causal effect whatsoever. We do not know because they are both endogenous. They are both symptoms of poverty. All of these things and any intervention like UN peacekeeping or foreign aid, are also symptoms of poverty.

Thus, as social scientists, what can we conclude from statistical associations with endogenous variables? I do not think we can conclude anything. There is no basis for making these kinds of statements. These statements are made very confidently but they are based on foundations of sand. They do not hold up to scrutiny.

What hold up better are correlations between democracy and per capita income, as demonstrated in the attached graph (see Figure 1).

On the horizontal axis is the famous Kaufmann and Kraay measure of "voice and accountability", which is a measure of democracy,

Figure 1   Democracy and Per Capita Income (correlation=.68)

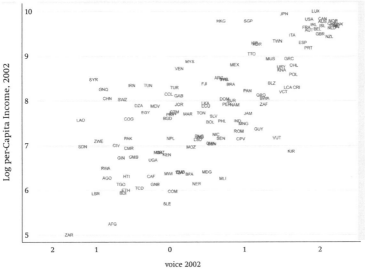

and on the vertical axis is the log of per capita income, both measured in 2002.

The obvious fact that democracy and development show a very robust correlation is a fact that has stood the test of time. This is the forest and we should not lose sight of the forest by trying to run regressions on the individual trees. Of course, this relationship does not fit perfectly.

It is interesting that the variation is a lot larger when you have low democracy. With low democracy you may get a benevolent autocrat who makes development more possible, or you may get a really awful autocrat like Robert Mugabe, who destroys everything. Dictatorship is thus a huge gamble because it all depends on the personality of the dictator, while democracy is consistently much more reliable in attaining a higher level of per capita income.

Of course, I have to admit that I have the same problem I have just mentioned, both of these variables are endogenous, democracy and per capita income. We must therefore formulate strategy to solve this, deciding what causes what. Does per capita income cause democracy or does democracy cause per capita income?

There has been much research within the profession to find good instruments for democracy and other institutions, to demonstrate that this relationship does indeed seem to be causal, that the endogamy problem has to some extent been solved, that people have found exogenous variables that predict democracy. You can then use this as a natural experiment to say: "Under the exogenous conditions in which democracy appears, what is the effect on per capita income?" and the relationship appears to be strong and positive.

I think that the endogamy problem, rampant in the other literature I just mentioned, has been solved. The same goes for economic freedom. What I am trying to argue is that free markets and democracy go together. They both reinforce each other, which is an argument that has been around for a long time. Democracy is more valuable when you have many different centres of power and, under free-market capitalism, there are many different centres of power, because you have many different people who manage to become successful and attain some wealth, which allows them to influence policies. Because it is a free market and there is free entry, new centres of power are continuously created. There is never a concentration of power and this also contributes to the consolidation and stability of democracy and prevents it from being overthrown and dominated by any particular political elite group.

Economic freedom, some measure of free markets, is also strongly associated with per capita income, as demonstrated in the following graph (see Figure 2).

Again we have had some success in resolving the causal direction of this relationship, in which economic freedom can be predicted by some exogenous variables and exogenous variation of economic freedom does seem to generate a higher level of income.

Figure 2   Economic Freedom in the World, 2002, and Log per-Capita Income

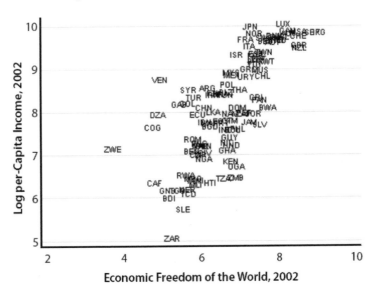

There is another interesting relationship that makes a lot of intuitive sense, which is that democracy is highly correlated with the quality of government service delivery (see Figure 3).

Figure 3   Democracy and Government Service Delivery

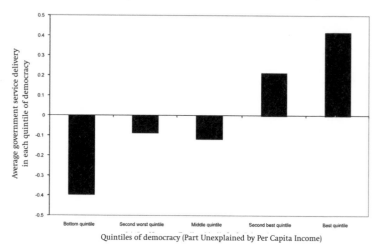

Quintiles of democracy (Part Unexplained by Per Capita Income)

Here, I am arranging countries and the quintiles of democracy. To the bottom quintile of democracy belong the most authoritarian, the most dictatorial countries. in the top quintile are the most democratic countries. On the vertical axis I have an index of the quality of government service delivery, which is again from the Kaufmann and Kraay data base.

You may say that of course they are correlated because they are both correlated to per capita income, but this shows you the residuals: the part of democracy that is unexplained by per capita income. This thus removes the spurious correlation because both are correlated to per capita income. Even when controlling for per capita income, we find the strongest association between democracy and government service delivery.

These are all examples of why having democracy is important. Both the theory and the evidence say: what you should do if you do not know what to do is have more freedom and democracy, to allow people to figure it out for themselves. This makes a lot of sense theoretically and then empirically, we indeed find that the big picture is that democracy is associated with prosperity. Democracy is associated with achieving economic development.

Democracy also means freedom from foreign control: it is no good having democracy if you are under the occupation of a foreign army. Iraq is occupied by a foreign army; that is not democracy. Colonialism is not democracy. There is a lot of debate about the economic impacts of colonialism. Let me throw out for you another stylised fact, which is that there was virtually no economic growth under colonialism and since independence, developing countries have had much higher levels of growth.

Another form of foreign control is foreign aid that comes with lots of conditions, which is called structural adjustment. Economic growth under structural adjustment has been very poor. Most successful examples of growth are not countries that had heavy interference by foreigners, but countries that achieved their own home-grown path to development. Not all of them were democracies by any means but they were free from foreign interference and of any form of structural adjustment. They just followed their own path to development like China, India, Vietnam, Turkey, Chile, Singapore, Taiwan, South Korea, Mauritius and Botswana. The list is endless. These are countries that seem to have figured it out for themselves. They figured out their unique path to accommodate dynamic individuals. They were not told what to do by international organisations or by invading armies.

Some of these are very far from being democracies at the moment but all have made some movement in the direction of greater freedom for individuals. They have moved away from a totalitarian state to a state that is less totalitarian. They moved away from state planning and state socialism towards free markets and individual freedom.

Economic growth is associated with change. Economic growth is therefore quite well explained by the change in freedom. Societies that move towards more individual freedom have shown rapid economic growth and this seems to be characteristic for all these societies.

The opposite side of this is when the donors are in charge and are telling you what to do. I have read this horrifying document, called the Ghana Joint Assistance Strategy. The official donors said to Ghana, which happened to be celebrating the 50th anniversary of its independence from Great Britain, that it was totally up to the government what they did and then gave them about 100 pages of advice. "Partners advised the need for the investment plan to be fully consistent with macro-economic stability, debt sustainability and principles for public finance management". "Partners were committed to an overview of the investment plan and then will approve it..."

You see: you can devise your own investment plan but then we will approve it! There are also all kinds of specific recommendations. Somehow, the donors knew better then the Ghanaians what was the best path forward. It had something to do with public-private partnerships and transportation, energy and ICT, flexible markets, etc. All of this violated freedom from control. This is not democracy.

It is also time for far more caution with military intervention. Operation Iraqi Freedom has not accomplished much freedom for Iraq. There is much literature on Cold War regime change that has propped up corrupt dictators and worsened democracy in the long run, regardless of whether they were Soviet or American interventions. Nowadays, people say the situation is different from the time of the Cold War. The great powers no longer have geo-political interests. They are now acting purely out of humanitarian concerns when they send military forces into other countries.

How many people believe that? I am not convinced that military intervention is there to achieve development or is motivated by humanitarian concerns. That could be a good thing if there were

68

some kind of neutral humanitarian military force, but there is no such force available to fix failed states or that can provide economic development.

In conclusion: it is all about freedom. Nobody is too poor to be free. Let us stop the patronising attitude, which is also not supported by theory or empirical evidence, that some people are too poor to be trusted with democracy. I think everyone deserves democracy. Everyone deserves the indivisible bundle of freedom that combines democracy with individual rights and human rights, individual freedoms and free markets and is empirically associated with prosperity in the long run.

There are complicated issues about the transition from here to there. Frankly, the state of knowledge in this area is that we do not have this knowledge. Our knowledge is not great enough to make prescriptions and recommendations about transition paths. But this lack of knowledge is another argument for freedom. When the experts are in doubt and are fighting with each other and cannot agree, then just let the ordinary people, the free market entrepreneurs, the democratic activists, the intellectual dissenters, the political activists, let them figure it out for themselves. Development will come, to echo the lofty words of Martin Luther King, when poor people are "free at last, free at last, thank God Almighty, free at last".

Reference

William Easterly, *The White Man's Burden, Why the West's Efforts to Aid the Rest Have Done so Much Ill and so Little Good*, Oxford University Press, New York, 2006.

Part II

Democracy versus stability

Democracy, Nation Building and Development

Bernard Berendsen and Cor van Beuningen[1]

In January 2004 the Dutch monthly *Internationale Spectator* published a number of articles on democracy and development, providing comments on the publication of "The Future of Freedom. Illiberal Democracy at Home and Abroad" by Fareed Zakaria[2]. Zakaria distinguishes between true democracies in which the rule of law is respected and individual constitutional rights are guaranteed on the one hand and illiberal democracies where formal democratic institutions are present but only serve as a façade, as summarised by Andre Gerrits in his contribution.[3]

The relationship between democracy, nation building and development was also the central issue in the series of lectures organised by the Society for International Development in the autumn of 2006 and the first half of 2007.[4] In this context, the question came up as to whether external interference and the promotion of democracy are at all reconcilable. One may very well say that development assistance in its conventional form would rather undermine than actually promote democracy. Because such assistance is often provided under conditions that are not legitimised by, for example, making them subject to discussion and decision making in a national body like a parliament, as was pointed out by Ineke van Kessel in her contribution about the future of democracy in Africa.[5]

Democracy is generally recognised as the form of government that is best able to facilitate decision making and resolve internal conflicts in a peaceful way, as well as to provide the conditions for social and economic development and the reduction of poverty. Similarly, the human rights of citizens can best be realised through the development of democratic institutions, procedures and values.

The advancement of democracy is thus considered to be not only an essential goal in its own right, but is also linked to peace building, the consolidation of human rights and to growth and development.

Development co-operation and the promotion of democracy; delicate questions

The promotion of democracy within the broader framework of international co-operation has become a heavily disputed subject both in academic and policy-making circles. Many complicated issues have been raised and not a few of them seem to point to devilish policy dilemmas that cause uneasiness amongst politicians and policy makers in the field of international relations.

Some of the questions involved already have a history, like those related to what comes first, democracy or development? Is democracy a precondition for economic growth and social development; or will democracy only be viable and sustainable when a certain level of development has been attained? Should societies be made fit for democracy, or do they become fit through democracy? Is economic development sustainable without political development? – and *vice versa*?

Then there is the dilemma of democracy versus stability. Do they go together or do stability, law and order, rule of law and security really come first? Is there a case for the need of a dictatorial-development state in certain stages of economic growth – because necessary but unpopular changes will not be produced via elected governments? And is democracy sustainable in societies characterised by huge income disparities?

There is the fundamental question of whether democracy promotion from outside is possible; is it legitimate and can it work? How to avoid its counterproductive effects, which are heavily looming, to the extent that the cure (aid for democracy) might become the poison?

On an even more practical note, there is the structure – culture debate. There is a broad recognition of the fact that outside assistance on hardware and institutional make up will not produce sustainable outcomes without effective change in the political culture; but can culture really be changed through outside intervention?

If democracy promotion is to be seen as essential, how should it then relate to existing development co-operation practice? Is it just another sector, next to education or drinking water; or does it require a new approach, a new professionalism?

Should democracy promotion be mainstreamed in the whole of development co-operation? As any outside intervention produces effects on the parameters for political development, mainstreaming seems desirable or even unavoidable, first in order to avoid negative or even destructive effects, secondly to steer and optimise the positive effects of the whole of development co-operation on democratic-political development. Does this imply a new concept – and another institutional set-up – for development co-operation?

Such questions are posed in a global context dominated by September 11, international insecurity, the crises of Muslim societies and the US-led war on terrorism, including the US-led regime change approach to promoting democracy in the Middle East; i.e., a context in which the meaning of democracy promotion will have as many connotations as there are perspectives on the current state of international affairs.

In what follows, a few of the concepts involved will be clarified and some background information will be given on the issues raised above. We will also turn to what we call the soft side of democracy and conclude that the soft power approach to democracy promotion might be preferable to the imposing way, where democracy promotion has become an integral part of US foreign policy and as such associated with the war on terrorism.

What is democracy?

In contemporary usage, the term "democracy" refers to a government chosen by the people.

Thus, in a democratic regime the citizens in charge of government are selected by electoral competition, and while in power they are disciplined through various checks and balances. In fact, elections serve as such control mechanisms, through the prospect that those in power may not be re-elected. Checks and balances are also involved in formal mechanisms like referenda and plebiscites; in the classical separation of powers in the *trias politica*, e.g., by enabling parliamentary control and independent court action; in relatively autonomous agencies like the central bank, or the ombudsman; in informal and adversarial mechanisms like extra-parliamentary pressure groups, civil society organisations and, especially, the mass media (press freedom). The principles of legality and legitimacy urge democratic governments to respect the rule of law and democratic principles, be responsive to the voice of citizens and to foster human rights.

At the same time, a democratic government has to govern, i.e., exercise authority, and to perform the essential state functions, which are:
- to provide external and internal security, maintain law and order and provide safety and stability (to which end it holds the monopoly of force);
- to facilitate social interaction and to regulate financial, economic and commercial interaction;
- to give directionality to societal development and to allocate values;
- to supply basic public services.

Here, the focus is on the effectiveness of governance: to what extent does the democratic government fulfil its tasks, while making the most effective use of scarce resources?

Legitimacy and effectiveness; governance and governability

In short, democracy is a particular mode of organising the power question in society, involving, on the one hand, mechanisms to install authority and exercise power, and on the other hand, mechanisms to control, limit and disperse power through checks and balances. Democratic governance is to be judged by its effectiveness, i.e., by the effective use of authority and other scarce resources (acting responsibly), as well as by its legitimacy in terms of respect for democratic principles (being responsive).

Of course, both sides are intricately intertwined. A particular government will most probably enhance its legitimacy (in the eyes of the population; i.e., legitimacy understood as societal approval) when it performs its functions in a more effective way. Inversely, a government that is lacking legitimacy will find it increasingly difficult to govern without reverting to coercive and oppressive means, and then risks getting involved in a downward-spiralling process – losing control and legitimacy at the same time.

The popular notion of (good) governance comprises both of these quality dimensions, legitimacy and effectiveness, while addressing the government. Inversely, the notion of governability addresses the society to be governed as well.

In order to be able to govern in any effective way, a government needs the acceptance of its authority and the recognition by at least a broad majority of the population, of its right to monopolise the use of force, to enforce its laws and to allocate values – if it is not to revert to large-scale coercion and thus lose its legitimacy. Furthermore, a democratic government needs to be able to count on citizens that are able and willing to respect democratic principles, to exercise their democratic rights and to fulfil the corresponding (republican) duties.

Thus, with the notion of governability the focus shifts from the government as such (and its governance qualities) to the dynamics between government and the citizens that make up the society to be governed.

Democratic politics

Free elections are essential but not sufficient for the make up and well-functioning of democracy. In order to avoid perversion, respect for human rights – especially for minorities – and for the rule of law is indispensable, as are effective institutions and checks and balances. In democratic politics, different proposals for the directionality to be given to the development of society (through the authoritative allocation of values) compete for electoral support. This presupposes both voice and choice, i.e., an electorate composed of citizens; a number of different proposals for public or collective action, embodied by competing political parties (multi-party democracy) and free elections. Ideally then, democratic politics involves a number of political parties with different proposals for development, competing for the electoral support of engaged citizens.

However, it will be clear to anyone slightly familiar with reality in developing countries that the factual functioning of politics here does not comply with this ideal description. This is also true for most democracies (and even, for that matter, for most democracies in the first world).

What can be observed in reality, is – for example – that political entrepreneurs compete for electoral support, not in order to obtain access to state power and to serve development and the common good, but aiming to obtain access to the loot constituted by public resources, in order to administer them as their own patrimony and distribute them amongst themselves and their clienteles (state capture, patronage and clientelism, corruption).

And inversely, the electorate is constituted not by engaged citizens that choose the best proposal for the development of society, but by persons that act as clients looking for compensation by their patrons through the redistribution of the public loot.

In fact, what is involved here is a perversion of the logic of democratic politics; a perversion which to a greater or lesser extent is observable in many if not most of the developing countries (and elsewhere).

Democracy and the (Nation-)State

Over a period of at least two centuries, the principles of human rights, the rule of law and democracy have firmly embedded themselves in Western nation-states and their political-legal consciousness. The uncontested position of these principles in the West is matched by their universal appeal and their dissemination throughout the world.

Two more recent developments stand out, however.

Firstly, the past decades have witnessed a transformation and erosion of the role of the state in the creation and development of policy and law. Both internal (see below) and external factors, such as globalisation and internationalisation, are to be held responsible for this. The state is in danger of losing its quality as the focal point of public decision making. To the same extent, the principles of human rights, democracy and the rule of law are in danger of losing their traditional centre. They are developed and defined in relation to national and sovereign states; their relevance, implementation and operation are dependent upon mechanisms (such as the separately functioning powers of the *trias politica*) that are associated with a particular constitutional design within the framework of a state. Without a relevant sovereign state, the future of democracy seems to be unclear.

Secondly, the connection of democracy and state with nation is becoming more and more troublesome. Remember that democracy is a form of government; state a geopolitical entity; and that nation refers to a cultural and eventually also ethnic community. Historically, in Western Europe the three coincided geographically and they evolved simultaneously – strengthening each other. Accordingly, the nation-state and nation building have long been on the agenda of the new states after decolonisation.

Actually however, phenomena related to culture (including religion and language) and ethnicity, seem to have mostly divisive effects in the context of state and politics. Paradoxically, democratic procedures are even instrumentalised by politicians who expressly promote and capitalise on religious or ethnic conflict and hatred, thus rendering society unviable and undermining the idea and purpose of democracy as such (cf. Zakaria's illiberal democracy).[6] Ethnic and religious strife are at the heart of many of the armed conflicts and civil wars in the past years, and more generally, issues related to uniformity and diversity with regard to identity will surely continue to affect the viability of democracy and the State for a long time to come.

Identity matters

Historically, the double project of a unified state and democracy is connected to the coming about of a collective identity in nation-terms; people sharing a common national founding myth, language, religion and *ethnos* (blood, land and history).[7]

If such a "thick" national community nowadays is an unfeasible (or even undesirable) project in many cases, still it is hard to see how a society composed of multiple communities (kinship, ethnic, religious...) might constitute a viable state and democracy without a substantial part of the population sharing a sense of loyalty or collective identity – albeit in the form of an imagined political community. What is required then, is that at the level of the personal, subjective identity, people are prepared (able and willing) to identify and commit themselves as members of a political community, as citizens of the *republica*, together with all the other citizens; and to act accordingly, i.e., 1. to perceive a collective interest or common good; 2. to match the individual interest with collective interest, and 3. to comply with established democratic principles, procedures and outcomes.

The soft side of democracy

In the words of Robert Putnam: it is civic engagement, trust and social capital that make democracy work.[8] The viability of the democratic and constitutional state depends on the extent to which citizens are prepared and willing to co-operate, both amongst themselves and with their government. If the state does not want to revert to large-scale coercion, it is required that the great majority of the population more or less voluntarily complies with the most important rules, which again presupposes their civic engagement, horizontal and vertical trust, a set of shared values and a sense of a common fate.

In fact, democracy is about moral attitudes and the moral or ethical capacities of the people, of the individual persons both in society and in the government; about their willingness and ability to transcend the immediate me/here/now and to care for others, the environment and the future.

How do these moral attitudes come about? This question has been raised in Western philosophy since the days of Socrates. Socrates defended the thesis that with regard to good and evil, the individual person – in the end – has the final say. Morality cannot be enforced; it can only be guided or supported. Moral attitudes cannot be organised; a sense of shared responsibility cannot be imposed; trust cannot be enforced. Moral insights can only be found through reflection and consent of the person involved. What makes for the vitality of a society and for the viability of democracy cannot be produced on purpose. If moral attitudes are to come about, they come about only as a by-product of social interaction.

Government is meant to serve and facilitate this interaction and the coming about of these moral attitudes – on which it depends for its own functioning, as well as the sustainability of society as a whole. But government can also and easily frustrate the coming about of moral attitudes and propel a downward-spiralling movement. Too much and wrongly directed government intervention may frustrate meaningful social interaction, substitute social ordering mechanisms and the coming about of moral attitudes.

Culture, democracy and development

In fact, these same soft attributes – moral attitudes; civic engagement, trust and social capital – might not only be necessary preconditions for making democracy work, but for economic progress as well. Illustratively, Fukuyama distinguished stagnant low trust economies from successful high trust economies.[9] Though the evidence he presented was not completely convincing, the relationship between trust and social capital on the one hand, and economic development (and democracy) on the other, has since then been the object of a great deal of research, and seems to be corroborated by the work of, e.g., D. Landes and L. Harrison.[10]

At the aggregate level, values, beliefs and attitudes are the defining components that make up for a society's culture. The above, then, suggests that some societies, characterised by determinate cultural patterns (sets of generalised values, beliefs and attitudes), are more prone to make political and socio-economic progress than others. That is exactly what L. Harrison is trying to demonstrate in *The Central Liberal Truth*: some cultural values and attitudes propel democracy and development, while other sets of values and attitudes retard or resist them.

Though one can have doubts regarding the simplicity of the causality chain that is presupposed in his reasoning, Harrison's case for a relationship (in the sense of co-variance) of determinate cultural values and moral attitudes with economic and political progress seems to be rather strong.[11]

Democracy promotion in the present global context

The advancement of democracy is a relatively new goal in development co-operation, if it is understood in its strict sense, i.e., political development. Democracy promotion should clearly be distinguished from the field of strengthening the public administration system, the latter having a much longer history in development co-operation (cf. institutional engineering). Much of what presently is labelled democracy promotion in the context of good governance programmes still is, in fact, of a rather technical nature: electoral assistance, expert and material support to relevant institutions such as the parliament or the electoral court.

Democracy promotion in its strict sense is, of course, a quite sensitive matter.

82

Non-democratic governments might feel that pro-democracy activities in their countries undermine their hold on power, and the fact that these activities are sponsored by external agents may provide them with sufficient argumentation for repressive measures, adducing threats to national sovereignty and stability.

On the other hand, it should be noted that pro-democracy activists and their Western sponsors might not in all cases have managed to clearly separate this goal from more immediate and profane partisan objectives; thus providing substance to the autocrats' claim of illegitimate political meddling. The case against democracy promotion has, however, received its strong momentum by the way the present US Government applies the concept in its foreign policy and especially in the war against terrorism. Many observers, democratic and non-democratic alike, feel uneasy about the motives behind the hard power used by the US to promote freedom and democracy abroad, and this has greatly fuelled the present backlash against democracy promotion as such (Carothers).[12]

The generalised scepticism on external democracy promotion might also explain why the EU behaves so cautiously in this field. The former Minister for Development Co-operation of the Netherlands, Mrs A. van Ardenne, noted this in her contribution to the SID lecture series.[13]

She stated that the democratic shortcomings of internal EU governance is also reflected in the weak external positioning of the EU *vis-à-vis* third countries on issues of democracy. As a consequence, the EU finds it hard to respond properly to the hard power approach to democracy promotion of the US. This contrasts strikingly with the way the Copenhagen Principles are applied to its new member states.

While many observers, especially from the South, would like to see the EU actively apply its alternative soft power approach in democracy promotion, the EU refrains from doing so and limits itself to mostly techno-institutional good governance interventions and electoral support. The EU should come forward with a clear vision on why and how it wants to promote democracy outside the

EU, while it has apparently no doubt on the importance of democracy within its borders, given the attention the subject gets in the negotiations with aspiring new member states.[14]

The soft power approach applied

The relevance of the soft power approach can be demonstrated with help of a number of examples given in the *Internationale Spectator* referred to above. To start with, one should recognise the paradox that is implied in any initiative aiming to promote political change processes through external intervention in other societies. This paradox is most clearly present in political co-operation aiming at the promotion of democracy. Co-operation intends to introduce changes in the political culture, changes at the intersection of government and political systems, concerning civic engagement, trust and social capital, culture and ethics: sets of generalised values, beliefs and attitudes.

The recognition of this paradox and of the wide range and unavoidable complexity of the task of democracy promotion should not discourage but, on the contrary, stimulate the policy makers to observe more clearly and be more creative. First of all, one should begin to recognise what is already available; signal initiatives that are already undertaken and processes that are ongoing and one can build on.

Secondly, one should look for possibilities to organise programmes in areas that seem to be dealing with completely different subjects such as drinking water and education, in such a way that they have optimal effects on civic engagement, trust and social capital, on the promotion of civil society organisations and the co-operation between them and the government.

In the Arab World one should look for possibilities for engagement with movements within Islam aiming at modernity and for initiatives in the academic world and civil society; priority should be given to education, from alphabetisation programmes to higher education, and to the development of an economic middle class and initiatives of women's organisations.

In Eastern Europe and in the newly created states of the former Soviet Union, the soft approach of democracy promotion should try to link up to mechanisms and traditions that find their origin in forms of pre-communist democracy, sometimes also religious traditions, and should support the development of a strong civil society through programmes promoting faith based education and private-sector initiatives on a non-commercial basis in social areas such as the health care of physically and mentally handicapped people.

In Africa one is inclined to look for connexions with existing communal groups; but it is equally worthwhile to engage in initiatives that try to promote a new public domain and a political system that is not related to tribal organisations. Furthermore, all programmes in the area of poverty alleviation should be reoriented and redesigned to include the objectives of civic engagement and civil society development. One should recognise that extreme income inequality undermines the feasibility of sustainable development; this in itself implies the recognition of a certain trade-off between economic liberalism on the one hand and democratic political development on the other.

In Indonesia the soft power approach would imply linking up to initiatives that came up as a result of the political changes in the late nineties (*reformasi*), including free elections, constitutional reform, the fight against corruption, etc., by strengthening the independence of the judiciary and the introduction of checks and balances at the local level, in a way that makes the decentralisation process contribute to putting an end to traditional centralism in Indonesian society.

In Latin America finally, the soft power approach would mean linking up to the new social and political movements, beyond the old politics of exploitation. One should make sure that priority is given to legitimising democracy by making sure that it results in achievements that are socially acceptable and not only benefit the elite.

Notes

1   The original version of this article was written by one of the authors as a general introduction to the lecture series on democracy and development, organised by the Society for International Development in 2006/2007 (Internationale Spectator, Jaargang 58, nr. 1, January 2004, pp. 2-38: articles by Tromp, B., Berger, M., Gerrits, A., Kessel, I. van, Buve, R., Schulte Nordholt, N. and Zeeuw, J. de.). This first version was revised and published in the Dutch monthly on international affairs Internationale Spectator in February 2007 (van Beuningen, C. and Berendsen, B.: Democracy, Nation Building and Development, in Internationale Spectator, Jaargang 61, nr. 2, February 2007).
     The present version contains elements of both, including a general introduction to the theme "democracy and development", but also focusing on what it considers to be the best approach to democracy promotion. It also illustrates this so-called soft approach by a number of concrete examples.

2   Zakaria, F.: The Future of Freedom. Illiberal Democracy at Home and Abroad. 2003, W.W. Norton & Company.

3   Gerrits, A.: Between Democracy and Dictatorship in the former Soviet Union. In: Internationale Spectator, Jaargang 58, nr. 1, January 2004.

4   See www.sid.nl for the programme of the lecture series.

5   Kessel, I. van: The Future of Democracy in Africa. In: Internationale Spectator, Jaargang 58, nr. 1, January 2004.

6   Zakaria, F.: o.c.

7   Böckenförde, E.-W.: Zum Begriff der Verfassung. Die Ordnung des Politischen. 1994, Ulrich Klaus Presse.

8   Putnam, R.: Making Democracy Work. Civic Traditions in Modern Italy. 1993, Princeton University Press.

9   Fukuyama, F.: Trust. The Social Virtues and the Creation of Prosperity. 1995, Penguin.

10   Landes, D.: The Wealth and Poverty of Nations: Why Some Are So Rich and Some So Poor. 1999, W.W. Norton & Company.

11   Harrison, L.: The Central Liberal Truth: How Politics Can Change a Culture and Save It from Itself. 2006, Oxford University Press, USA.

12   Carothers, T.: The Backlash against Democracy. In: Foreign Affairs, March/April 2006.

13   Ardennne, A van: Development Starts at the Ballot Box, first SID Lecture, October 2006, see this volume.

14   Gerrits, A.: Is There a Distinct European Democratic Model to Promote? In: Doorn, M. van, and Meijenfeldt, R. van (eds.): Democracy. Europe's Core Value? Eburon Delft, 2007.

Fragile States

Paul Collier

B y the 1990s it had become clear that something had gone wrong with the African development process over and above Africa being a victim. Something was going wrong internally in Africa, which stagnated the development process. The obvious diagnosis by around 1990 was to say: "It is dictatorship. It is these awful autocracies that are more prominent in Africa than anywhere else. If only we could get rid of them and bring in democracy, things will be alright".

Most of these dictatorships, not all of them, were got rid of through the wave of democratisation that spread in Africa and other low-income, fragile states following the collapse of the former Soviet Union. That was a pretty hopeful period and I was part of it hoping that now that we have democracy, this will basically fix the problems. They were not foolish hopes, but they were not right. I am going to look at two sets of questions: does democracy resolve the problem of violent conflict in Africa? Does it resolve the problem of economic stagnation?

Democracy and Violent Conflict

It is quite clear why we thought that democracy would reduce the incidence of violent conflict. At least two things would make democracy peace-promoting in these societies. One is that it would end exclusion and the other is that it would confer legitimacy on governments. Both of these things, one would imagine, would have a stabilising effect and reduce the incentive for violence. Is that what actually happens? To answer this question, I will draw on *Beyond Greed and Grievance*, an unpublished paper which extend the work in *Greed and Grievance*, and on my latest book *The Bottom Billion*, While *Greed and Grievance* looks globally at all the large-scale violent conflicts and civil wars from the mid 1960s to 2000, *Beyond Greed and Grievance* updates this work with data on the 5 most recent years, up to 2005, but, more importantly, it doubles the data set of observed civil wars and it massively increases the number of possible explanations that can be measured. Finally, *The Bottom Billion* brings all this research together in order to provide concrete solutions.

The following approach in trying to understand civil wars is statistical. Potentially anything could be the underlying cause of civil war, thus whatever one can measure should be taken into account until one is left only with a core of significant variables.

What comes up first of all are the same economic drivers of conflict found previously. That is, the propensity to conflict is much more likely if your country is low income, if you have stagnation or, worse, economic decline, and if you are dependent on primary commodities. The cocktail of all three – poverty, stagnation and primary commodities – is a dangerous combination, increasing the risk of conflict.

A number of variables have been found to proxy the feasibility of conflict. For example, terrain: is it as flat as the Netherlands? Or as mountainous as Nepal? It is now possible to say categorically that the reason why the Netherlands has not had a civil war for a long time – besides the fact that it a high-income country – is that it is flat. On the other hand, one of the reasons why Nepal has conflicts is that it is not flat. The risk of conflict goes up considerably if the terrain is conducive to rebel armed groups.

This sort of causal explanation, things like mountainous terrain, does not fit very naturally into an explanation based on motivation. Yet, according to my research, motivation does not provide a great deal of explanatory power. Of course, there are always stories about what motivates the rebels and in one sense that accounts for what they have done, but it does not account for why it is possible for large-scale organised violence to occur in some societies, whereas in other societies it is just not feasible, no matter what people's motivation is.

Where does democracy fit into all this? How do we measure democracy? Political scientists have a scale to measure democracy. From extreme autocracy – North Korea – to all-singing, all-dancing democracy – the Netherlands. Is there anywhere on that spectrum that makes a difference to the risk of civil war? The answer is: it depends. Unfortunately, it depends upon the interaction with the level of per capita income.

In rich societies democracy makes things much safer. In poor societies it has the opposite effect. What do I mean by rich and poor? There is a level of income at which democracy makes no difference and that is about 2,500 dollars per capita per annum. Above that level, democracy makes things significantly safer and below it, significantly more dangerous. All the countries that my research focuses on, the Africas of this world, which include not just Africa but central Asia as well, are impoverished countries with way below 2,500 dollars per capita income. Unfortunately, therefore, they are all in a range where democracy appears to increase the risk of civil war.

Yet, one needs to be more precise because half of all civil wars occur in post-conflict situations gone wrong. Post-conflict situations are very fragile: 40% of post-conflict situations revert to civil war within a decade. Looking at all the available post-conflict situations, 66 of them, at the risk of reverting to conflict during the first decade, I assessed what role democracy played in this. Using a 21-point scale between the extreme autocracy of North Korea and the Netherlands, I look for the existence of a cut-off point anywhere along the spectrum where there is change. There is a point about mid-way along the autocracy part of the spectrum where the risks on one side look different from the risks on the other side.

The results are as follows: the risks of going back into conflict are lower in the severe autocracy part. Outside the range of severe autocracy, the risks are pretty high along the whole remaining spectrum. The risks overall for these countries are 40%, but if one rules out the range of severe autocracy, the risks are around 70%.

The democracy agenda we naturally and rightly promote in these post-conflict situations – and that I do not wish to oppose – cannot be sold as peace building, unfortunately. The fear is that we have to face up to the fact that we are actually building extremely fragile situations by insisting on democracy. The message is not "do not promote democracy" but "recognise that it is not the solution to those highly fragile post-conflict situations". We had better do something else to restore peace.

As well as insisting on democracy and democratic constitutions and suchlike, we are also, as an international community, very clear about how we implement democratic legitimacy and that is: by post-conflict elections. Thus, my research studies what post-conflict elections do to the risk of reversion to conflict.

There are two schools of thought on this in political science: one thinks that post-conflict elections bring the risks down, the other thinks that post-conflict elections increase risks. While they cannot both be right, they can both be wrong, and, according to my research, they are. The reason is that post-conflict elections shift the risk from the year before the election until the year following the election. In the year before the election the risks go down a lot and in the year after the election they go up even more.

As soon as we start to think why this might be the case, it becomes blindingly obvious. In the year before the elections there are incentives to take part in the electoral contest – you might win. So all the different players struggle politically and then, after the election, there is a winner and a loser.

There are two groups that see the election as legitimate – one is us, the international community (we are the people who thought this was a good idea in the first place, it makes the government legitimate). The other people who think it is legitimate are those who win. What they tend to say after they have won is, "we have won and we can do whatever we want – and we will."

What about the losers? They tend to say, "you cheated and we are worried because we see that this government can do whatever it likes and we see our friends, the international community, getting on planes and flying away. So we will defend ourselves in the one way we know that works." That is why they tend to get into another conflict after an election.

Now, we are the friends, we are the peace keepers in this and what do we tend to do? Unfortunately, we use this post-conflict election as the milestone for withdrawal. For instance, let us look at the Democratic Republic of Congo. Here, we had a big peace-keeping force and we insisted on democracy and also insisted on an election. The date of the second round of the elections was October the 29th last year and the date for withdrawal was October the 30th. Late in the day we discovered that we had to send out more troops instead of flying them all home. That approach does not work. If we are going to have democracy and we have to have elections, then we need to keep our international peace-keeping forces there for a long time.

In my analysis there is a package that to some extent works. I think of it as "politics plus". My research, which makes use for the first time of United Nations data on its peace-keeping missions, shows that international peace-keeping forces are effective in bringing the risks down. However, the risks in the post-conflict period do not fall very rapidly, they fall decade by decade. Time does heal but it is a very slow process. Within that first post-conflict decade there is no statistically significant reduction in risk over time. We therefore need these peace-keeping troops for at least a decade.

On the other hand, the exit strategy is not political design, it is economic development. Economic growth significantly and substantially brings post-conflict risks down, both in the year in which the growth occurs and cumulatively, because it is raising income. The higher the level of income, the safer the society.

The problem with economic growth is that it takes a long time. It is going to take a decade before growth at 10% accumulates to something that is significant enough to bring risks down in low-income countries. This is a complementary package: the economic development needs the external peace keeping and the external peace keeping needs the economic development. Peace keeping needs economic development because without it there is no credible exit strategy. But economic development needs the peace keepers because without them, the risk of going back to conflict is so high that you will not receive any investments and if you do not obtain any investments you will not achieve economic recovery. External peace keeping and economic development are thus complementary.

Regarding the achievement of economic development, this is a mixture of what we can do and what governments can do. What we can do is provide large aid packages post-conflict. They do work but they need to be sustained for much longer than in the past. They need to be sustained through that decade, not just for the first couple of years, which is technically what we have been doing. Also, there needs to be very vigorous economic reform because post-conflict countries come out of conflict with terrible economic policies.

There is a very simple reason for this: during a civil war governments simply grasp at whatever resources they can find, with very short-term economic policies, in order to win that war. So the inherited economic policies are terrible and need to be reformed quickly, otherwise it is impossible to sustain rapid growth. For example, Mozambique managed to sustain 10% growth a year for a decade. However, typically, everyone is so focused on political design in the first years, that economic policies go on the back burner.

Democracy and economic development

Let me turn now to the democracy and economic development story. Suppose that we are managing to keep the peace, is democracy going to be helpful in promoting economic development? Firstly, does democracy help the process of policy reform from initially very poor policies and governance? There are windows of opportunity for policy and political reform. Yet, all of these reform policies have to happen within the country: they cannot be externally imposed by donors, as with policy conditionality for 20 years, which has been simply a failure.

In all these societies with very poor policies on governance there are reformers and, periodically, these reformers come to power. Elites become weakened because the economies collapsed catastrophically, and so even corrupt elites become desperate and are willing to support some reform. But does democracy itself speed up that process? Unfortunately, this is not the case. In fact, elections during these incipient processes of reform actually chill the reform process, they slow it down.

There is one simple reason for this, which is very low-income and very low-education environments. Elections tend to be overtaken by populist agendas. Populism is going to technically win out over more sophisticated strategies in environments with very low income and very low levels of education.

Most of these societies do not have an informed media and do not have educated citizens. They do not even have very educated elites because from the 1990s onwards, the donor agenda on education has been focused on primary education and has neglected tertiary education. Hence the tertiary education systems in these countries, universities, are falling apart. Educated elites have actually withered in these societies, there are many fewer than they were. And yet a critical mass of well-educated people is necessary for the society to undertake serious reform. It cannot be done externally but has to be done through internal debate, criticising what is going wrong in the society.

For example, China and India have had policies that were as bad as anything you could find in Africa. The difference is that India and China were able to turn themselves around much faster than Africa. The difference here is scale. India and China have large, educated societies. If there are enough educated people one can sustain an informed media, one can have, for example a financially literate press. A newspaper that has a large circulation.

In Africa, other than South Africa, you will not find any financially literate press. When I was in Angola, there was not a single newspaper, never mind a financially literate one. If you go to the Central African Republic, you can put all the people who know how to read a financial newspaper under one roof. There is just no market for such a newspaper in these societies since these societies are tiny. In that context, democracy is very prone to a populist agenda.

Resource-rich low income countries

What has been said above may not apply to resource-rich low-income countries. Resource-rich countries are at the moment becoming more important among the low-income societies. Two related processes have jacked up resource revenues: one is very high prices, the other is the US and Chinese agenda of diversifying away from the Middle East into Africa and Central Asia for additional supplies of natural resources. Due to both new discoveries and higher prices, a lot of these societies are now becoming resource rich: low-income, small, low-education, but big resource rents flowing into the government.

Historically, they have used those resource rents very badly. If we go back to the last big wave of resource rents in the 1970s, there were missed opportunities. Looking statistically at the effect of all the resource rents on growth over the last 45 years, one can identify a global pattern. If prices go up for oil exports, for the first five years growth goes up, but 20 years later, the society is poorer than it was before prices went up. If the historical pattern over the last 45 years continues, simulations for the effects of the present resource booms show that Africa's growth will be 10% up, but after 25 years it will be 25% down. It is therefore vital that we do not repeat history.

The question is therefore will democracy be the change that enables us not to repeat history? In the 1970s Africa was not democratic, now it is much so; is that going to make things better? Unfortunately, there is evidence globally that democracy, uniquely in resource-rich countries, makes things worse. The global evidence is that outside resource-rich countries, democracy actually accelerates growth, but in resource-rich countries it reduces growth. Something about resource richness contaminates democracy.

If this were the end of the story, it would be too depressing for words. Yet, one needs to distinguish between two kinds of democracy. In a mature democracy, like in the Netherlands, of course one is very aware that democracy means one thing, which is electoral competition. But democracy is not just that. After someone wins, the other aspect of democracy kicks in.

Elections just determine how governments acquire power, but then there are a whole lot of aspects about democracy which determine, constrain and limit how governments use that power. They are called checks and balances. A mature democracy has lots of checks and balances. A free press, scrutiny by parliament, the courts and due process. Thus government performance does not just depend on the electoral contest. It depends on these other aspects of democracy: the checks and balances.

We can measure checks and balances and we can decompose democracy into electoral competition and checks and balances. Some societies have a lot of electoral competition but no checks and balances. Others have lots of checks and balances but only modest electoral competition. So let us see whether that matters for this unfortunate effect of democracy on resource rents. The answer is – it does. Uniquely in the resource-rich societies, electoral competition is actually dysfunctional, whereas checks and balances are extremely useful. If a society has enough checks and balances, it can make democracy work very well, harnessing those resource rents for growth. If it has no checks and balances at all and intense electoral competition, this analysis predicts that the society is in deep trouble. Why is that?

So far, we have talked about the dangers of societies turning to populism as a result of low education. The other danger that democracy can encounter is patronage politics. Imagine there are two political parties in a resource-rich country, the Netherlands minus checks and balances. One political party is honest and the other is not. Let us not play this scenario in the Netherlands, let us play it in Africa, which is more real. Patronage politics in a low-income African country or in a low-income Asian country looks like the following. The political boss thinks: "There is a village, how am I going to win the votes of that village? I could offer lots of public goods, I could say you are going to have a school, you are going to have a health clinic. In fact, since I have been in power for 5 years, I could have actually done that but I did not because it is a very wasteful strategy.

If I go for national public goods like health and education, it is wasteful because everybody benefits. I do not need that to win, I can get all the votes in this village because that fellow in the middle is actually the power in this village. He is the chap who tells everybody how to vote and they follow him. It will cost me $50,000 to put a school and a health clinic in this village, but I can buy his support for just $500.

I simply give him the cash and he tells everybody to vote for this guy, he's good". That is patronage politics. In most of these societies it is unfortunately more cost effective in attracting votes than the honest party strategy: health, education, good policies and the rest. Leonard Wantchekon, an ingenious political scientist from Benin, managed to persuade political parties to run randomly in different campaigns in different parts of the country: patronage politics versus public good politics. Patronage politics won! That is the bitter reality of democracy in these societies at the moment.

If patronage politics is a winner why does it not happen everywhere? Why is it associated with resource rents? Why does democracy become undermined by resource rents? And can democracy work without resource rents? Here is the explanation I propose. When you have a lot of resource revenues coming into the government, the government does not need to impose taxation. If it does not need to tax, it does not provoke citizens to scrutinise what it is up to. Scrutiny by ordinary citizens is the life blood that makes reality of the checks and balances. Checks and balances are not just a set of legal rules, they are people actively enforcing them. Scrutiny is what is called a public good, everyone benefits from it. The tragedy of public goods is that because everybody benefits from them, it is in nobody's particular interest to supply them. Thus, it is high taxation that provokes citizens to scrutinise the government.

Let us take the case of Nigeria, which is a federal system with 36 states. In a meeting with the economic advisor of the President of Nigeria, he told that he had visited the states to look at what state governors are up to, and some of them are deliberately avoiding any taxation because they just do not want to provoke any scrutiny. They want a quiet life. That is the on-the-ground reality of the relationship between big resource revenues, low taxes and low scrutiny. If there is no scrutiny, one can embezzle the resource revenues and then one will not just build palaces but also finance patronage politics. If patronage politics is the electoral winning strategy because it is cost effective in obtaining votes, the only way to stop it is to make it infeasible to embezzle public money, so that although parties would like to have patronage politics, they cannot finance it.

What we need in resource-rich Africa is lots of checks and balances and what we get is intense electoral competition. Electoral competition is very easy, and it can even be done in Afghanistan and Iraq. The reason is that it is not a public good. Private incentives to participate in an election are overwhelming, that is how one comes to power. It is especially overwhelming if there are no checks and balances. The message is then: 'democracy, yes, but...'

Democracy and ethnic diversity

There is evidence on democracy and economic development that is more hopeful in one sense. It is not so much a message of hope, it is a message of necessity and that is: in ethnically diverse societies, autocracy and dictatorship are economically ruinous. There is a very simple reason for this. A dictator always has a specific power base in the society. This power base is the military and the military is the ethnic group that he belongs to and that he has to look after. That is how a dictator stays in power, by looking after his own people. Thus, the dictator has incentives to change the size of his ethnic group relative to the whole society.

As the diversity of the society increases, the dictator's ethnic group in power becomes increasingly smaller. The dictator can follow two strategies to benefit his ethnic group. He can deliver national public goods like good policies and health and education, which benefit everybody, not just his ethnic group. Or he can adopt predatory policies that transfer resources to his own group. In the process, he will kill the economy because this grabbing is so damaging that it has huge costs.

Depending on the size of the dictator's group, he will implement one of the two strategies. If his group is large – for example, 70% of the whole society –, even if the dictator does not care about the other 30%, there is not enough of them to take from. Thus, the dictator will deliver the public goods for the 70% of the people that he cares about. This strategy will also benefit the other 30% of the people he does not care about, but this is the winning strategy to benefit his group.

Now, let us shrink the dictator's group to 10% of the society. The winning strategy is for the dictator to grab from the others without wondering about the consequences because they are much larger.

Thus, in ethnically diverse societies, democracy becomes much more important, and, as it happens, the typical African country is much more ethnically diverse than anywhere else on earth. This implies that the typical African society does not have a choice: it has got to make democracy work. Unfortunately, this does not make it any easier because all that has been said so far still applies. Democracy is going to increase the risk of conflict, it is going to make reform processes slower but there is no alternative to democracy because if one turns to a dictator one could get a Mobutu.

Conclusion

Where does this leave us? I think democracy has been oversold, mis-sold and undersold. It has been oversold because we used the paradigm of the East European revolutions as a model for what would happen everywhere else. Eastern Europe was most peculiar, it was at the extreme end of the democratisation process most likely to work. In Eastern Europe there had been democracies before, they were European cultures, they had a middle income, the prospect of European Union membership if they abided by specific aspects of democracy and, if they could get into the European Union, they would then be saved from the menace of Russia. The incentives to get democracy right and its feasibility in those societies were overwhelming.

Just because democracy could work in Eastern Europe however does not mean it could work elsewhere, but that was part of the oversold image. This is also true in Iraq: in those first few days television broadcasted the statue of Saddam Hussein being pulled down, but this was echoing the statue of Lenin coming down. Iraq was supposed to be like Eastern Europe. But it was not, and nor will low-income Africa, unfortunately.

Thus, oversold in this sense and oversold in an even more disturbing sense. Typically we have promoted the sequence to first democratise and then do the economic reform, yet this might not work. It may be that by democratising these low-income societies whilst they still have very bad policies, we lock them into this trap with a high risk of conflict and great difficulty in getting any policy changes. We might need the sequence that China is adopting. First do the economics and the political reform will then come down the line. For example, while the Democratic Republic of the Congo is more democratic than China at the moment, this will not necessarily be true in 30 years time – and my guess would probably be China.

So it is oversold in the Eastern European image and it is oversold in that sequence of politics, politics, politics, let the economic baggage come later. We might even sometimes have to settle for less than democracy and rather settle for stability. So it is oversold and it is mis-sold.

It is mis-sold because the image that we push down the throats of developing countries has been that of elections. That is not what we mean by democracy in Western societies, we mean something much more than elections, we mean checks and balances. But the image we have presented and the money we have donated has been virtually entirely for elections. We have to rebalance this because elections are easy but checks and balances are really difficult, because nobody is their champion – they are public goods. We therefore need to get behind an agenda of building the checks and balances into these societies.

It is also being mis-sold in that elections are being presented as the solution to the problem of violent conflict. The message here is not against elections, but rather that we need some complementary policies that are effective in containing the risks of reversion into violence. The key strategy is peace keeping. If we are going to have elections we better have troops in there and have them not pulled out the day after the elections: as it turned out in the DRC, instead of the troops being flown out on October the 30th, more troops had to be flown in.

Thus, it has been oversold, it has been mis-sold but it has also been undersold. In ethnically diverse societies like Africa and various other places, there is no alternative to democracy. Unfortunately, African leaders at the moment think there is an alternative. They think that China is not only an economic model, it is a political model. They think it justifies African autocracy. As sad as it might sound, autocracy has worked pretty well in China. China is a much more homogeneous society in which the leadership has ambitions for the national good of China, and that is simply not true in Africa. African autocracies are always ethnically divisive and economically costly. We have to make democracy work and, in practice, this means avoiding the twin deformities into which democracy in these low-income countries turns: one of them is populism and the other is patronage.

Fighting populism and patronage

How can we help the heroic people who are struggling against populism and patronage politics in these societies? In all of these societies there are heroes, truly courageous people. One of my friends in a major African government at a senior level has this year had 21 death threats targeted against him and his children, so he moved them within the country. He then got letters saying "we know you moved your kids, we know where they are now." So now his wife and children are living in a little flat in London. He is an asylum seeker! He was a major figure trying to implement reform in his own country, and that is the bitter political reality of being a reformer in these societies, it is clearly very dangerous.

We need to get behind these reformers and we have not done so as yet. A defence against populism in the medium term is education, which may be financed by aid, and not just primary education, but rebuilding Africa's tertiary education system, universities, and its think-tanks, so that there is an informed elite able to navigate their societies out of their present difficulties.

It is also a case of technocracy. For example, over the last 30 years in Europe we have moved towards some decisions which we recognise are better taken by technocrats than by electors. This is why we have created independent central banks. It is why the European Union created something called a fiscal stability pact.

Africa needs these types of institutions to take some key decisions one step away from the populists. It needs more independent central banks and fiscal stability. For example, in Nigeria they have tried something called the fiscal responsibility bill. Yet, a role model may be needed and the Transparency International initiative is an example. We can build models of governance, which they can then follow. That is guarding against populism.

There are also safeguards against patronage, yet the way to strengthen checks and balances in these societies may be more controversial. Policy conditionality on the part of donors has been deeply dysfunctional because it has confused the lines of accountability. African governments must be accountable to their citizens, not to donors. If donors start telling these governments which policies they should adopt, that just confuses who is really responsible for the policies that governments are implementing.

However, there is sharp distinction between policy conditionality and governance conditionality. Donor governments should actually insist on some conditions of governance. What these conditions should be is basically insisting that governments are accountable to their own citizens, not to ours. We should be part of that struggle to bring accountability.

References

Paul Collier and Anke Hoeffler (2004), "Greed and Grievance in Civil War". *Oxford Economic Papers* 54: 563-95.

Paul Collier, Anke Hoeffler and Dominin Rohner (2007), "Beyond Greed and Grievance: Feasibility and Civil War", mimeo, University of Oxford. http://users.ox.ac.uk/~econpco/research/pdfs/BeyondGreedand Grievance.pdf

Paul Collier 2007, *The Bottom Billion. Why the Poorest Countries are Failing and What Can Be Done About It*. Oxford University Press, Oxford.

Leonard Wantchekon 2003, "Clientelism and Voting Behaviour: Evidence from a Field Experiment in Benin". *World Politics* 55: 399-422.

Democracy Meets Development

Bert Koenders

In this day and age we must realize that structural poverty reduction cannot be attained without substantive democratization. By that I do not mean imposing democracy by force, or promoting democratization as a quick fix for complex development problems. Development cooperation should encourage and support home-grown processes of political change and emancipation in developing countries, which will ultimately contribute to a sustainable world with less poverty and more equality. To do so, it needs to focus on increasing access to and participation in these processes by the poor themselves. It's time for democracy and development practitioners to combine their efforts. This kind of development cooperation requires political intuition, modest ambitions and a strategy that corresponds to the political realities on the ground. In fact, it requires an eye for the necessary democratic reforms and for the quality of democracy. And especially in the turbulent international context we live in – one that is far from perfectly democratic – Europe has an obligation to do much more than it has done to date. The credibility of our development efforts is at stake.

Today most countries have governments resulting from elections in which all adult citizens could vote. Hierarchies are breaking down; closed systems are opening up. At the same time, in many places in the world democratization has stalled. In these cases the danger exists that democratization will be reduced to formal election of warlords, separatists or racists. Democracy is making headway, but it is still often illiberal democracy, not yet accompanied by the rule of law, separation of powers and basic liberties. In Pakistan, for example, the struggle for democracy has been enhanced by the enormous growth of the free press and the courage of an independent judiciary in a still largely feudal society. Only completely free and fair elections can create the broader legitimacy that is needed to fight extremism and poverty.

Substantive democratization is not easy, and neither is supporting it. Copies of Western models can be extremely counterproductive for democratic change. The irony is that our models are being exported at a time when our own democracies in Europe are under pressure and going through major changes. On the European continent, where democratic change made a leap forward after 1989, the long and violent road to democracy is often forgotten.

The European experience

England experienced a slow transformation from an agrarian society to a parliamentary democracy. In France, a revolution was needed to remove obstacles to democratization. In the twentieth century, all over Europe, the labour movement and civil society fought to beat back fascism and communism. In the end, military action was needed to defend democracy. The German socialists' struggle led initially to the Weimar Republic, a fragile attempt at parliamentary democracy that proved unable to withstand the Great Depression and the Nazis. In Germany, the struggle for a more substantive democracy continued after the war with the Federal Republic, resulting in one very successful model of democracy and a social market economy. In his case studies Barrington Moore[1] sheds light on the historical conditions in which these transformations took place, in Europe and elsewhere, and the decisive role that social groups played in these political processes.

The struggle for democracy is not only about establishing a political system. Achieving substantive democracy is crucial. There was no universal suffrage in the Netherlands until 1919; it was only in 1922 that women's right to vote was enshrined in the constitution. And today the position of women is still being debated in the strict Calvinist SGP party. Until the 1950s diversity in the Netherlands was managed through "pillarisation", whereby society was compartmentalized along religious and ideological lines. While the old pillars have long since collapsed, globalization and above all increased immigration have created a new diversity.

In 2006 the Netherlands carried out a "State of Democracy Assessment", using the methodology of the International Institute for Democracy and Electoral Assistance. One of the conclusions was that traditional political parties are losing their roots in society. At the same time involvement in politics, especially among young people, seems to be increasing. And populism, both left-wing and right-wing, is on the rise. Political parties now play a different role in our democracy, a role in which individual personalities are central and the ability to project an image is crucial. Also, the Assessment showed once more that social cohesion and the integration of new citizens into a common identity – a new "us" – is one of the biggest challenges in deepening Dutch democracy. Democracy requires a community, a polis – this is something that European democracy and its parliament still have not fully achieved. And in the Netherlands, we constantly have to reassess who our polis consists of.

Challenges in the international debate

This is of course also the case in many developing countries. In developing countries as in richer ones, the economic and political complexity of societies is a given. You can't plan a market; you can't plan democracy. At the same time, economic growth and a functioning democratic system are essential to ultimately achieving sustainable, equitable development, independent of foreign aid. In a democracy that functions well, the government looks for ways to supply the services that citizens demand. In many countries, however, citizenship cannot be taken for granted. It requires respect for the political and civil rights of all individuals and groups in society, and conditions in which people are able to make use of their rights. Citizenship also means that people must want to shoulder their responsibilities as citizens. It means that they must be aware of their rights and duties – and above all of their opportunities as citizens to improve their own living conditions.

In this connection, I support William Easterly's call for "searchers", who look for solutions that reflect the reality of the poor themselves. I agree that in many cases the dynamism of the poor has much more potential than the plans of those at the top. In my opinion, however, the challenge is not to shift all our attention from plans at the top to the dynamism of the poor. It is to translate the dynamism of the poor into plans at the top. They must be flexible plans; but we cannot reduce poverty without sensible plans to improve service delivery, create safety nets, foster pro-poor growth, improve the educational system and construct energy systems and infrastructure that benefit the poor.

Of all the dimensions of poverty, the economic dimension may be the one that is most often discussed in relation to democratization. This is partly because economic growth, and the distribution and redistribution of the benefits of growth, are necessary to reduce poverty in practice. But the popularity of this topic is also closely related to the high growth rates of countries like China and Vietnam, whose democratization lags behind their impressive economic growth. Their high growth has lifted millions out of poverty. At the same time other countries with high growth rates, like India and Brazil, have functioning democratic systems. Clearly there is no one-to-one relation between growth and the political system. Growth is a result not only of governance but of economic policy, climate, regional stability and other factors linked to place and time. I am convinced, however, that the type of political system in a country and the quality of its performance do have an impact. It is no accident that 95% of the worst economic results over the past forty years were furnished by non-democratic governments. Compared with autocracies, democracies are structured to take account of a broader range of interests. The separation of powers also serves as a constant reminder, as argued in *The Democracy Advantage*, that "the central government's powers are limited. Thus, it encourages the expansion and the independence of the private secto[2]. This, in turn, fosters a climate of innovation and entrepreneurship, the engines of economic growth." Democracies produce better development indicators on average "because they tend to be more adaptable". In a functioning democracy, corrupt and ineffective leaders are more likely to lose their jobs. Finally, thanks to their adaptability and "quality of steadiness", democracies are better able to respond to economic and humanitarian disasters. And for large parts of the population, this can in fact make the difference between life and death.

Countries that have not yet been able to plug into the global market will have an especially difficult task in catching up. In Europe, the poorer EU countries have grown more quickly than the rich ones, so that the gap between the relatively rich and poor has narrowed. By contrast, globalization makes it harder for the poorest developing countries to bridge the gap with the rest of the world. Money and highly educated and enterprising people are draining away from these countries. With China, India and Brazil occupying their potential niches in the global economy, the latecomers to the world market have been forced to the sidelines. The challenge presented by this perverse globalization is to see that these countries too experience an economic take-off.

Can democratic developments spark economic growth in the countries that need it most? If so, what democratic developments, and under what conditions will they lead to a take-off? Despite everything that has been written about democracy and economic growth, there is still no answer to this question. Case studies present unique patterns of social, economic and other factors that cannot be easily summed up with generalizations. True, more substantive democratization can undeniably favour economic growth. Substantive democratization is necessary to distribute and redistribute the benefits of growth and ensure universal access to and participation in that growth. And undeniably, poverty is not only economic; poverty also has political, human and sociocultural dimensions. By definition, effective poverty reduction means working to change the nature and quality of governance, because these things shape the conditions in which comprehensive poverty reduction takes place. They therefore have a decisive influence on the results that can realistically be achieved.

In a functioning democracy, democratic principles are respected. Democratization is a never-ending process of negotiation between state and society to ensure this respect. Democratization is therefore not a quick fix for poverty. Both the state and the society have to ensure that formal institutions operate democratically in practice.

Paul Collier and others rightly state that low per capita incomes, the presence of oil and other natural resources, and serious inequality and ethnic divisions are not conducive to democracy. Collier has also said that democracy is misunderstood. Revolutions in one part of the world are too often seen as models for other parts of the world, and democracy is wrongly portrayed as a panacea. And democratization is equated with holding elections, while hardly any attention is paid to ensuring checks and balances. When this superficial kind of democratization fails to produce positive effects, the value of democracy as a political system can easily be dismissed. The unique case of China, with all its short-comings, is then taken as a model for Africa. But the Chinese model does not work in Africa, or in the Middle East or Latin America. In fact, I'm convinced that the Chinese model isn't even working well enough in China. China's economic growth has come at the cost of an alarming increase in social inequality and unacceptable harm to the environment.

We have yet to see the big socioeconomic benefits of the wave of democratization in the 1990s. At the same time, we have seen that young democracies can relapse into conflict. But I firmly believe that this is not the fault of democratization. More often it's the fault of stalled democratization. First and second elections can be accompanied by violence. As Jack Snyder emphasizes[3], elections give political elites a chance to exploit ethnic tensions and nationalist and religious sentiments. Therefore in any process of democratization, power-sharing mechanisms and strong civil society organizations and state institutions need as much attention as elections. Thomas Carothers maintains that it is not substantive democratization but a one-sided emphasis on state-building that fuels most wars. I too think that the failure of worldwide democratization to pay dividends in terms of peace or development is due not to the failure of democracy as a concept, but to the failure to deepen democracy. It was in fact "democratic deficits", not democratization, that plunged Côte d'Ivoire in 2002 into the hopeless crisis that it's been in ever since.

Should democratization be postponed until certain preconditions have been met? The "sequencing" debate is all the rage at the moment. Carothers rightly says that sequencing is not a solution to the challenges facing societies engaged in democratization. There are very few autocratic leaders who are sincerely development-minded. As Carothers says, "Prescribing the deferral of democracy – and consequently the prolongation of authoritarian rule – as a cure for the ills of prolonged authoritarianism makes little sense." But is it really a good idea to support democratization in sub-optimal conditions? Here I would like to cite Sheri Berman: "The main drivers of democratic development are generally internal rather than external. But on the margins, taking the side of the local democrats and reformers rather than their authoritarian overlords makes more sense both morally and politically. The construction of stable liberal democracy generally requires breaking down the institutions, relationships, and culture of the *ancien régime*, a process that is never easy and about which the *ancien régime* itself is rarely enthusiastic. Yes, achieving a full transition to consolidated democracy is difficult. But it cannot be completed if it never starts."

Global trends

There is another problem with the stability argument. Stability in the Middle East for example is either mostly superficial or, at best, fragile. Carrying out democratic reforms would enable countries in this region to link up with a globalising world. As it is elsewhere, in the Middle East, democratization is a precondition for justice and prosperity. Today, after the failures in Iraq, we are seeing the reassertion of stability as a chief goal. But stability can only be meaningful when it is based on development, peace and security. Therefore substantive democratic reforms from within societies will ultimately increase true stability.

Anwar Ibrahim has elegantly disposed of the bromide that Islam is incompatible with democracy. In fact this is a non-issue. After all, no one asks whether Christianity, Judaism or other religions are compatible with democracy. The supposedly non-Islamic character of democracy is however used too often by autocratic rulers in Arab countries to ward off democracy, and by the West as an excuse for maintaining a double standard.

The UNDP Arab Human Development Report 2005, published in December 2006, says that public freedoms have been further restricted in Arab countries in recent years and that oppressive systems of rule have remained in place. At the same time, small steps have been made "towards widening the margins of freedom in the region". For example, democracy and human rights have been made required subjects in the state school curriculum in Bahrain. The Justice and Reconciliation Commission in Morocco has recommended legal, institutional and cultural reforms. In nine Arab countries, women occupy prominent positions at national, provincial and municipal level. "With a few exceptions," the report says, "no Arab country is now without a parliament or a cabinet or a local council in whose assigned tasks at least one woman participates in an able manner." Participation by women in public life is slowly increasing in the region, even in Saudi Arabia.

The report also notes that announcements of reforms and pseudo-reforms are used as a cover for maintaining the status quo. Respecting the singularity of democratization in the Arab world should not mean accepting indefinite postponement of reforms due to lack of commitment by its political elites. In the Arab world and outside it, rulers' fears of the possible effect of democratization – effects that might be unacceptable to them – are the greatest obstacle to democratization. Yet as the Arab Development Report 2004 says, "widespread and thoroughgoing political reform, leading to a society of freedom and good governance, is the means of creating a free society, in the comprehensive sense, which in turn, would be equivalent to human development". Therefore, democratization needs the broadest possible support base.

When the discussion turns to Africa, governance is often spoken of in Patrick Chabal's terms of façade and reality. I prefer to find out what democracy really means in Africa. It is a fact that more leaders are coming to power by democratic means and that there are fewer violent changes of regime. This is one aspect of the trend that Daniel Posner and Daniel Young have so aptly described as the "increasing institutionalization of political power in Africa".[4] As they write, "the formal rules of the game are beginning to matter in ways that they previously have not." Between 1960 and the 1980s, most African leaders met their ends through coups, murders or other violent forms of regime change. Since the 1990s, periods in office have usually come to an end in accordance with democratic rules, through electoral defeat or voluntary departure at the end of a constitutionally limited term. While formal institutions alone are no indicator of how well governance works, they do determine what strategy is used to gain or retain power. This is a fundamental change in the way power is exercised.

Surveys by Afro-barometer show that large majorities of Africans prefer democracy to any other form of government. The people of Ghana, Kenya and Senegal have the greatest confidence in the functioning of democratic institutions. But even in countries where confidence is lower, like Tanzania (especially Zanzibar) and Madagascar (after outbursts of violence there), this does not mean that citizens prefer some other form of government. The surveys also show that formal institutions are beginning to matter to people's perceptions of democracy. The changes to the electoral system in Lesotho have greatly increased popular support. Relying on the surveys, Michael Bratton writes[5] that formal institutions seem to matter even more than informal ones, and that Africans generally think they are not getting what they expect from democracy. "People continue to think that presidents ignore constitutions, that legislatures are unrepresentative of popular desires, and that multiparty competition all too easily spills over into political violence," Bratton says. "As such, Africans estimate that the key elements in a well-functioning democracy – notably institutions that check the executive – are performing below par."

One particularly interesting conclusion from Bratton's work is that informal institutions are used to fill gaps in formal democracy. "Because the performance of all formal institutions systematically falls short of popular expectations, people will plug ensuing institutional gaps with informal ties." What does this mean? Like other people, Africans prefer democracy to other forms of government. Democracies are becoming more institutionalized and the functioning of democracy, particularly in Africa, is affected by both formal and informal institutions. And finally, in Africa as elsewhere, the effectiveness of democracy determines how much space is left for informal institutions to undermine sustainable, equitable development.

In Latin America, inequality and the rise of institutionalized crime – such as the political power of drug lords, state capture, violence and corruption – are the biggest challenges to ongoing democratization. As far as individuals can see, democratization has not improved their lot. When governments fail to deliver social and economic goods or ensure justice and reconciliation, their credibility suffers. This has increased tensions and led to the emergence of new nationalist movements. These movements in turn have radically altered the relations among states.

What is the significance of the swing to the left in Latin America? What does it mean for the future of democracy? Hector Schamis talks about different varieties of "post-socialism" and "post-populism" in the region[6]. He argues for a deeper analysis of the quality of party systems, however, because these are more important for determining a democracy's effectiveness than a regime's exact political leanings. The institutionalized party systems of Chile, Brazil and Uruguay are the main explanation for these countries' success, he says, while dislocated systems explain the failure of Menem and Kirchner in Argentina and Toledo and Fujimori in Peru. Schamis also says that oil distorts the entire political and economic picture, "whether in a collapsed party system such as Venezuela's or a disjointed and fragmented one such as Bolivia's". The role of political parties cannot be emphasized enough. As the African surveys also show, there is a substantial gap between what parties are supposed to do and how they actually function in practice. Worldwide, confidence in political parties is much lower than in any other democratic actor.

I don't have any quick fixes for complex development problems. I certainly don't have quick fixes for the inequality, social exclusion, violence and impunity that plague Latin America. But the democracies in the region will have to find solutions to these problems soon if they want to survive. When large numbers of young people cannot share in economic progress, they have no confidence in the formal institutions that are the bearers of democracy. If left unchecked, marginalisation will lead to more violence and more institutionalised criminality. Preventing this is the biggest challenge to substantive democratization in Latin America.

Development cooperation and democratization: lessons learned

In supporting democracy, we need to learn from the mistakes of the past. Democratization cannot be strengthened by relying on Western models. Effective support for democratization should focus on the operation of universal democratic principles in a specific context. Democratization should not be left to technocrats, because that means losing sight of its essential political significance. And those of us in the field of development cooperation need to take more account of the impact of our working methods on local politics. It is also time to stop being afraid that paying attention to democracy will undermine stability. As I said earlier, it is not "excessive" concern for legitimacy that ultimately undermines peace and security, but rather the lack of it. Finally, the role of women has been neglected for too long. In the area of substantive democratisation too, women can make a difference. What is needed therefore is a more political conception of good governance; a democracy test for our development agendas; and more focus on fragile states and women's rights.

1. A more political conception of good governance and deepening democracy

Because poverty is not only an economic phenomenon but also a sociocultural and political one, good governance has become less a precondition for development partnerships and more an objective. Experience shows that poverty reduction does not have sustainable, equitable results unless there are genuine improvements in the political realm. We therefore need a more explicitly political conception of good governance if we want development cooperation to have a positive effect on governance problems like corruption and insufficient rule of law and their underlying causes. We have to shed more light on democratic deficits. To do this we need more political analyses of the context, which should lead to a more political strategy for good governance and a more political strategy for poverty reduction. This means making greater efforts to deepen democracy – not only in government-to-government cooperation but also in cooperation with NGOs and through intergovernmental networks and organisations. I refer in particular to the work of International IDEA, the Netherlands Institute for Multiparty Democracy and the Association of European Parliamentarians for Africa, as well as efforts by the EU, OSCE and UN.

2. A democracy test for our development agendas

Wherever development aid is given, and especially budget support, the role of local politics in development cooperation requires more attention. Too often, because we see the implementing government as our natural counterpart in a recipient country, that government accounts for its spending and policies mainly to donors. Accountability by national governments to donors should never come at the expense of political accountability in the country itself, however. And too often, the ownership of national poverty reduction strategies by recipient countries still means in practice ownership by a small elite that can speak the donors' jargon. Ownership should be in the hands of ordinary citizens, not donors. So we need a reality check to ensure that poverty reduction addresses the real causes of poverty and not merely its symptoms. Harmonization and alignment with national poverty strategies and budget mechanisms are important principles of the Paris Declaration. They are essential to avoid putting too heavy a burden on the limited capacity of governments and partner organizations in recipient countries. However, they can also give legitimacy to procedures that are insufficiently democratic. We need to take a critical look at governments' and donors' actions, and where necessary, take steps to ensure that development cooperation does not further weaken national democratic institutions. If this is the side effect of our development cooperation, our aid is in fact irresponsible.

3. *Fragile states*

When dealing with fragile states it is a fatal mistake to ignore the importance of legitimacy – either because lack of legitimacy is a cause of the state's fragility, or because a viable and thus legitimate state has to be built in a post-conflict country. Of course essential services have to be provided immediately after a conflict; but it makes a difference who does what and how. So we have to do our best to avoid creating parallel responsibilities and parallel mechanisms of accountability. At the same time we have to ensure that the institutions receive the signals from society and are sufficiently responsive to them. So it is important not only to support parliamentarians' technical capacities but also to help them increase their legitimacy as representatives by accounting to their constituency for their actions and by keeping their feelers out. And it is crucial not to underestimate the risks of outsourcing key government tasks and responsibilities. Of course basic services are urgent; but legitimacy must be taken into account in ensuring their delivery. After all, our aim in fragile states is effective governance that is also legitimate. We must forestall the institutional collapse that insufficient attention to this goal can lead to.

4. Women's rights

Finally, in a functioning democracy, all citizens have equal rights and in principle equal opportunity to exercise their rights. In practice, where democracies fall short in this regard, ensuring that women participate equally with men is an enormous challenge. Giving women more rights and opportunities leads to higher economic growth by raising national productivity. More rights and opportunities for women also means that girls and women are more likely to speak up and take part in local administration and national politics. So investing in women is a way to achieve both maximum economic growth and substantive democracy.

Persistent marginalisation of girls and women has deep-rooted social and cultural causes. Exclusion and discrimination also simply reflect the realities of power. Often women cannot afford the costs of becoming candidates for parties with a real chance of being elected. Nor have they usually been trained in organizing themselves politically. Increasing women's rights and opportunities requires sociocultural and political transformations and girls' and women's empowerment. Political transformation is necessary for sustainable, equitable development, especially to attain MDG's three and five. For example, we need to invest in expanding women's role in local government as a means of improving their sexual and reproductive rights and health. In Guatemala, women are often members of local committees, especially those related to healthcare issues. Committees are represented in community councils which set priorities for the community. The community councils are in turn represented in municipal councils, where the financial decisions are taken. We should support women in the committees not only with training in their particular field, but also in having a say at different levels of government. Learning better meeting and negotiating skills strengthens these women's position in their communities and in government. This leads to enduring gains for women's reproductive health and rights.

The international dimension

It makes no sense to talk about democracy and development without discussing the political climate in which we try to work on these issues. As I said, that climate is far from perfectly democratic. There are unequal relations of power at intergovernmental as well as national level. The international political arena is a domain of constant political competition and negotiation. Geopolitical interests count for more in the world than development. There are tensions between international agreements and national sovereignty. At international as at national level, crooks are rewarded, and loyalty is a crucial informal factor. Therefore efforts to deepen democracy at national level must be accompanied by efforts to democratize international organizations, strengthen the international legal order and ensure more coherence between the words and actions of non-state actors, countries and organizations. Serious efforts are needed to reach agreement about democracy and support for democratization, for example within the EU. We should also share our experiences and push for standards of governance in intergovernmental and other networks. And we can push for broader accountability of NGOs and businesses.

I want to conclude with another reference to the State of Democracy Assessments. The Netherlands is of course not the only country that has assessed the state of its own democracy. Many other countries did it before we did or have done it since, from Mongolia to Mexico, which recently announced its intention to carry out such an assessment. This is an excellent way to show commitment to democracy, not only in other countries but also in one's own, and to launch an inclusive debate on deepening democracy. It goes without saying that the discussion of democracy and development has many sensitive aspects. I am convinced, however, that the sensitive political points must be addressed to make a fundamental difference in the world. At stake is not only the functioning of other people's democracy, but democratisation and development everywhere.

Notes

1   Barrington Moore, Jr, 1966. *The Social Origins of Dictatorship and Democracy: Lord and Peasant in the Making of The Modern World*. Beacon Press.
2   Halperin, M., J. Siegle and M. Weinstein, 2005, *The Democratic Advantage: How Democracies Promote Prosperity and Peace*, Routledge, New York, p. 13.
3   Snyder, J., 2000. *From Voting to Violence: Democratization and Nationalist Conflict*. W.W. Norton & Company, Inc.
4   Posner, D., and D. Young, 2007. "The Institutionalization of Political Power in Africa". In: *Journal of Democracy* Vol. 18, No. 3, pp. 126.
5   Bratton, M., 2007. "Institutionalizing African Democracy: Formal or Informal". Paper prepared for *The Journal of Democracy* Vol. 18, Issue 3. pp. 83.
6   Hector Schamis, 2006. "A 'Left Turn' in Latin America? Populism, Socialism, and Democratic Institutions" Paper prepared for *The Journal of Democracy* Vol. 17, No. 4, pp. 20-34.

References

Berman, Sheri, 2007. 'The Vain Hope for "Correct" Timing. *Journal of Democracy* Vol. 18, Issue 3, pp. 14-17.

Bratton, Michael, 2007. "Institutionalizing African Democracy: Formal or Informal?" In: *The Journal of Democracy* Vol. 18, Issue 3, pp. 81-95.

Carothers, Thomas, 2007. 'Misunderstanding Gradualism', *Journal of Democracy* Vol. 18, Issue 3, pp. 18-22.

Chabal, Patrick, and Jean-Pascal Daloz, 1999. *Africa Works: Disorder as Political Instrument*. Indiana University Press.

Collier, Paul, 2007. *The Bottom Billion: Why the poorest countries are failing and what can be done about it*. Oxford University Press, Oxford.

Easterly, William, 2006. *The White Man's Burden: Why the West's efforts to aid the rest have done so much ill and so little good*. Oxford University Press, New York.

Halperin, Morton H., Joseph T. Siegle, and Michael M. Weinstein (eds.), 2007. *The Democracy Advantage: How Democracies promote prosperity and peace*. Kindle book.

Ibrahim, Anwar, 2006. 'Universal Values and Muslim Democracy'. *Journal of Democracy* Vol. 17, Issue 3, pp. 5-12.

Snyder, Jack, 2000. 'From Voting to Violence: Democratization and Nationalist Conflict'. W.W. Norton & Company, Inc.

UNDP, 2006. 'The Arab Human Development Report'. New York: Oxford University Press.

Part III

The promotion of democracy

Does Democracy Promotion Have a Future?

Thomas Carothers

W hen the organisers contacted me about this lecture, they essentially asked me to sum up the entire field of democracy promotion in thirty or forty minutes. This is actually an impossible task, but in a way, I think it is the right task now because many people these days are asking new but fundamental questions about the overall enterprise of democracy promotion. They are searching for some understanding of just what this endeavour really consists of and what it means.

I frequently travel to different parts of the world to speak about this subject, both in countries that are trying to promote or support democracy elsewhere and those that are on the receiving end of these efforts. When I do that, and I have been doing it for about twenty years, I always encounter a great deal of wariness, doubts and suspicions. This is partly because I am from the United States. As a global power on the world stage, the U.S. provokes many doubts and suspicions about its efforts to promote democracy. But I think the questions that people tend to ask when confronted with this subject are deeper than that.

The very act of one society trying to engage itself in the political affairs of another society naturally provokes concerns: what are the real motives and the methods, what is this really all about? In the past several years, I have encountered a qualitatively greater level of concern – in fact substantial amounts of bewilderment, suspicion and sometimes open hostility and anger – than ever before with respect to this subject. The subject of democracy promotion has become intensely controversial.

To some extent the reason for this is obvious. The close association of the concept of democracy promotion with the war in Iraq has alienated many people in the world. They hear the U.S. administration equating democracy promotion with the war in Iraq and, understandably, they react badly. But I think there are other factors at work as well and what I would like to do here is to explore the overall picture.

I believe that this shift, this fundamental questioning of democracy promotion, reflects a broader shift, occurring in this decade in international affairs, away from the immediate post Cold War period into a new period of international politics, one whose basic features are only starting to become clear but which is going to be quite different from what came before it in many important ways. In short, I believe that democracy promotion is significant not only in and of itself, but also more generally as a window to understanding the state of international politics.

In order to look through this window, I need to go back briefly and trace the evolution of work in this field in recent decades. You may feel that you did not come for a history lecture, so bear with me. It is just a brief tour. We have to look back a bit to understand this present decade because it is only by seeing the present in the light of recent history that I think we can understand its principal features.

The Start of the Third Wave

In looking backwards we could go far back if we wished. If we had enough time, we could go back to 1848 and talk about the spread of different ideas about democracy in Europe in the middle of the nineteenth century. We could also talk about World War I or World War II: both wars having been fought, at least on one side, in the name of democracy. We could talk about colonialism and the ways it contributed to, as well as detracted from, democracy in the world, and so on. Our time is limited, however and I wish to focus on what I consider to be the contemporary period of democracy promotion, which is roughly the mid-1970s up to the present day. It is a period that began with what Samuel Huntington called the third wave of democracy.

Much contemporary democracy promotion is a response to the third wave of democracy. Democracy promoters often like to feel they are leading democracy in the world. In fact, in my experience they are often trailing behind, trying to catch up and support what has already started. We saw the initiation of this contemporary period of democracy promotion in the mid-1970s, with the efforts by German political foundations and some other European organisations to involve themselves in democratisation in Southern Europe, especially in Portugal and Spain. Then in the 1980s, as democratisation spread in Latin America and parts of Asia, democracy promotion began to emerge as an identifiable policy and aid domain.

It was in those years that assistance for elections began to spread in the world, both election observing and technical aid for election administration. Political party strengthening assistance also began to be broadly pursued. Rule-of-law aid emerged, as did legislative strengthening programs and other basic elements of what soon became a standard menu of democracy aid.

It was not just democracy aid. In the 1980s, pro-democratic diplomacy grew, such as European human rights diplomacy in Central America, pressure against Apartheid in South Africa and pressure on some Eastern European countries' human rights practices. The human rights agenda of the 1980s started to become a pro-democratic agenda and merged with movements for political change.

The 1980s were an essential start-up period. But in those years democracy promotion was deeply and in some sense fatally, entangled with Cold-War politics. Efforts by the United States and other Western powers to shape political events in other countries were often motivated by strategic anti-communist objectives and conflicted with democracy or often even undermined it. What was done "in the name of democracy" was in reality often anti-democratic, either in its intentions or its results.

As a result, in the Cold-War years, democracy promotion was regarded with a great deal of suspicion by people in most parts of the developing world and by many people in Europe and North America. It was not until the 1990s that democracy promotion really took off. Why did this occur?

The 1990s – A New Consensus

There are several reasons why democracy promotion gained significant ground in the 1990s. The first was the rapid global expansion of democracy in those years. The third wave caught fire in the 1980s and early 1990s with the fall of the Berlin wall, the break-up of the Soviet Union, a rush of democratic or at least attempted democratic transitions in Africa, further democratisation in Latin America and Asia and so forth. Suddenly, the expansion of democracy was a dominant theme in the world and democracy promotion was the response. This was thus one driver of positive change.

The second cause was the end of the Cold War. The struggle with the Soviet Union fell away and was not replaced by a single overreaching security theme in Western policy circles. This had a tremendously stimulating effect on democracy promotion. Suddenly, it was no longer the case that when the United States or another Western country crossed borders trying to affect the politics of another country, the first assumption was that this was part of Cold War tactics. That sort of initial reaction was replaced with a question: "If you are not here for that, why are you here?" I remember vividly, when I started my work for the U.S. State Department in the mid-1980s, working in Latin America as a North American, I could not walk into a room with Latin Americans and use the term democracy promotion without people bursting into laughter or tears at the idea that the U.S. was at all serious about it.

In the 1990s there was instead a sort of puzzled silence: "You are still talking about this? What do you mean now?" There was at least the possibility of a real conversation about democracy promotion. People in the developing world in the 1990s began to think, "Well, if this is not about containing the Soviet Union by subverting the left, what is it then about?"

A third driver of democracy promotion in the 1990s was a new attachment of democracy promotion to the development agenda, as practised by the Western donor community. In the 1960s and 1970s and through much of the 1980s, there was a strong idea in the development community that countries do not need to have a democratic government in order to develop. In fact, the view was, strong-hand governments are really the best for economic development. What developing societies need to do is put up with authoritarianism for a generation or two and only then give democracy a try.

That began to change in the late 1980s. In those years, we saw the World Bank issue an important report on Africa, identifying governance problems as a key obstacle to African development. In the 1990s, this insight broadly emerged as the good governance agenda, which, when you looked at what governance included – accountability, transparency, participation and governmental responsiveness – had many pro-democratic features.

Although there was certainly still a gap in the 1990s between economic developmentalists and democracy promoters, there was, at the rhetorical level but also at the policy level, the idea that democratisation will promote development and development will promote democratisation. In short, there arose the powerful idea of a common unified donor agenda, political as well as economic.

The result of these three drivers, the spread of democracy, the detachment of democracy promotion from the Cold War framework and the merging of the donor agenda, gave a tremendous impulse to democracy promotion in those years. The result was the significant growth of the field. There was a multiplication in the number and type of organisations working on different aspects of democracy building. Bilateral aid agencies created offices for democracy and human rights. Multilateral organisations began entering the field: the United Nations Development Programme (UNDP), the Organisation of American States (OAS), the Organisation for Security and Cooperation in Europe (OSCE), the Commonwealth Institute, the Council of Europe and so forth. While democracy promotion was a kind of "boutique" activity in the 1980s, by the end of the 1990s it had become something of an industry, with some good and some bad elements of that term. It was absorbing well over 2 billion Euros a year, with a slightly larger share from European actors than North American ones.

We began to see greatly increased activities in the diplomatic realm as well. Foreign ministries added offices of democracy and governance and began to put forward strategies on democracy promotion. Many small- and medium-sized diplomatic interventions were initiated, supporting elections, pushing for political openness and supporting pro-democratic, post-conflict reconstruction and so forth.

There was the emergence at the diplomatic level of regional standards – the democratic charter of the OAS, the Copenhagen criteria of the OSCE and other attempts to create democracy at the normative level on the international plane. And of course, in these years there was the expansion of the European Union and the idea of a democratic threshold for entering the EU, which proved to be a strong positive force for democracy in Central and Eastern Europe.

Taken together, the changes in democracy aid and democratic diplomacy resulted in substantial pro-democratic engagement by the United States and Europe, particularly in Central and Eastern Europe, Southern Africa, Central America and Southeastern Europe, somewhat in the former Soviet Union and in a few other parts of the world. It came to a point by the end of the 1990s that if you travelled to a country attempting a democratic transition, every single sector in that country's political or public life was in some way touched by democracy assistance. You could not visit the judiciary, the legislature, the local governments, the civil society organisations, media and so forth, without tripping over people from the other countries, trying to promote democracy.

Two striking, positive features characterised this pro-democratic activity. One was its growing legitimacy. The Cold War suspicion certainly did not disappear but people began to see that there was something potentially legitimate about this work, that it represented a set of values in and of itself, rather then simply being an instrument for something else. Democracy promotion, or at least certain parts of it, came to be accepted as somewhat normal. Election observation, for example, became to be something of a norm and standards began to emerge around it. It got to the point by the end of the decade that, for example, if a country refused to allow international observers at an election, such a refusal raised a serious question mark. The same was true of civil society development. Outside support for civil society began to be seen as sort of a norm.

Another striking feature was the fact that the United States and Europe began to converge to some extent in the activities they were carrying out. I remember in those years nothing used to anger European audiences more than if I stood before them and said, "You are basically doing the same thing in many of these programmes as the Americans." The same thing happened if I told an American audience: "Actually you are duplicating or moving in parallel with what the Europeans are doing," because both the U.S. actors and the Europeans liked to think they each had their own distinctive superior methods and ways of doing things. However, in those years I saw considerable convergence. This was very clearly evident, for example, in Serbia in the late 1990s. European and American actors worked very closely together in their efforts to support pro-democratic actors and processes in that country.

Flaws and Limitations

I do not wish to idealise the 1990s. We can find all kinds of flaws in the democracy promotion of that period. It was a crucial period of expansion but it certainly was not democracy-building paradise. I want to highlight two limitations here. First, although the U.S. and Europe did begin to take this subject seriously in those years while committing more resources to it, their interest in the subject was often secondary to other interests. Both the U.S. and Europe maintained warm, sometimes very cosy relationships with non-democratic governments for all kinds of reasons: trade, access to oil, security cooperation, or other things. One saw the West on the one hand promoting democracy fairly seriously in certain parts of the world, but in China, Vietnam, Central Asia, the Middle East, substantial parts of Sub-Saharan Africa and elsewhere, the West really was not very interested and did not do very much about it.

The second limitation was that the actual effect of all this activity, both the assistance and the diplomacy, were actually pretty modest. I believe that outside actors can be helpful in encouraging democracy in other societies, but the externally-sponsored work we saw in those years was rarely very decisive. There was a frequent tendency on the part of democracy promoters to take too much credit for democratic advances, to believe that they could be or should be the agents of change in other societies, rather than just the facilitators of change.

The greatest successes of democracy, both in the late 1980s and the 1990s, were driven by people within the democratising societies themselves, despite the credit-taking that sometimes went on outside, whether in South Africa, Poland, Chile or Mongolia, or many other places.

Unexpected Trouble

By the end of the decade, it looked as though the world was moving into a period marked by a growing consensus on political values. It appeared that in the new century, democracy promotion would probably continue, either with a little bit of growth or reduction, but in a fairly steady pattern. That has not proven to be the case. Democracy promotion has instead, in these last six years, been going through turbulent times, surrounded by controversy, doubt and uncertainty.

What happened? If we look back at the drivers of change from the 1990s: an advancing democratic trend, disconnection from a geo-strategic framework that often conflicts with democracy and a growing connection between democracy and economic develop-ment, we see that all three of these are being challenged or partly reversed.

The global democratic trend has gradually slowed down and in many places stagnated. The evidence is everywhere before us. In the former Soviet Union, Russia has moved backwards in the last six years, away from the political openness that it started to enjoy in the 1990s, and it has cast a chilly political spell on its neighbours in the Caucasus and Central Asia. The former Soviet Union is very short on successful democracy, despite encouraging experiments in a few places.

China has been in a process of de-liberalisation in the last several years in which political reform gains of the 1990s have been steadily reversed, despite continued economic development. Even Central and Eastern Europe, which made such notable political progress in the 1990s, is facing a number of vexing political stand-offs and challenges, such as the recent problems of forming a government in the Czech Republic, the dispiriting political conflict in Hungary, worrying signs on the right in Poland and trouble with respect to reform in Slovakia.

Latin America has been going through a self-conscious crisis of democracy in the last five or six years. Its citizens, although still loyal to the idea of democracy, are tremendously frustrated with the political systems that they have, and some are opting for politi-cians from outside the system, who are promising or in some cases threatening, to break the existing system in some way. In the Middle East, a shaky political reform agenda is being overwhelmed by a rash of bloody conflicts.

Of course, there are also positive events that have occurred over the last five or six years, such as the noteworthy democratic progress in Indonesia, the pro-democratic breakthroughs in Georgia and Ukraine and the new political settlement in Nepal. Nevertheless, the overall democratic trend has stagnated.

Why has this occurred? Several factors are at work. First, there is a natural slowing down of any political trend of this sort. Those dictatorships that could not cope with the surge of democratic impulses have already fallen. Those dictatorships which remain are the adaptable, clever ones, often ones that have oil or other valuable natural resources. These dictatorships have learned to navigate the waters of international democratic pressures. In short, the easy cases are finished, the harder ones remain.

Second, democracies are struggling in many places to deliver the goods to their people. People in many countries are saying, "We have been trying democracy for five or ten years, I do not see my life becoming any better. In fact all I have seen are corrupt politicians trading amongst themselves. I do not like it and I want to try something different". They are therefore trying something different in some places.

Third, and this is extremely important, rivals to democracy are growing. A striking feature of the 1990s was the absence of any alternative to the liberal democratic model having any significant legitimacy on the international scene. But the success of Russia's and China's economic development over the last five or six years, which in China's case of course extends back for several decades, has greatly strengthened the idea of the strong-hand model once again. One sees a return in some places to the notion that development requires a strong, i.e., non-democratic hand, which puts off democratisation until some indefinite future, and focuses on economic development and perhaps a little rule-of-law development.

These two countries have been actively promoting this model. Chinese officials invite African officials and activists to come to

China and study the Chinese model. Russia puts both positive and negative pressures on its neighbours to follow its political and economic path.

You thus have a model that is actually very appealing, especially to non-democratic elites in the Middle East, South East Asia and other parts of Asia and Africa, who can use it to argue that their being in power is necessary for their country's development. In many places, citizens frustrated with the democratic experiments they have lived through are going along with this new trend.

The fourth reason for the slowdown of the democratic trend is a simple but powerful one – the high price of oil and gas. The massive flow of oil and gas revenues has been a tremendous benefit to many non-democratic governments because most oil-rich countries are not democratic. Kazakhstan, Azerbaijan, Saudi Arabia, Kuwait, United Arab Emirates, Iran, Russia, Venezuela – these are countries awash in oil money. And concerns about energy supplies weaken Western willingness to put pressure on any of these governments regarding their non-democratic practices.

The War on Terrorism

A second change in this decade, one completely unpredicted in 2000, has been the reattachment of a democracy agenda to a geo-strategic agenda. I refer of course to the U.S. war on terrorism. President Bush has set forward democracy promotion again and again as a central element and theme of the war on terrorism. This has had a major effect on democracy promotion. This is a complex topic with many facets, but let me just highlight a few parts of the picture.

First, as I mentioned at the outset, the war on Iraq, which President Bush holds out as a central part of the war on terrorism, has closely associated democracy promotion with a war that is almost universally reviled, rejected and regretted around the world. This association of democracy promotion with what is widely viewed as unauthorised military force, violations of rights and a horrendous level of violence in Iraq, has been devastating to the legitimacy of the concept of democracy promotion.

Second, President Bush's more general association of democracy promotion with regime change has taken the associational damage of Iraq and broadened it. For many people in the world, democracy promotion has become a way of describing efforts to get rid of governments that the United States does not like and a cover for ouster efforts. In other words, this is a reattachment of security interests with the democracy concept, whether *vis-à-vis* Syria, Iran or other countries.

Third, it may sound good when the administration in the U.S. says, "We have to promote democracy as part of the war on terrorism because it is only through democracy that we will undercut the roots of terrorism." The reality that many people in the world see, however, particularly in the Islamic world, is that actually the war on terrorism involves closer relationships between Western governments and non-democratic governments for the sake of security cooperation. The United States has reversed its policies towards Pakistan, for example. While it used to give Pakistan's military dictatorship somewhat of a cold shoulder, the U.S. suddenly became a major aid donor and warm friend to Pakistan in 2002. Pakistan is only one example. The U.S. war on terrorism includes closer relationships with the intelligence services of Egypt, Saudi Arabia, Jordan and other non-democracies.

Adding to all of this is that American legal abuses abroad, above all the violations of rights of prisoners and detainees in Iraq, Afghanistan, Guantanamo, off the streets of European cities in some cases and in the United States itself, have done devastating damage to the concept and the practise of democracy promotion abroad. They have badly hurt the status of the United States as a model of democracy and as a legitimate democracy promoter.

So the three drivers of positive change in the 1990s, the advance of democracy, the detachment of democracy promotion from a conflictive geo-political security framework, and the positive idea that economic development and democracy necessarily go hand in hand, are now in question in the world. The result is new doubt about the legitimacy of the concept of democracy promotion itself, as well as a renewed questioning of the Western democratic model. When I speak to audiences in the developing world, whether in Asia, the Middle East, substantial parts of South Asia or Sub-Saharan Africa, the first question I often hear is now: "Why are you so sure that your model of democracy is right for us?" That question had faded considerably in the 1990s but it is now very much back.

In addition, for the first time there is serious resistance to democracy assistance activities. The Russian government has been setting out a very strong line on this. The Russian government has decided that it is going to oppose Western democracy assistance. President Putin openly criticises U.S. democracy aid programmes. The government is making it more difficult for Western democracy promotion organisations to operate in Russia and warning its neighbours about the purported dangers of such activities. The Russians are trying to block the OSCE's democracy assistance functions, such as election observation. In short, Russia is carrying out a systematic, sophisticated campaign against Western democracy assistance.

But the backlash does not come just from Russia. As I described in a recent article in *Foreign Affairs* called "The backlash against democracy promotion," one sees this phenomenon in many places.[1] Ethiopia kicked out some U.S. democracy promoters recently. So too did Bahrain. Nepal has made it harder for international NGOs to operate there. Peru recently passed a restrictive law limiting funding of NGOs. One can name many points on this new map. There is a rising sentiment in the world of: "We were uncertain about this democracy aid in the 1990s but we have woken up to what it is all about and we are not sure we like it." There are many open statements articulating a fear of foreign-backed colour revolutions.

A Growing Lack of International Political Consensus

This troubled situation of democracy promotion is a manifestation of the fact that the overall state of international relations has changed significantly from the 1990s. We are no longer in a world in which there is a growing international consensus on political values. We are in a world in which there is less consensus on basic political values and increased conflict about them. We are in a world in which consensus on even the ability or right of other countries trying to promote certain parts of a political consensus is now in question.

What does this mean for democracy promotion? Well, obviously it means harder times. It is harder to establish trust with partners and with governments. Let me give one example. It is a microscopic example but an indicative one. I was in Indonesia doing some research a couple of years ago and working with me was an Indonesian man, who was working with the Netherlands Institute for Multiparty Democracy. He told me he had just seen a couple of Indonesian parliamentarians about a programme his organisation was hoping to develop in Indonesia. One of these parliamentarians had said to him: "This is part of a democracy promotion programme, isn't it? We don't want that sort of thing in our country." This fellow was a bit surprised and said, "I am an Indonesian, working for a Dutch organisation, I am not part of the war on Iraq. I am not part of the American security project." This parliamentarian replied, "Yes, but now we know what this democracy promotion business is really about. We didn't understand it before. Now we do and we don't like it."

So, in many small conversations in many different parts of the world people have to work harder to establish trust when they walk through the door and say, "I am here for democracy." There are also more disagreements among democracy promoters about basic methods. Should you push harder in such situations? Should you back away? What is the right response? And there is less of a sense of momentum in many countries about the advancement of democracy. Instead, there is, as I said, greater scepticism about democracy itself.

How to React: the U.S. Perspective

The fact that democracy promotion is harder and more in doubt does not mean that we should give up. But it does mean that those interested and involved in the field need to take stock and do some things differently. For the United States, this has some serious implications. In the U.S. there is now a new debate about democracy promotion. As we enter into the early stages of the presidential campaign in the U.S., it is clear that one of the issues will be, "Should we be doing democracy promotion anymore? Iraq has been horrendous. Maybe this push on democracy was a mistake?" For the first time in decades, public opinion surveys show only a minority of Americans believe the U.S. should be involved in democracy promotion. This is a significant change for American society. The U.S. faces the choice between moving significantly away from this domain or instead trying to do it differently, while still preserving the basic intention. If we are to preserve the basic endeavour, which I think we should, I think we need to decontaminate American democracy promotion. What do I mean by decontamination in this field? I mean several simple things. The U.S. needs to self-consciously begin to rebuild its own credibility of democracy promotion work itself. There is no one way to do this but rather, a series of approaches or steps.

If the U.S. wishes the world to take its own actions seriously in this domain, it has to first say that democracy promotion will not be pursued via unauthorised military force against another country. Secondly, it means that the U.S. must stop associating democracy promotion with regime change generally. I believe that the U.S. and other countries and democracies can still be critical of dictatorships and can still apply pressure, whether it is to the government of Burma, Zimbabwe or Belarus. But this has to be done on the basis of democratic principles, not near-term national strategic interest. And it has to mean pressure that is based on democratic ideas and principles, encouraging positive developments in other societies, not ousting particular governments.

Third, it means not intervening in elections for the sake of favouring certain groups. Last year the U.S. was engaged in trying to tilt the Nicaraguan election away from Daniel Ortega. That is not an appropriate form of democracy promotion. It has to be put aside. Similarly, in the Palestinian elections in early 2006, certain American assistance programmes were used to try to help Fatah before the elections. Intervening in elections under the cover of this idea of democracy promotion undercuts the field.

Fourth, the rhetoric on democracy promotion coming out of Washington has to be reduced to a manageable level. The rhetoric is simply counterproductive at this point. Not only because it comes from a president who is immensely unpopular around the world, but simply because the rhetoric is out of sync with the reality of the policies. When you are cosy with the Pakistani government, the Saudi government, the Egyptian government and so forth, you cannot tell the world that freedom is what principally motivates you. It only produces cynicism.

Fifth, America has to clean up its own legal act with regard to the rights of detainees and prisoners abroad and at home. Unless the U.S. starts setting up a positive example of how a war on terrorism can be conducted with respect for the rule of law, both at home and abroad, it will not be taken seriously as a democracy promotion actor.

A European Response

What about Europe? I think Europe also needs to take some steps. The current situation is a difficult one for a number of European governments and non-governmental actors. On the one hand they do not wish to be closely associated with the American agenda on democracy promotion. On the other hand, they do not wish to be perceived as trying to cash in on anti-Americanism and dissociating themselves from the U.S.

I think there is an important opportunity for Europe right now to step forward in the domain of democracy promotion and show a doubting world that democracy promotion is not one and the same as the pursuit of American strategic interests. For Europe to be effective in such an effort, several things have to happen. First, European organisations involved in this field need to define for themselves, in a group sense, what the distinctive principles of the European approach really are. There is a lot of belief among European actors that "we do things a lot differently than you Americans." Now is the time to come forward and tell the international community what those things are and what is distinctive about the European approach. I think there is the instinct on the part of European actors that Europe has greater belief in a real partnership in democracy work, that it draws on multiple models of democracy and does not offer the world a single model, and that Europe has more humility than the U.S. because Europe has had a lot ups and downs with democracy in the twentieth century. These are all part of the picture. They need to be put together to advance a European democracy agenda that the world could listen to and understand and believe in.

To do that, some of the mechanisms of European democracy promotion need to be strengthened. The response of the European Commission to the challenges of democracy promotion in the last ten years has at times been surprisingly and disappointingly weak. The Commission has struggled to create effective instruments in this field despite ample funding. Europe can do better than that and I think it has to.

Third, the major powers in Europe, and here I am pointing to Germany, the UK and France, need to get together at least on a couple of countries and show that they are serious about this. The world is watching European policy towards Russia and towards the Middle East for example, where there are quite productive and friendly relationships between all three of these countries and governments of dubious democratic fidelity and asking, "How serious is Europe about this? Where is Europe pushing hard?"

In short, strengthening European democracy promotion has to involve defining an approach, creating effective mechanisms and attaching some real diplomatic weight to the words.

Challenges Ahead

The United States has a challenging agenda ahead of it, if it wishes to re-establish credibility in this domain. I think the challenge for Europe is a serious one too. Looking ahead in international politics in the next ten to twenty years, the core questions about democracy's future are of fundamental importance: whether or not Russia finds at least a somewhat reformist and democratic path. Whether Latin America gets through this shaky period and avoids returning to authoritarianism. Whether China is able to establish a political reform dynamic. Whether or not the encouraging democratic experiments in some parts of Sub-Saharan Africa really take root and succeed. Whether or not the Arab world finally finds a way to translate some of its modest political reforms to something more far-reaching. These are not just issues about how democracy is doing in the world. These are issues that will define what kind of world we live in, what kind of relationships exist among states, what kinds of conflicts occur in the world.

Thus, I sincerely believe that despite these serious problems, democracy promotion has a vital place in the world for the next several decades. But it is not an automatic or an easy place. It is a place that we have to earn through the seriousness of our purpose and the excellence of our efforts. It is up to all of us concerned with the state of democracy to engage and earn that place in the years ahead.

Note

1   Thomas Carothers, 2006. "The Backlash against Democracy Promotion," *Foreign Affairs*, March/April 2006, pp. 55-68.

Alternatives for Liberal Democracy

Kim Campbell

My perspective on the question you have asked me to address, "Alternatives to Liberal Democracy", is based on three aspects of my life. I started my career as an academic political scientist, specializing in the study of the government and politics of the Soviet Union. In the early 1980s I left academic life to begin the study of law, so I do not claim to be an expert on modern day Russia. However, I have a deep knowledge of the base on which contemporary Russia is trying to construct a democracy.

The other aspect of my life that has shaped my outlook on this question is the time I spent as a practitioner of democracy in Canada, where I held elective office at all three levels of government. My experience in trying to make the institutions of democracy work was an extraordinary education in the reality of politics. Like many former politicians, even out of office I feel a sense of responsibility for my community and a desire to promote and protect democratic values.

Thirdly, in 2001 I returned to teaching at the John F. Kennedy School of Government at Harvard University, where I taught courses based on my political experience. In 2002 I was a founding member of an organization of former presidents and prime ministers called the Club of Madrid, and from 2004 to the end of 2006 I served as its Secretary General. Our 66 members – the majority of whom have led democratic transitions in their own countries – employ our resources, knowledge, experience, access and convening capacity to promote democratic transition and consolidation around the world.

The end of the cold war

At the turn of the 21st Century, supporters of democracy felt a certain optimism. The end of the Cold War had led to changes that were unforeseeable a decade or so earlier. Eastern European members of the former Soviet Bloc were engaging in such rapid political, social and economic change that some of them would soon qualify for membership of the European Union. Russia had the first democratic change of leadership in its history and there was a record number of democracies in Latin America.

The democratic transitions of the "third wave", which began with the end of dictatorships in Portugal and Spain and of military government in Greece in the mid 1970s, had created consolidated democracies whose addition to the EU laid the groundwork for the post cold war accessions. Even China, still ruled by its Communist Party, had turned towards a liberalized, market economy, which held the promise of profound social and political changes to come.

Certain realities, however, have dimmed this optimism. Research conducted by the UNDP early in the new century showed that in Latin America, while 60% of people thought democracy was a good idea, only half that number, 30%, thought it could make their lives better. In a short period of time, "caudillismo" – the rise of the all powerful, charismatic leader – has re-emerged as a style of leadership in the region and has led to the erosion of democratic liberties supposedly in the name of a greater justice to be provided by a powerful but increasingly unconstrained government. A similar centralization of power is taking place in Russia, and post-apartheid South Africa is seriously threatened by rising crime.

Perhaps most devastating is the unravelling of the efforts to create democracies in Afghanistan and Iraq. In these countries one is reminded of the importance of local governments and the provision of basic services – filling potholes, providing sanitation and clean water, reliable law enforcement and fire protection – in order to create the environment where democratic forms of decision making and problem solving can take root. As with the Latin American responses to the UNDP survey, where people do not see democracy as something that can make their lives better, they will turn to whatever form of authority can deliver on that promise. So discouraging has been the result of "regime change" in these two countries that I am finding an increasing number of people who are disillusioned with, or even outright hostile to, the whole idea of democracy promotion.

What does this mean for those of us who are committed to the notion that democracy provides the best framework for the realization of human potential and dignity? Is it naïve to think that democracy can take root in non-western societies or in countries that are economically underdeveloped?

What do we mean by liberal democracy?

Let us go back and asks ourselves what we mean by liberal democracy. Probably the easiest thing to define is democracy itself. Scholars Juan Linz and Al Stepan, both of whom have worked with us in the Club of Madrid, identified four central questions that help to define democracy:

Does the government accept the constraints of the Rule of Law?
Do institutions of civil society operate free of government control?
Are there free and fair elections with mass suffrage?
Is control of government held by officials accountable to the electorate, either directly or through a representative parliament?

Increasingly, we see political legitimacy being personalized rather than coming through the rule of law. In totalitarian societies, civil society is anathema; people do not have the right to organize themselves independent of the government. Societies that have lived under this sort of rule lack the skills of organization and one of the most important aspects of a democratic mindset – the understanding that opposition does not equate with disloyalty. Electoral fraud undermines faith in the democratic process but equally damaging are elections in the absence of rule of law. Where there is no effective constraint on political leaders and institutions, elections simply serve to provide a spurious legitimacy to authoritarian regimes. The holding of office holders to account is a complex process, requiring not only a functioning legal system and a legal framework that penalizes corruption and abuse of power, but also a free press, which is the cornerstone of a right of free expression and is essential to enable citizens to be vigilant about their rights.

There are those who claim that democracy is a "western" value – not transmittable to other cultures or belief systems. However, these basic values can be expressed in a myriad of institutional designs and the policy outcomes of democratic processes are enormously varied. Multi-party parliamentary systems, coalition governments, single member constituency systems, proportional representation, run-off majority systems, weak presidential systems, strong presidential systems, separation of powers, parliamentary supremacy, constitutional monarchy, unitary, federal, confederate – all of these terms can apply to existing political systems that are highly democratic. Free market, social democratic, mixed ownership, laissez-faire, welfare state – these terms all reflect approaches to how government is used in a democracy that produces very different policy outcomes – all of which are democratic. However, the four characteristics that Linz and Stepan identify – rule of law, independent civil society, free and fair elections based on mass suffrage and accountability – are the non-negotiable characteristics of democracy.

The question you asked me to address was "alternatives to liberal democracy". Where does the concept of "liberal" fit into this discussion? The word "liberal" is used in two quite different ways. In North America, "liberal" has been used to refer to the tradition of an optimistic use of government to improve human life and behaviour. In other words, political liberals are people who believe that government and the policies that democratic governments create can actually improve human society by changing human behaviour. Conversely, conservatives believe in a philosophy of imperfection. No human effort could improve human nature. In this view, the purpose of the state is to create order and allow people to function with security.

Americans use the term "liberal" to indicate an activist role for the state and this has the corollary of casting liberals as big spenders. Liberals want to make people better through education, healthcare and other sorts of policies. In the United States, liberal is seen by some people as a pejorative term, sometimes modified by the phrase "tax and spend". But liberalism in this sense also reflects an open, magnanimous and inclusive view of society, one that is tolerant of differences. Liberals tend to be at the forefront in advocating social policies that remove social and economic barriers to the fulfilment of human potential.

So, on the one hand, when we talk about liberal democracy, we are referring to a notion of democracy that focuses on the protection of liberties and sees a role for the state in creating equal opportunity. If on the other hand the term is used pejoratively, it is because its critics see liberals as naïve in their expectations for the transformative potential of social policy and wasteful in their faith that "inefficient and bureaucratic" government can implement policies that in the view of critics are better managed by the discipline of the private sector in a free market environment.

The Washington consensus

In Europe, liberal has come to signify the values of its North American critics. It is associated with "liberal" economists who elevate the market and denigrate governments as mechanisms for creating wealth and allocating value in an effective manner. Liberal has come to be seen as consistent with what is sometimes called the "Washington consensus" because it represents the philosophy of the major Bretton Woods institutions, the World Bank and the International Monetary Fund, based in Washington, as well as recent American governments. For its supporters, it is seen as the common sense value of small government, free markets and privatisation that unfetters the capacity for economic growth and wealth creation. For its critics, it represents the shrinking of government in the context of economic globalization in the name of corporate wealth at the expense of national economic sovereignty.

So, when we are talking about "liberal democracy", we really have to be clear about what we mean when we say "liberal". If you were to call President George W. Bush a liberal, he would object, but if you called him a "small government, free trade, market economy kind of person", he would say: "Yes, that is me!"

This notion of what we have called the Washington consensus was not always the governing philosophy in the US government or in the World Bank or IMF. For much of American history, starting with the growth of regulation in the early 20th Century, the application of Keynesian principles during the Great Depression and policies such as the GI Bill of Rights and the Marshall Plan after World War II, among others, represented a belief in the transformative power of government policy to improve the economy either by balancing the power of corporations or by investing public funds to compensate for what the market alone could not accomplish.

Beginning in the 1980s, many industrialized democracies began to rethink the efficacy of government ownership of industry and, starting with New Zealand and quickly followed by Great Britain, Canada and others, countries began to privatize their public sectors. In all of these cases, the national economies were robust and there was abundant capacity in the private sector to both finance and manage the privatized enterprises. Moreover, where there was a public stake in the exploitation of a natural resource or other previously state-managed activity, these countries could ensure that the public continued to share in the value of the activity through licensing fees, royalties and taxation.

However, with the fall of communism, many began to equate market economies with democracy. This sort of Washington consensus, that a liberal democracy must also have a free market and not a lot of government involvement in the economy, came to be seen by a lot of Americans as being part of the definition of democracy, rather than the experience of some but not all democracies and not for all times.

The view, after the fall of the Berlin Wall, that statist economic views were dead once and for all, has been an unfortunate one. The fall of the Berlin Wall was accompanied by a sense of triumphalism and it was seen as the final proof of the superiority of capitalism

144

as an economic model. Capitalism operates in many different ways and with many different formulas for the balance between public and private sector economic activity. However, the "Washington Consensus" became the model of capitalism that was to be recommended and supported for the newly emerging post-communist societies, notwithstanding that they lacked any of the preconditions that had enabled the older industrial democracies to reduce the size of their state-owned sectors.

While these new regimes needed to create market economies, the American model was not the only viable one. What is important to understand is that the role of the government in the economy is not just a political decision; it is a decision based on practicalities. These are decisions based on competence, public interest, investment needs, profitability, national interest, etc. In other words, there is nothing about democracy that says there can be no economic role for the government. One does not insist on the other.

As a former Soviet specialist, I was horrified to watch the privatization of the Soviet economy to a public where there was negligible business acumen and no legal framework to provide regulation and protection. This was not a society full of people who had gone to the Harvard Business School or London Business School, people who knew how markets function and how to manage. No, not at all.

Who were the people who were capable to engage in those privatizations? They were the people who, under communism, had operated in the areas were there was a certain amount of freedom of manoeuvre and the capacity to build networks – the Communist Party and the KGB.

In addition, I remember thinking when I travelled in the USSR in 1972 that if they could ever tap the energy of the "informal economy" they would be world beaters. Living out of the legal framework in the Soviet Union was how people made a lot of money, but they were fundamentally iconoclastic. These were not people just waiting for democracy to come in with the Rule of Law. These were people whose whole approach to being entrepreneurs was to get around the government. These are not people who are going to be paying taxes and helping to build this wonderful structure of commercial law, that we in the advanced democracies take for granted.

The rule of law

I can enter into a contract with you although we do not know each other because we have legal systems and cultural values that enable us to do business together. We take for granted that we have these institutions and structures and that they function. Unfortunately, neither the "black market" entrepreneurs of the Soviet era nor the members of the Communist Party or the KGB are imbued with the understanding of how to create legal systems that constrain the excesses of the market.

I have had a lot of debates and discussions about what might have been better than the privatization process that took place in Russia. There are some people who say that just as the Americans went through their "robber baron" period at the end of the 19th century, the Russians just have to grit their teeth and endure this phase of "buccaneer capitalism". There may be no neat way to make this economic transformation, but it was certainly a process that undermined support for democracy in Russia by associating democracy in many minds with economic insecurity and criminality. As with the Latin Americans who responded to the UNDP survey, many Russians came to believe that democracy could not make their lives better.

Without the rule of law, democratic electoral choices mean very little. Moreover, in the former Soviet Union, social welfare in all its forms was a state monopoly. With the disappearance of the Soviet state, many people were left with nothing and the emphasis on economic reform in the new countries seemed to be on privatization rather than on keeping the healthcare and education systems functioning.

146

Many successful mature democracies have also incorporated a large economic role for government. Canada is one of the most entrepreneurial countries in the world but it also has a public healthcare system. Canada has a constitutionally protected system of equalization payments to make sure that all people throughout our country get basic levels of social services, even if the provinces that they live in are not among the wealthiest provinces. There are certain things, like the public airwaves, that are considered to be a public resource. They are allocated to broadcasters through a public authority and broadcasters have a responsibility in return to provide some public service broadcasting.

In other words, you can be an entrepreneurial country, a very successful country but that does not mean there is no role for government. Yet, in many of these countries, public companies were being privatized based on a model that reflected the most mature democracy, the most mature development of an industrial economy when they really were not ready for that. The result was that in many cases it turned people off democracy.

Economic liberalism in a democracy is a function of philosophy, choice and interest. It is not something that you must have to have a democracy. I am living in Paris now and if you are watching the television coverage of the French elections, this is still a big issue in France: what should be the role of public regulation in determining how long people work? I am not saying that they all sit around like great thinkers arguing purely as philosophers. Of course, there is private interest and there are conflicts of interest and special interests in the country but it is the argument that is at the heart of the kind of policy competitions that characterize politics in a democracy.

What is also interesting is that economic liberalism can occur without democracy. China is a very good example of that. There is no democracy in China. I go to China and meet people and talk to them. They talk about democracy, but that does not necessarily mean that they want to have a democracy. They have created some opportunities for elections (e.g., local councils).

When I was there in 2005, I was told by many people that those elections were really rigged, but sometimes even rigged elections are better than none. People get into the habit of having elections and eventually they will not put up with having them rigged any more. The economic opening of China has not been accompanied by democratic development. It may turn out to be a useful platform for creating democratic development, and the need for legal structures becomes more acute in the context of global trade, but democracy is about much more than markets and, as the Scandinavian countries have shown, it can operate at a high level of integrity with a large public economic sector.

The tolerant aspect of liberalism

Finally, the tolerant aspect of liberalism is something that raises some interesting questions. The tolerant aspect of liberalism that we know and understand in our own countries really arose out of the Enlightenment. If you remember, Europe was not a very tolerant place: people were killing each other over the differences between Protestants and Catholics. This perplexes people outside the Christian tradition, just as we cannot understand why Shiites and Sunnis would kill each other. To us, they are all Muslims. But what role does freedom of religion play in a democracy?

In Western societies tolerance or the practise of allowing religious freedom has become more and more identified with democratic values. In democracy the rule of law means that rights that people enjoy should be enjoyed by everyone and there should be no basis for excluding anyone. In the early days as our countries were growing, there were distinctions and there was discrimination based on religion. I can remember as a very young girl when John F. Kennedy was running for President of the United States (he was the only Roman Catholic ever to be President of the United States), his religion was a big deal. People were saying "the Pope is going to tell him what to do".

Religion has certainly played a role, although more in some countries than in others. I astonish Canadians when I say that I was the first non-Catholic Prime Minister of Canada since 1963. People are surprised, because they do not even think of what the religion of the Prime Minister is; they just assume that if you are an Anglophone you are probably Protestant and if you are a Francophone you are probably Catholic. However, we had a couple of Anglophone Prime Ministers who were Catholics and most Canadians did not even know about it – it is not an issue in my country.

However, the issue is coming up again in a different way as we have a growing presence of Islam that is complicated by the implications of "political Islam" or "Islamism". Secular states are not necessarily irreligious. The US is a very good example of this. Rather they do not enshrine any particular religious view as the basis of policy. The British Monarch is also head of the Church of England and a Catholic is barred by law from sitting on the throne. So, there are still religious elements that are important.

But the question with respect to Islam is where it fits into the Enlightenment tradition. In 2004 I attended a Congress of Democrats from the Islamic World in Istanbul. These were people who were actually involved in public life. They were elected people from Indonesia, members of Shura councils from the Emirates in the Gulf. They insisted that there was no conflict between the values of Islam and the values of democracy as I described the fundamentals (the rule of law, free civil society, etc.).

This is one of the issues that is important here in Holland. This question of whether there are religious traditions that are inconsistent with the secular premise of democracy, is not that religion does not matter, but that religion will not dominate the institutions of government or be enshrined in the institutions of government. Fundamentalists of every kind reject secularism. It is conceivable that you have a democracy that does not support religious toleration, but that would only be feasible if you have a very specific and uniform society where the people would still be able to choose through universal suffrage their representatives who make the laws freely.

National identity and democracy

The question is: where is liberal democracy today? First of all, how do we characterize the growth of ethnic identity as a basis for political identity in mature democracies – Canada, Spain, the United Kingdom? Is this illiberal? I was watching a television conversation about the upcoming Scottish elections. The devolution of the United Kingdom is based on ethnic or national identity. It is not regional in the way that the Canadian provinces or the American states are regional. It is Wales and the Welsh identity and this one language and it is Scotland, the Scottish identity and the Scottish language. How should we see this if we see ourselves as exponents of liberal democracy?

Perhaps the Scots and the Welsh would argue that this is a regional division based on ancient kingdoms, which happened to be incorporated into the United Kingdom and that their diversity is within. Should this trouble us or is this a good thing? I am actually troubled by it because I think that the doctrine of national self-determination that was articulated after World War I was a dangerous doctrine because it suggests that ethnicity or nation is the absolute default fundamental identity, as opposed to the way you think.

In the European Parliament, members of parliament do not sit by national group; they sit by ideological group. The Greens sit together, the Conservatives sit together and the Socialists sit together. Yet now we are seeing political developments that seem to go back to ethnicity and nationalism as a more fundamental basis for political identity. You can argue that maybe it is not so much that these groups, such as the Catalonians in Spain, want to exclude some other people but rather that they feel as a territory and as a region, that they have a tradition of creating their own political community.

I am interested to hear what you think of that, because I think it is a very interesting question. Is there intrinsic value in multi-ethnic politics? What do these developments mean for the future of liberal democracy? Secondly, what are we to make of the rise of indigenous movements in Latin America? In many cases, they are using democratic methods to reduce the constraints on the power of the leader. Again we see this notion of legitimizing things through democratic elections and the rewriting of constitutions even though the ultimate result is a weakening of democratic principles in practice.

Writing a social contract

Some of you may know the work of the American philosopher John Rawls. In his book "A Theory of Justice," Rawls used the idea of social contract in a way that illustrates one of the dilemmas in actual democratic practice. In his view, the only truly fair social contract is one that would be written behind a "veil of ignorance" where the people who were writing the social contract had no idea what their personal characteristics were. They did not know if they were tall, short, fat, thin, black, white, smart, stupid, musical, whatever. He said that only those people behind this veil of ignorance about their own qualities could write a just social contract because they would then create a social contract under which they would be prepared to live if, when the veil of ignorance was lifted, they found themselves among the least advantaged.

What that means is that people who write the rules know exactly where they fit into society and what their characteristics are and so they write rules that they know they can live by. That is the case with constitutions. Who is participating in the writing of the constitution? What we are seeing in some countries, particularly in Latin America, are indigenous groups who have felt themselves excluded from the power structure of their countries and particularly from the sharing of the natural resources in their country, wanting now to rewrite the constitutions.

It will be very interesting to observe the formerly privileged groups. They are not behind a veil of ignorance but they will want to create constitutions that will not disadvantage them. They will now be the minority and having to think what it means to protect the rights of a minority. It is a very interesting challenge that these countries face. Will they create new and fair constitutional arrangements that will be just and fair to everyone who lives there or will they simply empower one group at the expense of another?

To conclude

Can democracy be exported? In our fourth General Assembly in 2005, The Club of Madrid examined the transitions in Eastern Europe. We concluded that the role of the EU in the Eastern European transitions was even greater than many people had thought.

I know that you can not export democracy. I can use the expression in English: "Democracy cannot be imported or exported, but it should be supported". There are ways in which people who are making democratic institutions work successfully can share that knowledge. If you have never had a Parliament before, how do you even know how to be a member of Parliament? If somebody who has been a member of Parliament somewhere else comes by and says: "Here is what we did and here is what I learned and I found that this worked", yes, you can do that, but that does not mean you can create the institutions or the love of those institutions externally.

Will the Eastern European transitions last? There is still some nostalgia for illiberal elements there. I am told that in Bulgaria many of the new leaders are the sons and daughters of the old communist hierarchy, but maybe they are a whole different generation, who knows? Much depends on what was there before. We know that totalitarianism is the worst basis on which to found a democracy because of the lack of social trust, the lack of a capacity to organize, the command economy and what that means in terms of developing efficient economies.

In Russia recently, I had a meeting with President Putin's party, United Russia – Putin has two parties now. To show that they actually have contested elections, he has created another party. His two parties will fight each other – I went to meet a group of 150 people from United Russia. These were people from all over Russia, provincial governors, high-level people. They were having a training session and I was invited to make a presentation to them. They used this concept which they called "sovereign democracy" and they were sure that Canada also talked about sovereign democracy. I said: "I have held elected office at all three levels of government and I have never heard anybody talk about sovereign democracy in Canada". But basically what sovereign democracy means is "we will do it our way". I told them: there are a gazillion ways you could make a democracy work, but there are some values that are non-negotiable, and if you do not have those values, you do not have a democracy. You can have eight Houses, two Houses, you can be Federal or Unitary, you can have proportional representation, you have variations, but there are some things like the Rule of Law, open civil society, accountability and free elections, that are not negotiable.

Economic development is not a function of a political system and democracy is no guarantee of economic development. In a globalised world, there are pressures to adhere to norms but not all countries have to in the same degree. When China goes into countries in Africa and says "we want to buy your oil, we do not care if you are democratic or not", that is a problem. In other cases, if you are in the World Trade Organization and you have to respect certain norms for the protection of intellectual property, that becomes a way of using economic development and those international norms to push people towards the fundamental values on which you can begin to build democratic institutions. I actually think that is the best hope for China.

I think if China had elections tomorrow, it would be a disaster. They are not ready for it. But if they can begin to create a culture of the Rule of Law and some capacity to make local institutions work on a democratic basis, I think they could build something without having huge chaos. And of course, they look at the former Soviet Union and do not want to be like that.

As Max Weber said: "Democracy is not essential for the Rule of Law, but Rule of Law is key to a democratic political culture". Perhaps the low voting turn out in the US is a reflection that people are so comfortable with the Rule of Law that they think it is more important than elections.

Finally, some surprises. I started out this discussion looking at some of the disappointments that have followed the initial optimism that followed the fall of the Berlin Wall. There are, however, some surprising success stories in the world of democracy as well. Here are a few examples.

In Pakistan, the lawyers demonstrating against the firing of the chief justice, are a very interesting reflection of a democratic value in Pakistan. Pakistan is a funny little dysfunctional democracy, but there is a Rule of Law. That the legal profession would take those risks, demonstrating, suggests that there is a value there. That is good.

Africa. I do not have time for more than one example so let us look at one of the poorest countries, Mauritania. Mauritania had a coup and they set some standards for a series of elections. They fulfilled those standards. I have been invited to the inauguration of the new President this week and though I am not able to go, I am impressed with what they have accomplished, including exceeding their seemingly unattainable goal of getting 20% female representation in the government.

I will conclude by saying that liberal democracy – in both its senses – is alive and well. There are different degrees of economic liberalism that are compatible with democracy and we need to understand the importance of building on local values and traditions, but the key democratic values are not negotiable. The philosophical liberalism that we associate with democracy, liberty, equal rights, toleration, equality under the law, etc, is the form of "liberal democracy" for which there is no alternative. Reaching the ideals of liberal democracy in that definition is always a process, a goal. How we see human society changes over time and new forms of liberty emerge to be protected. The cost of liberty is, indeed, eternal vigilance.

Democracy is important not just for the quality of life within a country, it is also important to the architecture of international law. It does matter to all of us whether other countries get it right not only so we can travel and do business in other countries in comfort and security, but also so that other countries can be players in a world that supports the "globalization" of democracy's non-negotiable values in an architecture of international law. Ensuring that we do not discredit these values is the duty of all who have the good fortune to live under them.

Democracy Building Globally: How can Europe Contribute?

Vidar Helgesen

The lecture series has been a timely initiative on an increasingly important subject: that of democracy and development. It is equally timely and important that the Government of the Netherlands puts such an emphasis on the role of democratic politics in development policies and development cooperation.

I will concentrate today on three issues. Firstly, the current global situation of democracy building. Secondly, how democracy building and development communities must come together in new ways. Lastly, I will give some considerations on how Europe could approach democracy and development.

Democracy Building Globally

A number of developments have led to a less rosy situation for democracy globally today than only a few years ago. The rise and fall of the so-called Freedom Agenda in U.S foreign policy has had important implications with Iraq epitomising the problems. Western policies towards democracy and elections have been seen as unequally applied. Whatever position one takes on what was the adequate response to the election victory of Hamas in the Palestinian territories, it is beyond doubt that European and American responses have led to a serious legitimacy challenge when demands are put forward for democratic elections elsewhere. This adds to a broader situation of polarisation between north and south, as seen in the UN over human rights and democratic governance and as seen in the Doha trade negotiations. This polarisation is all but tempered by the global or regional rise of powers, often rich in energy resources but poor on democratic practice and with a willingness to project influence in their neighbourhoods or even globally. Such powers also seem to demonstrate that economic development can be effectively achieved through autocracy, while in many democracies people are increasingly frustrated by the lack of economic and social development delivered by political institutions.

Some of these trends affect development cooperation as well. The effectiveness of aid conditionality is weakened when some powers provide aid with no strings attached or when regional petroleum powers provide contracts with no or few questions about governance or transparency.

The picture is not all grim though. Democracy retains its popular support in all parts of the world. The African Union adopted in January this year a Charter on Democracy, Elections and Governance. In Asia, ASEAN is developing a new charter and democracy is an issue now openly discussed, something which would have been unheard of a few years ago.

Democracy and development

Nevertheless there is space for global actors to take a more effective leadership in democracy building. The obvious candidate is Europe but the EU has not yet articulated what it can bring to the world in terms of supporting democracy. I will argue that the EU is well placed to take up this challenge. I also believe that the way forward lies not least in bringing policies and strategies for democracy building and development cooperation closer together and to create a more dynamic interplay between the democracy building and the development of communities.

To exemplify, let me start with democracy building. More often than not, it has been conducted as a series of unconnected single activities rather disconnected from development partnerships. To take one example, elections were for a long time treated like events that needed to be observed by foreigners every four years, while too little attention was given to the need to build national capacity for managing the full electoral cycle. This is why IDEA has taken the lead in developing international standards for effective electoral assistance: bringing experts, election authorities and donors together to take a more developmental approach to elections.

Political party assistance, while critically important, has also to too large an extent been a world apart from the broader development cooperation. Much good has been done and much good is being done in this field, not least by The Netherlands Institute for Multiparty Democracy but political party assistance has not really been integrated into the on-going efforts of the donor community to coordinate and harmonise.

The democracy building community has developed less common language, common standards and harmonised actions than the development community. In brief, there is no Paris agenda for the democracy building community.

On the other hand, the development community has been rather anxious about democracy building activities. I do not know whether this has to do with a sense of naïveté which has led to resistance against engaging with politics but democracy *is* politics and *aid* is politics.

It is commonplace today to state that democracy cannot be imposed from abroad, it must grow from within. The same holds true for development. As William Easterly pointed out, there is no single recipe for development. No country can be developed from the outside. This is not to say that economic development in the globalised era can take place through protectionism and isolation but for a country to unleash the potential of its people and make use of the opportunities for development, national leadership is needed. Not only ownership, which we know so well from the development discourse, but leadership itself.

Good political leadership can only happen if people are able to hold their leaders and not only donors to account for the policies they implement. Development cooperation will not yield results if it is a technocratic add-on to bad national policies.

Democracy – development linkages

Let me turn to the question of what linkages exist between democracy and development.

Academic literature about the linkages between democracy and development is both abundant and inconclusive. This is really not surprising if we consider that both development and democracy have many definitions and are understood in very different ways (someone once said that economy was the only science in which one could get the Nobel Prize by defending diametrically opposed approaches).

In a nutshell, some scholars have claimed that there is a causal link. Others refuted its existence arguing that evidence was contradictory and that there were plenty of examples to substantiate different, if not opposed views. Finally, some scholars recognise that the link exists but it is not direct and causal but somewhat more complex.

The complexity of the relationship is also exemplified by the semantic evolution of the two terms – democracy and development – over the last couple of decades.

Evolving concepts

Development used to be understood as the synonym of economic growth. Today, it still includes growth, but is also broadly understood as a process that should lead to a significant and continuous improvement of the quality of life of the majority of the people, particularly the poor. It also incorporates the dimension of human rights – including civic and political rights and should ideally lead to the reduction of disparities in the distribution of income.

The way we use the term democracy has also undergone important changes: from liberal democracy – concerned essentially with individual freedoms, electoral mechanisms and the rule of law – towards participatory democracy and some would say also – towards social democracy: not in the sense of the programme implemented by a specific political party but as a system of governance expected to deliver on social and economic rights and development in the broadest sense. This should not, however, lead us to believe that people in economically less developed countries do not also care about basic political rights and freedoms. A survey undertaken by IDEA in Nepal earlier this year demonstrated that what people expected from democracy was, first and foremost, political freedom.

There is evolution towards a more common ground for democracy and development. In spite of the empirically ambiguous and not very conclusive findings of the impact of democracy on economic growth and *vice versa*, there is a growing consensus – almost a universal acceptance – of three points:
First, that both development and democracy are desirable –values to be pursued in themselves.
Second, that development is more than economic growth.
Third, that democracy is more than the institutions and the mechanics of democracy, i.e., that democracy is also expected to deliver in terms of a better quality of life.

Thus, it is clear that there has been a converging evolution of the two terms towards each other: democracy is more and more meant to include development and development is more and more meant to include the realisation of the basic human rights, including of course, civic and political ones.

Politics matter for development

Both bilateral development agencies and multilateral organisations have to a great extent accepted the thesis that democracy and good governance are key ingredients of development. This is reflected in the fact that bilateral development agencies of the

160

industrialised countries and multilateral organisations include democratic governance as an important criterion for aid allocation. This is also how governance and democracy building became important dimensions of development assistance.

The flip-side of this evolution is that, in developing countries, debates on national economic policies and economic priorities have become strongly influenced by mechanisms designed to facilitate economic cooperation with industrialised countries and, in particular aid allocation. In developing countries, policy debates on development objectives are greatly influenced by internationally led mechanisms for policy dialogue, for example the Poverty Reduction Strategy Paper (PRSP) process. Though negotiated nationally through what should be a participatory and nationally owned process, PRSPs are ultimately assessed by bilateral and multilateral actors in international policy fora and aid flows are influenced by their approval.

The very recognition of the link between democracy and development, paradoxically, has also led to the establishment of instruments and channels to verify the compliance with criteria and priorities determined by the donors rather than those established by the citizens of the developing countries concerned. In a way, responding to criteria established by donors (not necessarily wrong in economic terms) has limited the internal democratic debate on development and taken precedence over it.

International partners place a strong focus on executives and civil society organisations. While the role of such actors is certainly important, an excessive emphasis on it undermines the functions of other actors in political systems such as Parliaments and political parties. Focusing only on the executive effectively means that the principle of ownership is applied to the government, often through the ministries of finance or planning. In polarised societies, not least in post-conflict situations, such approaches by international actors risk exacerbating the polarisation. If in the eyes of the political opposition, the international community cares for the government party only, it will be hard to avoid a "winner takes all" political culture in which being in government means access to big resources while being in opposition means trying to block whatever effort the government makes and trying to reap the benefits of office at the next elections. The space for nationally owned, broad-based visions for development is thus hard to achieve and the international community may be part of the reason why.

There is a growing concern among political party actors in many developing countries that national development objectives are so constrained by international donor pressures and conditionalities that there is effectively little space left for competitive politics. Leaders in political parties in Africa have, for example, expressed that developing political platforms is not all that important because that responsibility is taken care of by the PRSP process.

These undesired effects of the PRSPs are coming into contradiction with the notion of national ownership. The problem has been identified on both sides of the North/South divide and there are debates on how to overcome it.

How can Europe contribute?

My starting points are the following two: the European Union is probably the most successful democracy-building project in history and the European Union is today the largest provider of development aid globally.

The success of the EU in democracy-building has largely been a European affair: inducing potential member states, supporting new member states, and active and ambitious neighbourhood policies. On the global scene however, there is less articulation and less ambition. The European Instrument for Democracy and Human Rights is well and good but it is detached from the much bigger and broader development cooperation programmes.

Bringing the democratic politics dimension more strongly into European development cooperation policies can, needless to say, have a big impact. As there is no longer an American leadership in democracy building, today is the time for Europe.

Europe should build on its own example for other regions of economical and political integration. This position gives Europe an attractiveness and legitimacy that are important in pursuing democratic development efforts globally. In an era of polarisation within global organisations like the UN, there are at the same time interesting and promising developments within regional organisations of the south, not least in the African Union. There is much to gain from a stronger, broader and deeper EU partnership with other regional organisations in the field of democracy and development.

Given the different dynamics of each region and each country there is a need to ensure that programmes are aligned with the development objectives of the countries and regions at hand. For example, in Latin America and specifically the Andean region, International IDEA has been working (sometimes in partnership with the NIMD) with political parties to discuss the development challenges their countries are facing as well as their participation in policy making that targets poverty reduction. Such an approach is imperative in a region where exclusion and huge gaps in wealth distribution have played a major role in weakening the credibility of key political institutions.

In Africa, challenges also differ across the continent and policies have had to respond to different environments and take into account extreme levels of poverty. Both democracy and development are key to ensuring lasting peace and security and despite the manifold complexities there are many positive developments across the continent.

Firstly, a significant number of African countries have recently seen the end of violent internal conflicts which undermined human rights, democracy and development and are moving towards democratisation. Secondly, a number of emerging democracies have been characterised by the peaceful alternation of power and are moving in the direction of other countries that are working to consolidate democracy through a culture of representation, participation and accountability. Africa's own development programmes such as NEPAD and the Africa Peer Review Mechanism (APRM) continue to inspire more African countries to take responsibility to shape their own destiny and to position Africa as a key player in the global arena.

Thirdly, the unanimous adoption of the African charter on Democracy, Elections and Governance earlier this year by the 8th ordinary session of the African Union Assembly was another major step forward despite the complexities of implementing such an ambitious document. Throughout the Charter there is a constant commitment of AU Member States towards institutionalisation of democratic social, economic and political governance. To this end, I will take advantage of this opportunity to announce that International IDEA has been requested by the AU to provide support to the organisation in determining a solid action plan for disseminating and implementing the Democracy Charter. To formalise this arrangement a Memorandum of Understanding was signed between both organisations in June and work on the Action Plan has already commenced. The role of national democratic institutions, including parliaments and political parties, will be key to ensuring the implementation of the Charter especially since the rationale behind the Charter is that it *further reinforces commitment of AU Member States to democracy, development and peace*" and that "*while democracy requires participatory and inclusive development; participatory development too cannot be realised without democracy.*"

In a global context of more polarisation, Europe should *not* develop democracy building policies that are confrontational but ones that are partnership orientated towards regional organisations, developmental in terms of taking a long-term perspective and building on a national leadership of democratic and development processes and not only on ownership of largely foreign-led policies.

Looking Forward

Lena Hjelm-Wallén

The "Democracy and Development" nexus has been and continues to be debated both in academic circles and in the international community. There is, however, a broad understanding that the linkages are multiple and very relevant, both for those who work in the field of democracy building and those who are involved in development policies.

Development is increasingly understood as a general improvement of the "quality of life" for the majority of the population and as such, it includes GDP growth, but also the effective fulfillment of human rights, including civic and political rights. On the other hand, democracy is not only a value to be pursued for its own sake, but also an integrated tool. It is a system of governance expected to deliver a better quality of life.

Let me admit that when I heard that a new theme in the development cooperation debate was "Democracy and Development" I was a bit puzzled. I asked if this is really something that has to be discussed. To me, development and democracy is part and parcel of each other. Perhaps a naïve idea from a long life in parliament and government but also perhaps from experience in the field of development cooperation.

Since long ago we know that development – in order to be sustainable – needs dedicated people who take the responsibility for projects and achievements especially when the external financing and engagement is over. To be very practical, I would like to highlight "maintenance". The water pump in the village, the road, the collective latrine – they all need to be maintained by someone. People in the village must shoulder responsibility collectively. Someone has to be entrusted to ensure the continued functioning of this common investment.

In some places, there are no structures for this. In other places, there are traditional structures, even if they cannot always be called democratic. This is the opportunity to take the first basic steps in building democracy at the village level. The need for a collective responsibility must be reflected in a council, a shura, a working group or whatever it may be called. This body should be elected in a democratic way, make decisions and be accountable for its activities. For most donor agencies or NGOs this has been a normal way of attaching democracy to development at the local level and to ensure that development has a better chance to be sustainable.

I believe that we too often start the discussion about democratic structures from above. The first basic steps at the ground level are often neglected. My firm belief is that the local level is underestimated: this is where people get direct experience of the meaning of democracy. It is also at the local level that the struggle for involvement of women in the decision making must start.

This is not to say that the nexus "Democracy and Development" should not be discussed. On the contrary – it is very important, not least to secure that this concept continues to be at the front line of development cooperation policies and theories. The ongoing debate on the importance of participation and ownership in the design and implementation of development programs is a reflection of this new awareness, as are demands for governance reforms. One proof of this is that good governance has been included in the Millennium Development Goals and that the international community includes democratic governance as an important criterion for aid allocation.

So for development to stay sustainable, participation, ownership, responsibility at all levels (from the village to the state) are needed as well as the necessary qualities all attributed to democracy. As for sustainability to be long-term, both development and democracy must be homegrown. Let us, for the future, when the tendencies in development policies come and go, remember this as the basic strategy! This is even more important to stress when we know that it is very difficult to measure in quantitative terms the concrete "impact" of democracy on development.

However, the thesis that authoritarian rule may be better for development is definitely losing strength, not least because development itself is no longer seen as something just reflected in economic growth. The case of China is frequently cited as a disturbing exception to the rule but please remember the way in which China's case is being presented. It is debatable whether the remarkable growth of the Chinese economy should be attributed to authoritarian rule or rather to other features, such as the growing pool of skilled human resources and the equally huge domestic market. Furthermore, is China more or less authoritarian today than it was in Mao's time?

China's political stage is still closed to multi-party elections but the margins of free economic initiative have definitely expanded and China is certainly a more open country today than it was thirty years ago. This is not to say that China is on the verge of becoming democratic – China is still far from that; the point is that one should be very careful in identifying causal relations in such complex developments. The development/democracy nexus in China will be of great interest to follow and should be closely scrutinized in the future. I hope that even in China we will be able to see that development will have a positive influence on democracy, rule of law and respect for human rights and also a growing understanding in China that development needs democracy in order to be sustainable.

Let me now turn to the question about the capacity of a democratic regime to make a better life possible for its citizens. I am sorry to say that there are ample evidences of the failure of democratically elected governments to deliver on economic issues and basic services. For example, in Latin America, democratic countries also show large income distribution disparities. This seriously affects the credibility of democratic institutions, including parliaments and political parties. Even if expressing an opinion about this is close to internal politics in these countries, I would like to argue that it must be debated more in the future as being an obstacle for democracy building.

Rule of law and respect for human rights are fundamental elements in a democracy. They constitute core elements in the development of a better quality of life, especially for marginalized people. Please note that even in democracies, millions of women are still expecting improvements in their daily lives, respect for their human rights and equal participation in political life. Therefore a lesson for the future is: democracies that do not deliver a better quality of life to poor people and do not even show efforts in that direction, will in the long run damage all democratization efforts. Unfortunately, I have to add that when governments in the West – the US as well as in the EU – decide not to accept the outcome of democratic elections, strong obstacles are also created to the struggle for democracy worldwide.

Political parties are necessary in a democratic system, but they face big problems globally. It is obvious that they lack the trust of the people. This is a challenge in the established democracies in Europe but is, of course, even more complicated in societies where a party system is relatively new and the development agencies do not always behave in a way that is supportive to political parties. Competition between NGOs and political parties and the unintended effects of the behavior of international donors are limiting the political space.

I wish to repeat what Vidar Helgesen mentioned earlier: development agencies place a strong focus on executives and on civil society organizations. Of course the role of such actors is important but an excessive emphasis on them can undermine the functions of other actors in the political system, for example parliaments and political parties. There is a growing concern among political parties in many developing countries in this regard. They argue that national development objectives, as important as they are, do not constitute issues that can differentiate their political platforms from those of their contenders. The political space is limited by outside actors such as international donors, their pressures, processes, and even conditionalities.

Also, there is often a perception that the recipients of development assistance are more accountable towards the donors than towards elected representatives in their parliaments and political parties. This situation may have several adverse consequences. Firstly, national political actors (parliaments and ruling political parties) lose a key opportunity to strengthen their roles and their credibility as representatives of the citizens by shying away from debating development issues and priorities. Secondly, development issues, by being absent (or insufficiently present) in the political debate, run the risk of becoming out of tune with the key expectations of a broad range of national stakeholders.

By the same token, political parties may lose motivation to acquire the necessary knowledge and capacity to aggregate the important demands of their constituencies and to express themselves through coherent economic and social programs. Let us be aware of these consequences. The donors should avoid measures that hamper a normal political life which must function in a democratic society.

Several development cooperation agencies have shifted or are shifting towards a stronger focus on Parliaments and political parties as key institutions that should be involved and supported in the reconstruction and development of their country. EU countries – such as the Netherlands, Sweden, Spain, the UK and Germany – are adopting this focus in terms of their policy making. This must also influence the wider development agendas of the World Bank and the harmonization agendas of the OECD.

It is also obvious that the EU should and could do much more. The EU should use its own experience from the enlargement process to enrich its development assistance and its support to democratization. The EU has experienced the positive interactions between democracy and development. The EU can and must use its "soft" power, not only in its development cooperation but also use its role as an important political actor on the international stage, for example in the UN and in the Bretton Woods institutions. This is even more important as the American way of dealing with issues of democracy is highly questionable. To express it diplomatically – Iraq and Afghanistan are not good examples of how to work with these sensitive issues.

It is now up to actors for democracy to ensure that the Democracy-Development nexus is translated into policies and actions by the international community. The landscape of democracy building is complex for all. Let us bear in mind that the ultimate purpose is to allow women and men at all levels, civil society and political parties to be real democratic actors in their own societies.

Part IV

Culture and democracy

Structural and Cultural Preconditions for Democracy

David Beetham

The term "democracy" can mean many things because there are many features that are required if a political system is to realise the basic democratic principles of popular control over government in conditions of political equality. For the purpose of this chapter, I shall take democracy to mean *an effective electoral democracy*, that is, one which not only has the outward form of elections for public office by universal suffrage, but where elections give citizens sufficient control over the personnel and policies of government that it works in the main to meet their expressed interests and needs.

Two basic preconditions for democracy

I begin with two basic preconditions for such an electoral democracy, preconditions which are fairly self-evident, though they are frequently overlooked.[1] The first is a functioning state, which has the capacity to enforce its law and administer its policy throughout its territory. In the absence of a functioning state in this sense, an elected government will simply lack the power to deliver on any electoral programme it may have put before the people. We could all cite examples of countries where the writ of the government hardly extends beyond the capital city, or where it is systematically incapable of ensuring that its legislation is enforced in practice. Such a country may enjoy all the trappings of "free and fair elections", but not an effective electoral democracy, since popular control or influence over government is meaningless where the government itself has little or no control over its own territory.

173

A second basic precondition for an effective electoral democracy is a minimum level of agreement on nationhood within the country's borders. If democracy means rule by the people, then there has to be agreement on who constitutes the people who are to be both the agents and the subjects of that rule. As the democratic theorist Rousseau recognised, this is logically a *pre-democratic* question: before you can implement a majoritarian procedure, you have to have broad agreement on the identity of the "demos" who is to be the subject of that procedure.[2] In the absence of such agreement, electoral democracy may serve to intensify rather than reconcile societal divisions, especially where it leads to the virtually permanent domination of one community over another. In such a circumstance, the electoral process, however formally "free and fair", cannot realise the basic democratic requirement of political equality between citizens.

Again, we can all cite examples where this has happened. In my own country, you need look no further afield than Northern Ireland, where the combination of fundamental disagreement about nationhood with the mobilisation of political parties around this division has made electoral democracy unworkable for more than a generation. Now, of course, we should acknowledge that when electoral democracy breaks down under such circumstances, it is to the *democratic* processes of discussion, negotiation and compromise, rather than forcible imposition, that we have to turn. But we should not confuse that sense of democracy with electoral politics, especially where that politics has strongly majoritarian, winner-take-all, outcomes. To put it at its simplest, there has to be sufficient agreement among the "demos" for it to be able to withstand the inevitable divisiveness of electoral competition.

That you cannot have an effective electoral democracy in the absence of these two prior conditions – a functioning state and agreement on nationhood – seems to have been overlooked by the authors of the project to impose electoral democracy on Iraq; since removing an oppressive regime simultaneously destroyed a functioning state apparatus; and radically altering the power balance between the country's communities undermined an already fragile sense of nationhood. Whether that error was inscribed in the project from the outset, as I would argue, or was the result of failures in implementation, is a question for another day. The advantage of the Western democracies historically was that these two preconditions of state and nation were largely established prior to the introduction of electoral democracy, whereas many new democracies have the difficult task of establishing them, i.e., democracy and its preconditions, simultaneously.

Democratic culture as precondition

This brings me now to my main subject, which is whether there is a further precondition for electoral democracy, something called a *democratic culture*, that is, a set of popular attitudes and dispositions without which democratic institutions cannot take root or flourish. I am sceptical about this precondition for two reasons: first because the academic literature has always been divided over precisely what that culture consists in. Some of you may be old enough to remember the controversy that was aroused in the 1960s by Almond and Verba's book *The Civic Culture*, which concluded that the culture necessary for democracy was just that combination of attitudes and dispositions only to be found in Anglo-Saxon countries – a controversy that was not stilled by the publication of a second volume entitled *The Civic Culture Revisited*.[3] I am sceptical for a second reason, and that is because the academic literature has also been deeply divided over whether a democratic culture – supposing we can agree on what it is – is more a *cause* or a *consequence* of functioning democratic institutions. For myself, I have tended to be convinced by those who argue that it is the opportunities available for political participation through which people develop the capacities to use them effectively, and that the education for democracy largely comes through practising it.

However, there is a negative version of this cultural argument, with a long pedigree, which holds that, whatever difficulties we may have in defining what counts as a democratic culture, there are certain characteristics inherent in some peoples and their belief systems, which make it exceedingly difficult, if not impossible, for democratic institutions to take root and become consolidated among them. In other words, if we cannot define a democratic culture, at least we can recognize a non-democratic one when we see it.

In the nineteenth century this argument took a liberal-imperialist direction with the thesis, typically expounded by John Stuart Mill in *On Representative Government*, that there were different stages of civilization through which all peoples had to pass, and that only at a more advanced or "higher" cultural stage were they capable of supporting self-government through democratic institutions. Before that time they were best suited to what Mill called a government of "leading strings", that is, a paternalist form of rule by those who had already attained this higher cultural level. Mill was thus dismissive of the more generalizing theories of his predecessors, such as Jeremy Bentham and his father James Mill, "who claimed representative democracy for England and France by arguments which would equally have proved it to be the only fit form of government for Bedouins or Malays."[4]

In the twentieth century, the identification of cultures that were supposedly hostile to democracy took a religious turn, and whole religions were anathematized as providing barren soil for the support of democratic institutions. At first this was expressed as a contrast between Protestantism on one side, especially in its non-conformist, non-Lutheran, form, which was seen as encouraging self-responsibility and opposition to hierarchical authority, and Catholicism on the other, which supposedly fostered a much more deferential and even anti-democratic culture. This culture was argued to be the reason why Catholic southern Europe and Latin America had such difficulty in sustaining democratic institutions. However, with the transition of Spain and Portugal to democracy in the mid-1970s and much of Latin America from the mid-1980s onwards, this argument wore rather thin; and Western Christendom as a whole came to be given a clean bill of health, so to say, in contrast to Eastern religions, which were the ones now identified as antithetical to democracy: Confucianism, for example, because it subordinated the individual to the collective good; and Islam, because it comprised a legislative project which allowed no separation between faith and politics. The fact that such arguments were appropriated by authoritarian governments to justify their rule in the name of "Asian values" did not make them any more credible, especially when a number of East Asian countries with a Confucian culture showed themselves capable of sustaining representative democracy.[5] And as far as Islam is concerned, it is a fact that the greater number of Muslims in the world now live under democratic institutions, including three countries where Muslims constitute a large majority of the population – Indonesia, Bangladesh and Turkey. Whatever defects there may be in these democracies would be difficult to assign to Islam; just as the obstacles facing democratization across the Middle East have more to do with the specific social and geo-political formations of that region than they have with Islam as such.[6]

What then should we conclude from this brief, and no doubt somewhat selective, survey? My first conclusion is a negative one: we should be sceptical of any attempt to categorize whole belief systems as either supportive of, or antithetical to, democracy *tout court*. As regards religions, these belief systems have been amenable to widely different interpretations and political implications according to the context and circumstances. So Christianity has historically supported both the divine right of kings and the most egalitarian republicanism; in its Catholic form it has supported both authoritarian government and principled resistance to it in the name of liberation theology. And so on. We need to understand the social and political reasons why religions take the form they do in a given context, not ascribe it to some inherent tendency *per se*, as is done for example in the "clash of civilisations" rhetoric, or even in explanations for terrorism embraced by some Western governments who should know better.

The question of trust

This does not mean that the prevalent attitudes and dispositions within a society have no consequences for the character of its democracy; only that we should not look to unchanging belief systems for their explanation. Here comes my second conclusion: a *political culture* – that is, the political attitudes and expectations that people have – is typically a response to their experience of social and political relations, and the way power is exercised and reproduced within their society; and it is to these more tangible features that we should look if we want to understand the interplay between popular attitudes and democratic politics. This is a conclusion that a careful reading of Robert Putnam's original work on Italy, *Making Democracy Work*, would also endorse.[7]

Let me take as an example the question of *trust*, which was given as a subject to include in today's lecture, no doubt because it is widely accepted that public trust in political institutions is important to the functioning of democracy. Now we know that in many of what the UN calls "new or restored" democracies, levels of popular trust in their political institutions and the political elites who occupy them is very low. I have been involved over the past eighteen months or so in a project at the Inter-Parliamentary Union in Geneva to produce a guide to good democratic practice for parliaments, in the course of which we looked at comparative figures from the various regional barometers of public opinion, measuring the levels of popular trust or confidence in parliaments – which are, after all, the key institutions of representative democracy. Almost everywhere, across all regions of the world, parliaments came bottom of the list of public institutions in which people expressed confidence, and they came, and come, particularly low in the new or restored democracies.[8]

What is the explanation for this low level of trust? Well, there is a cultural, or we could say culturalist, explanation, which holds that levels of trust in institutions are a function of the levels of interpersonal trust that pertain in society at large, such that, if people do not trust others in their everyday dealings, this is reflected in a low level of trust towards their political institutions. We can, I think, recognize this explanation as another version of the idea that in certain societies there are endemic cultural obstacles, at a pre-political level, to the operation of democratic politics.[9]

Richard Rose and colleagues have, I believe, convincingly refuted this explanation with a careful statistical analysis of the polling evidence, which shows, perhaps unsurprisingly, that the main reason people express low levels of trust in their democratic institutions is because their experience of their performance is so poor – that is, because they are not perceived as trustworthy. Poor performance leads, perfectly reasonably and predictably, to low levels of public trust or confidence[10] And if we assume that effective government performance requires a combination of *capacity* and *integrity*, then that expression of low confidence is a judgement, not only on the institutions, but also on the people who occupy them. The problem, in other words, lies not so much with the citizens and their supposedly endemic cultures, but with the characteristics and behaviour of their governing elites.

Richard Rose's analysis is largely based on data from the former communist countries of East and Central Europe, but his conclusion is also borne out from polling evidence from Latin America in the Latinobarometer, which shows that the vast majority of respondents across the continent believe that government and parliament serve the interests of a powerful and wealthy few, inside and outside government, rather than the public at large.[11] This is perhaps hardly surprising, given that most elected politicians are drawn from the wealthy strata of society, whose interests they are likely to seek to protect. This is a wider phenomenon that applies to most new or restored democracies, not just in Latin America. A recent study of election financing by the Washington-based National Democratic Institute involved a survey of parliamentarians in developing countries across all continents, and concluded: 'More than four out of five respondents state that they supply the majority of funds for their campaigns, often at the risk of personal bankruptcy... As a result, many resort to relationships with individual donors who expect preferential treatment once the candidate is elected.'[12]

Well, you may say, that is a good description of elections to the US Congress, where candidates require huge personal wealth to stand a hope of election, and put themselves under obligation to the various special interests, which help to finance their increasingly expensive campaigns (the so-called electoral 'arms race'). Yet this is a situation that is particularly damaging to democracy in countries where the gap between the well-off and the rest is so huge, and where elective office offers a standard of life that is far beyond the reach of the average voter, and indeed, where increasing the level of their parliamentary remuneration is under the control of the politicians themselves. In such countries it is much easier for elected office to come to be seen primarily as a means for personal advancement, and for the benefit of those whose financial support is needed to contest an election in the first place.

Now if you talk to the average taxi-driver in most cities in the world, and admit that you are studying politics or democracy, after an initial expression of amazement that anyone should spend their time doing such a thing, they will assure you that all politicians in their country, whichever country it is, are the same, and that they are in the business for what they can get out of it for themselves. That perception is commonplace. Indeed, there is a whole theory of democracy, by Jeremy Bentham and his nineteenth century utilitarian followers, premised on the assumption that everyone seeks to satisfy their personal interests before anything else, and that applies to politicians as much as anyone else. The question Bentham posed was: how could the personal interest of the politician in securing and maintaining office be aligned with a wider *public* interest, which he defined as securing the well-being of the greatest number of citizens. You cannot eliminate self-interest, ran the argument, but you can ensure that it can only be satisfied if a wider public interest is also served. And the only secure mechanism for doing that, according to Bentham, was the prospect of the politician losing office if he did not; and that required a regular electoral sanction in which the electorate was extended to the whole adult population, including women.[13]

The question we have to address is what happens when the electoral sanction does not work? Or when it does, all that seems to happen is the replacement of one self-serving elite by another, and the wider public interest as Bentham defined it gets lost on the way? What happens when elections themselves become part of the problem, because of who can afford the cost of securing election, and because of the favors that come to be owed to those whose financial support is needed to achieve office by the electoral route? What happens when we have elections, in other words, but not an effective electoral democracy as Bentham would have understood it, one which aligns the self-interest of politicians with the wider public interest?

How to make electoral democracy effective?

I want in the last part of this chapter to sketch out three different kinds of solution to this problem that have been tried over the past decade or more; and, since space is limited, I will only be able to give the most cursory summary of each. I will call these attempted solutions the institutional, the economic and the political, respectively.

1. The first, the *institutional* approach, will be familiar to you from the anti-corruption literature. It takes its starting point from the correct assumption that the electoral sanction – or what is called in the jargon the "vertical accountability" of office holders – cannot work on its own, but needs to be supplemented by a robust apparatus of "lateral" accountability, comprising published codes of conduct, registers of financial interest, legal limits on election spending and so on, together with independent institutions with powers of investigation and enforcement – commissions on standards in public life, ombudsmen and so forth. Now, what a number of commentators say about these institutions is that where the

problems are really deep-seated and chronic, these lateral bodies may achieve a clear declaration of standards, and sufficient transparency to identify some of the worst offences, especially with the help of the media, but they fall down at the point of sanctions because the bodies responsible, whether courts or others, can be simply bypassed or subverted in turn.

As one recent article I read expressed it, "there are no win-win anti-corruption strategies; somebody stands to lose, and those who stand to lose are on top." Or as another researcher put it, it is not just a question of identifying appropriate institutions of accountability, but also of *agency*, of who the groups are who are most losing out from corruption, and finding ways of mobilising them in broad-based campaigns within civil society, to bring pressure on governments and shame them into action.[14]

What all agree is that there are no quick fixes. If you look at the history of my own country, it took decades during the nineteenth century to bring to an end what was graphically called "Old Corruption" – the system whereby most public offices could be bought and sold, and where it was taken for granted that office would be used to advance the interests of one's family, clients or dependents. This does not mean that the institutional approach is mistaken, only that it takes a long time and requires strong reinforcement in turn from the agencies of civil society.

2. Where the institutional approach seeks to strengthen the mechanisms of public *accountability*, the economic approach aims to limit the *opportunity* for self-serving politicians by reducing the resources directly controlled by the state, and the amount of economic activity that is subject to political, as opposed to market, determination or decision. These are the well-known strategies of privatization, outsourcing, bringing the market into public service provision and so on. The rationale is that these are not only supposedly more efficient, but also radically reduce the opportunities for what is called "rent-seeking" by politicians. And unlike the institu-

tional approach, which works slowly, this approach promises a quick fix.

The trouble with this strategy is two-fold. First, if, as I have argued, effective government performance is a combination of capacity and integrity, then this strategy seeks to improve integrity by reducing government *capacity*. As Bentham put it succinctly, if you reduce the powers of those in government to do harm, by the same token you also reduce their power to do good. The second objection has been put forcefully by David Marquand in a recent book, *The Decline of the Public*. The distinctive achievements of the modern state, and above all the welfare state, he argues, have been the result precisely of protecting the state against the market, against its logic of profit maximisation and ability to pay. Against this logic has been a different logic, on the one hand, of equal citizenship rights and entitlements, and, on the other, an ethos of public service and public interest. The problem with marketisation, on this analysis, is that it erodes that protection by treating the public sector and its administration as interchangeable with the private. Marquand is writing about what has been happening in the UK, which had already developed a strong sense of the public interest and impartiality in service delivery, but his analysis is even more pertinent to countries where these have been only weakly developed in the first place.[15]

3. The third, *political*, route to a government which serves the public interest, in the Benthamite sense of a government serving the interest of the many not the few, involves a radical change in the political elite; and that usually only happens in countries where social and political movements of the disadvantaged throw up a leadership that remains embedded in the environment and character of the movement, but can go on to win political office through electoral mobilization. This is the route taken by European social democracy in what one might call its classic period in the mid-twentieth century; also the route taken in some countries of Latin America under leaders such as Lula, Chavez and

Morales, where public office is used to improve the lives of the disadvantaged, and so serves to consolidate an electoral base.

Now I know that this generation of Latin American leaders is often dismissed with the disparaging term "populist". There is not the space here to deconstruct this somewhat ambiguous concept. All I will say is that it is surely better to use a country's oil revenues to fund health and education programmes in the poorest communities than to swell the Swiss bank accounts of the ministers; and surely better to use public office for much needed land reform than to propel elected politicians into the ranks of the landowning classes. No doubt we shall never see again what might be called the "hair-shirt tendency" within social democracy – Clement Attlee, who when Deputy Premier in Churchill's wartime cabinet, used to go back to his suburban semi in the evening on the bus (a mode of transport whose use Mrs Thatcher declared to be a sign of social failure); or Stafford Cripps, who when Chancellor of the Exchequer, lived a life of almost monastic asceticism. Those times may well be over. What matters is that, whatever advantages elected politicians may enjoy from office should have wide public endorsement, and they should only continue to enjoy them if they also manifestly serve a wider public interest; because that is, surely, when electoral democracy is working as it should.

Conclusion

Let me conclude. My subject has been what I call an effective electoral democracy, one, that is, where elections give citizens sufficient control over the personnel and policies of government that it works in the main to meet their expressed interests and needs. Apart from the necessary preconditions of a functioning state and a minimum agreement on nationhood, we have been enquiring whether there is also a further precondition for such a democracy, namely something called a "democratic culture". I have expressed scepticism about such a precondition, and argued that low levels of popular trust in democratic institutions are a response to their performance, not the product of some pre-political cultural pattern. This then put the spotlight on the political elites, and on the question of how their desire for power could be harnessed to serving a public and not simply a private interest. I sketched out three attempted solutions to this dilemma: the long haul of institutional accountability, the quick fix of marketisation and the social-democratic mobilisation from below. Although the last of these depends on a favourable conjunction of social and political conditions which cannot be readily influenced from outside, it is the only one where the remedy for the defects of electoral democracy is achieved through the electoral process itself.

Notes

1 For a fuller analysis of these preconditions see Juan J. Linz, and Alfred Stepan, *Problems of Democratic Transition and Consolidation*. Baltimore, Johns Hopkins University Press, 1996, chapter 2.

2 Jean Jacques Rousseau, 1913. *The Social Contract*, Book 1, chapter V. London, Dent.

3 Gabriel A. Almond, and Sydney Verba, 1963. *The Civic Culture*. Princeton, Princeton University press.

4 John Stuart Mill, 1910. *On Representative Government*, chapter 2, esp. pp. 197-9. London, Dent.

5 See Hahm Chaibong, 2004. 'The ironies of Confucianism'. *Journal of Democracy* vol. 15, no. 3, pp. 93-107.

6 See Alfred Stepan, and Graeme B. Robertson, 2003. 'An "Arab" more than "Muslim" electoral gap'. *Journal of Democracy* vol. 14, no. 3, pp. 30-44; and the subsequent debate in *Journal of Democracy*. vol. 15, no. 4, 2004, pp. 126-146.

7 Robert D. Putnam, 1993. *Making Democracy Work: Civic Traditions in Modern Italy*, chapter 5. Princeton, Princeton University Press.

8 David Beetham, 2006. *Parliament and Democracy in the Twenty-First Century: a Guide to Good Practice*. Geneva, Inter-Parliamentary Union, pp. 109-112.

9 For an example, see Marta Lagos, 2001. 'Between stability and crisis in Latin America'. *Journal of Democracy* vol. 12, no. 1, pp. 137-145.

10 William Mishler and Richard Rose, 1998. *Trust in Untrustworthy Institutions: Culture and Institutional Performance in Post-Communist Societies*. Glasgow, Centre for the Study of Public Policy, University of Strathclyde.

11 The findings for 2004 are analysed in *The Economist*, August 14, 2004, pp. 35-36.

12 Denise Baer and Shari Bryan, 2005. *Money in Politics*. Washington DC, National Democratic Institute for International Affairs, p. 4.

13 Jeremy Bentham, *Constitutional Code*. In: *Works*, ed. Bowring, Edinburgh, William Tait, 1843, vol. IX, esp. pp. 95-100, 107-108.

14   See Alina Mungui-Pippida, 'Corruption: diagnosis and treatment'. *Journal of Democracy* vol. 17, no. 3, 2006, pp. 86-99.

15   David Marquand, 2004. *Decline of the Public*. Cambridge, Polity Press.

Democracy and Islam

Anwar Ibrahim

I have been asked to deal with the issue, contentious at times, of Islam and democracy. This happens to be one of the few extremely popular topics entrusted to me. At times, however, I get a bit depressed because the assumption is of course that there is an incompatibility between the two, that there is a problem. Islam and democracy is "problematic". Otherwise it would not be a topic for discussion.

We do not talk about Christianity and democracy or Hinduism and democracy or Confucianism and democracy. Islam and democracy is the political narrative of today and a subject for discourse. Let us then review this issue and look at its historical incidence.

At the Vrije Universiteit this afternoon, as a Muslim I made reference to the classical texts from Ibn Shaf to Abbas Mahazarah to the present-day scholars, about the higher objectives or the makassa or the Shari'a. In these texts, contrary to what we see in practice, the fundamental principle of freedom of conscience, of expression, sanctity of life, property and honour and dignity of men and women, is sacrosanct and cannot be compromised. These are basic principles that must be adhered to.

The question is of course, why are they not applied? That is what we have to grapple with today. But at least, at a foundational level, there is no issue. For a Muslim, for a believer, the principles are laid down in the high objectives or the makassa, or the Shari'a. They are to protect and defend the rights of freedom of conscience, freedom of expression, the sanctity of life and property and the honour and dignity of men and women. This is not my construct, this is what Ibn Shatlini, Uzali, this most prominent of Muslim thinkers, and the contemporary scholars Ibn Shaour and Mohamed Abu Zahra have said. These are the principles as they have been laid down and which I am trying to articulate, consistently with their views.

The case of Indonesia

Now look at it again from a political and historical viewpoint. You are familiar with the developments in Indonesia and of course I am also very passionate about the developments over there. Indonesia gained its independence after the second World War and then in 1955 they conducted their first elections. In my lectures in the United States, I often compare these elections with those in Florida in the year 2000 and consider them far more clean and fair. At least Al Gore agreed with me on that!

But what is amazing to my mind, is that even the Muslims participated at that time, by way of the Mashrumi party, a combination of the Nahdatul Ulama and the various other Muslim parties led by Mohamed Hatta, who later became Prime Minister. He was very Islamic in his views but very inclusive.

Then there was this contentious debate about whether to support the national philosophy of Pancasila or the Piagan Jakarta, the Jakarta Charter, proclaiming an Islamic State with the application of Shari'a law as one of its key objectives. The decision was clearly and categorically in favour of a national agenda, a national state ideology and not for the Islamic State and the application of Shari'a law. This decision was made by the Islamic party and by their Muslim leader.

You should therefore not confuse this Muslim movement in Indonesia with the so-called Islamists or fundamentalists or equate this experience with that of the Taliban and the other extremists and fundamentalists elsewhere and at later times.

188

That has really been the problem for this sort of narrative and so-called discourse here in Europe and the United States: experts and academicians tend to generalise, contrary to the teachings and training of their discipline.

Of course later, under President Sukarno, democracy was hijacked not by the Islamists but by the secularist nationalists under President Sukarno for a number of reasons. I will not dwell on them but the fact is that for the next 30 years Indonesia had to grapple with a form of authoritarian dictatorship until the end of the Suharto era, backed very strongly by many Western governments and more emphatically by the United States. They were supporting not a democracy but a dictatorship, as they did with President Marcos of the Philippines and many others.

However, we have seen in the last few years an amazing, phenomenal development, unprecedented in modern times, a peaceful transition of the largest Muslim country in the world, Indonesia, into a vibrant democracy. The media are free, the leaders are openly criticised, issues of corruption have surfaced, judicial decisions have been questioned and elections have been conducted in a very free and fair manner. Moreover, after democracy was in operation, were they able to resolve decades of contentious problems: civil wars from Aceh to East Timor.

I am, as I said, passionate about this and an optimist as far as Indonesia goes, although I have to acknowledge that they still have to grapple with two problems: development and corruption. They have huge problems with the marginalised, the poor living in abject poverty and also allegations of enormous corruption involving the leadership, the instruments of government and the administrative system or framework. I am, however, more optimistic about the future of Indonesia because, given the institutions of governance and democracy, with these institutions in place, including the free media, you can be assured that these excesses will be exposed and no leader in a functioning democracy will survive or would dare to ignore this huge barrage of criticism against the excesses.

The case of India

Let me turn to India, the second largest Muslim community in the world. It is a vibrant democracy where, because they are not the majority, the Muslims are not represented in government. There is a recent report by a commission in India, appointed by President Mahmohan Singh, a man of high integrity. He installed a commission on the plight of the Muslims in India and found that the Muslim community happens to be the least developed, the poorest and most marginalised of all minorities, worse then the untouchables or the Dalids, the lowest caste.

The immediate response of President Mahmohan was that India has to deal with this, it will have to protect the minority rights of the Muslims. Now my immediate response was that if India under a non-Muslim Hindu leader could guarantee the rights of Muslims in India, it should be the duty of Muslim rulers all over the world to ensure that the rights of the minority non-Muslims in their countries are protected. This is the principle of reciprocity that I learned from Islam and also from the basic teachings of Confucius: "Do not do unto others what you do not want others to do unto you".

This is, by the way, the advantage of coming from a multicultural, multi-religious country like Malaysia: you survive by going from Shakespeare to the Koran to Confucius to Bagawawita and Mohamed Hatta. However, Indian Muslims participated in democracy. I was once with the Indian Finance Minister and we discussed this question. It was with great pride that he pronounced that India, because of this democratic experiment, has not seen any semblance of extremism or terrorist cells as you see elsewhere. They spring up endogenously within India. Yes, they have problems in Kashmir, but in India proper, it stands out as an example of democracy.

Turkey

Then we come to Turkey. I mention this because, why is it that at the end of a discourse like this, people do not seem to be impressed or convinced that there is a possibility of having democratic regimes in Muslim societies and countries? You have the largest Muslim country, Indonesia, the second largest, India and the economically more successful Turkey.

Turkey has to grapple with the issue, not so much between the Islamists and the secularists, as between democrats united in a democratic party, including some Islamic groups on the one hand and the threat of a coup d'état by the military on the other. Hence, the battle of the soul in Turkey is not a matter of Islam or secularism but a battle for vibrant democracy in Turkey on the one hand or the threat of military rule in Turkey on the other. I hope friends here, including Europe, make their positions clear that they are for freedom and democracy.

What about Malaysia?

Now you may make the following remark that these countries happen to be non-Arab countries. You should have an Arab speaker to answer for the Arab world. I am "safe", being from the region I come from, although Malaysia is certainly far from being democratic: there are no free media, the judiciary is corrupt, the corruption index has soared in the last few years, we have lost in competitiveness and we are still grappling with some of the problems of a racial and religious divide, which we have not had since 1965/70.

There are therefore quite some worrying signs in Malaysia but certainly, the situation is far better than in many other, African countries. I tend to be quite cynical in my lectures in Malaysia. This is, as you can understand, why the government does not quite approve of me. When they object and say: "Who says we are not doing well?", my answer is:"Yes, we are doing much better then Somalia and Zimbabwe...".

Unlike the Indonesian experience, a country like Malaysia has enormous potential because we started at a very high level. In the 70s we competed with Singapore, Taiwan and South Korea. This was the level of Malaysia in the '70s. Now Singapore's GDP is five times as high as that of Malaysia, the GDPs of Taiwan and South Korea are three times higher. I would then question why this is so. Is this because of the Islam we boast so much about? Or is it because of poor governance or poor accountability? No, it is because there are no free media to question the excesses and due to the corruption endemic in the system. My answer is therefore: there is a need for democracy as is demonstrated by cases like Indonesia, India and Turkey, where we have seen very impressive development indeed.

In the Middle East, Iran is currently a classic example of a country having experienced democracy at an early stage. As you know, in 1953 Mossadeq was duly elected President of Iran. But of course, the President was toppled by the CIA and the British. Fortunately, in that case the Dutch were not involved! There was a system, however. Now any Iranian, when you tell them you want them to be democratic, will say: "Look, you want to preach on behalf of the Americans"? Immediately the association is with the Americans, in particular the Bush administration, and this is not something to be taken lightly because they speak from historical experience.

The promise of freedom

My view is that this has to be distinguished from freedom, as promised by the leaders of those countries. Remember Sukarno and Mohamed Hatta at the time they were fighting the Dutch. What did they promise to the Indonesians: "We want to build you this "Golden Bridge", or in the words of Sukarno: "Jembatan Mas", in those backward days of destitute and colonised rule and build this new Indonesia, free, democratic and economically successful.

Nothing happened in that way but there was a promise!

What did Neru and Mahatma Gandhi promise the Indians? Freedom, democracy. How did they succeed? Through the free media. How was Sukarno able to disseminate this information to Hatta throughout Indonesia? Partly through free or even semi-free media in some other places in Indonesia. How can people in the West, after all that, 50, 60 years after independence, tell us: "You are not ready for democracy?" I think this a bit strange after such a basic promise.

The Islamic debate

The question of an Islamic debate, the Islamic debate about compatibility with democracy is more vibrant in the US and Europe then in Islamic countries. Do you see any discourse in the Arab world? Nobody says they are not compatible! The dictators do not want it. Period. The ruling autocracies do not want it. Period. There is no discussion. There is no one saying: "Well, in our country they are not compatible."

Some will use this argument of incompatibility while introducing draconian measures like Guantanamo Bay in the US. Then the Malaysian Prime Minister will say: "Look, that is why we need the internal security act. You know, even the US has it". And suddenly, the US has become the example!

When President Bush made what I consider one of his most disastrous policy decisions regarding the principle of freedom by suspending *habeas corpus*, suspending civil liberties, this was quoted by all the tyrants and dictators in the Muslim world.

Back to Iran: as you have seen, Iran is a clear example of a country that had some experience of democracy. This demonstrates that there is not something inherent in Muslim society that is not compatible with democracy. They have done it! Successfully! Had there not been that intervention, they might still have it.

On Indonesia again: one of the most perceptive studies of Indonesian society was done by a Dutch scholar, Snouck

Hurgronje. Had the Indonesian leaders read his classic two-volume account and study of the Acenese in the later part of the 19th century, I do not think the civil war would have taken place or have gone on for so long. Not that I agree with his thesis, leading to his final recommendation to the Queen to introduce and apply an ethical policy, but he was a great scholar in his own right and he was deeply perceptive of and understood the culture and religiosity of the Acenese. Which unfortunately, our semiliterate leaders do not have time to read!

How to deal with the Arab world

Now we come to the final point: how should the West deal with the Arab world? It is for the European Union to consider and try to support the institutions of civil society and not intervene through force of arms, as was attempted by President Bush in Iraq, which was clearly a disaster. This was more of a disservice to democracy and to Islam and to the Muslims then any other policy decision in recent times.

To my mind, the Iraq war, because of its faulty, fraudulent plan and implementation by brute force, has not only led to chaos in Iraq but to a complete disillusionment and distrust by Muslims of the US. However, this is not a fair account because President Bush is not the whole US. He happens to be the voice of the administration of the US. I have met many Americans who are deeply opposed to his views.

As with the war in Iraq, the US fails to resolve the Palestinian-Israeli conflict, which has enraged the Muslims even more in the Middle East and has given them a pretext and excuse not to undertake any changes in their policy.

The religious view on Islam and democracy

There have also been questions raised about the incompatibility of democracy and Islam because the ultimate authority lies in Allah. We are only his servants on Earth. Thus all laws and legal systems

194

follow from this and the people have no say in them. Therefore, democracy cannot function. In classical terms this means: *vox populi, vox dei*, a principle which was adhered to even by the Christians. This was of course articulated by scholars like Maududi in "Islamic Law and Constitution", or Said Kutu, the Islamic leader in "Milestones", where he said: "Where democracy has been introduced and exploited, serious transgressions of God's laws took place because decisions were motivated and determined by majority vote only".

Whilst I respect these scholars and some of their views, I insist they must be read in context. Their thesis of democracy is fundamentally flawed because it is based on the assumption that human beings will continue to err. These scholars are motivated essentially by all the excesses and examples of the Western experience with democracy. In their eyes, Westerners decide to transgress against God in everything: in liberation, in gender equality, etc. This is contrary to my understanding of Islam because I think gender equality is a basic principle of our religion. Who are we to determine and denigrate the status of women or whomsoever, Muslim or non-Muslim alike?

The important point is: are the views of scholars or ulama like Maududi or Said Kutu so pervasive in their influence that Muslims on the whole have rejected democracy? I do not believe this is tenable because given half a chance, if there were free and fair elections in Pakistan, people would still opt to participate in them whether they respect Maudidu or not. For that matter, Maududi's party Jamal Islami participates actively in democratic elections in Pakistan.

The next question

Then of course the next question – because for Muslims there are always series of questions to answer – would be: once they win, will they not hijack democracy? I do not know the basis for this idea. Whether this has happened somewhere once or whether they just say it is bound to happen. Maybe it is because of the application of

Shari'a law by the FIS in Algeria that they say we must not recognise democratic elections won by Hamas in Palestine. Then this is a recipe for disaster. This is a clear case of contradiction and hypocrisy.

In Malaysia, I worked with the Chinese opposition democratic party on the one hand and with the Islamic party on the other. The Islamic party is not the Taliban! They accept the constitutional provisions, including issues like freedom of conscience, freedom of expression and the rule of law. They accept and call for a reform agenda.

Once countries adopt and accept constitutional guarantees, the West must be prepared to work with them whether they like it or not, even if these countries do not fully conform to the theoretical philosophical construct accepted by the West. The Europeans and the Americans cannot and must not dictate the *language of discourse* in other societies.

Universal principles? Yes, we all call for freedom, we cannot detain people without trial. We cannot ill-treat our women and children, condemn whole societies and marginalise them. These are central issues, but what they want to wear or choose to wear, whether they choose to wear a long beard or a short one or no beard at all, whether they prefer to be bald or have a lot of hair, is their own damned business.

This is a fundamental principle to me as a democrat and a person who believes strongly in freedom: it is not the business of Muslims to dictate the lifestyle and decisions made by European and American governments. You can question them, of course. After all, this is a free country in a globalised world. However, the language of discourse cannot be dictated.

This is the present problem: the language of discourse is being to a large extent dictated. Take the example of Indonesia again being strongly criticised. This country has been under a dictatorship for thirty years. It has moved toward democracy, it has free media, free elections, a remedy against judicial indiscretion, etc. There is also a debate about pornography and laws affecting pornography. There was a huge outcry because the ministers apparently did not understand democracy because they wanted to curb pornography. "I mean, give them a break, for heaven's sake"!

The right to navigate

This is the problem in my view: the right to navigate. This also applies to Turkey. I am not pressing my own personal views but allowing people navigate, find their own way. What cannot be compromised is when hundreds or thousands are detained without trial, when we suspend *habeas corpus*. Then you must voice your strong opposition against inhuman practices, not only in the Muslim world but in the USA, when there are excesses against fundamental universal principles. It does not matter whether they are Christian, Muslim or Hindu. You cannot pick and choose. One person who reads the Koran and talks about violence is condemned. Why don't you re-read Saint Augustine's "City of God"? You will find excerpt after excerpt that is not acceptable in modern parlance. I was a professor in a Jesuit university, so I am quite familiar with this text.

As you have found out: I speak with great passion. As you know, being in solitary confinement for six years teaches you a lot. That is why I can refer to so many books: the Koran and Shakespeare and Ahmatova and John Locke. I had all the time in the world to read. Many of you doing your doctorate do not have the time. You can always go on to become a politician and find time, like I did!

Don't compartmentalise

I make reference again to Amartya Sen, the great Nobel laureate, economist, a great friend of mine, who finally said: "Don't compartmentalise people". I think this also applies to Muslims. Don't compartmentalise Europeans and say: "They are conspiratorial, they are anti-Islam."

Then, to whom do I speak? Who do I represent? Yes, I am a Muslim. I am a Malaysian, I am an Asian, I can quote Shakespeare, I read Ahmatova, I associate myself with the Bill of Rights and the Jeffersonian ideals, I consider Tocqueville's "Democracy in America" a great piece of work, I consider Shakespeare as the centre of the universal canon.

How then do you describe me? East? Yes! West? Yes! Lover of Shakespeare? Yes! Lover of the Koran? Yes! Muslim? Yes! Admirer of religions? Yes! A great fan of Confucius? Yes! So how do you compartmentalise me? Of course, in essence I am a Malay. I am an Asian, I can associate myself very much with Europe. After all, I am a Malaysian colonised by the British for a hundred years, and I love to be in London. I tell you, most Indonesians that I meet, when they go to Europe, if you ask: "Where to?" they say "Amsterdam, Bak, Amsterdam!" Immediately, for Indonesians it must be "Belanda". For a Malaysian it must be London, of course.

I mean, if you do that and if you encourage people through education and development, half the problems of the world would be solved. Our main problem is lack of education and development. This is the point: it is not Islam and democracy, it is essentially and finally: education and development.

Between Theology and the Law: Reconsidering the Islamic View of Democracy and Rights

Vincent J. Cornell

You [Americans] are the nation who, rather than ruling by the *Sharia* of God in its Constitution and Laws, choose to invent your own laws as you will and desire. You separate religion from your policies, contradicting the pure nature that affirms Absolute Authority to the Lord and your Creator. You flee from the embarrassing question posed to you: How is it possible for God the Almighty to fashion His creation, grant men power over all creatures and land, grant them all the amenities of life, and then deny them that which they are most in need of: knowledge of the laws which govern their lives? (Osama Bin Laden)[1]

Although it has often been overlooked, this statement by Osama Bin Laden reminds us that despite the emphasis on the Shari'a in contemporary Islamic discourse, theology remains important. Today, just as in the past, theological questions cannot be artificially separated from legal or political questions in Islam. In fact, whereas theology might be practiced without recourse to the law, legal questions about religious belief or practice in Islam cannot be answered without recourse to theology. The assertion by Tariq Ramadan that "there is no Islamic theology" makes a good slogan but it is just as mistaken nowadays as it would have been several centuries ago.[2] In premodern Islam, the question of whether one's faith was "pure" or "impure" was often decided by jurists; however, many of these jurists also doubled as theologians and *vice versa*. When the famous Sunni theologian Abu Hamid al-Ghazali (d. 1111) helped his patron, the Seljuq vizier Nizam al-Mulk (d. 1092) define orthodoxy (Pers. *niku i'tiqad*, "right belief") and "pure religion" (Pers. *pak-din*), he fully expected his writings to be used by jurists.[3]

199

In medieval Islam, it was often better to be branded as an apostate (*murtadd*) than as a heretic (*zindiq*). Although both accusations were often politically motivated, the theological concept of apostasy left open the possibility of recanting one's beliefs and thus regaining one's liberty. No such option was offered to the heretic, who was likely to suffer the death penalty. The frequent abuse of the concept of heresy prompted Ghazali to write a famous theological treatise defining the limits of heresy and unbelief and led the later Hanbali jurist and theologian Ibn Taymiyya (d. 1328) to assert that theological questions should not be adjudicated in the courts.[4]

Theology and Democracy

Although Osama Bin Laden uses legalistic language and faults the American people for not following the Shari'a, his problem with the U.S. political system is mainly theological. In the United States, civil society is based on a democratic pluralist view of civic organization. According to this view, in the words of Alexis de Tocqueville (1840), "The people reign over the political world as God reigns over the universe."[5] In a liberal democracy, popular sovereignty is exercised through self-government, which promotes the common good by expressing the will of the majority.[6] Democratic values are nurtured by a political culture that develops out of local voluntary associations where citizens of similar social standing, education and temperament practice the skills of self-rule. This principle can be seen in the following statement by Thomas Jefferson: "I know no safe depository of the ultimate powers of the society but the people themselves; and if we think them not enlightened enough to exercise their control with a wholesome discretion, the remedy is not to take it from them, but to inform their discretion by education."[7]

For Bin Laden, Tocqueville's observation that in America "the people reign over the political world as God reigns over the universe" is proof that democracy is a form of infidelity grounded in *shirk*, associating partners with God. In Bin Laden's version of Islamic theology, democracy is anti-Islamic because it seeks to usurp divine sovereignty in the name of popular sovereignty.

Shortly before he was killed in a shoot-out with Saudi security forces outside of Mecca in June 2003, the Al Qaeda ideologue Yusuf al-Ayeri also portrayed democracy as a theological threat to Islam. According to Ayeri, democracy is based on the concept of the autonomous individual, whose participation in civil society shapes the nature of society as a whole. The concept of personal autonomy opens the way for other individualistic doctrines to enter society, such as religious pluralism or moral relativism. Individualistic doctrines like these undermine God-given moral standards by basing political relations on the lowest common denominator of human values. Even more, democracy also causes people to believe that they can change the laws that govern them whenever they choose. According to Ayeri, this leads the citizens of democratic states to reject God's determination of affairs and to imagine that they are the authors of their own destinies. If Muslims became liberal democrats, they would ignore the commands of God in the Qur'an and reject the Shari'a as the expression of God's will.[8]

Despite its radicalism, the Al Qaeda critique of democracy makes an important point. Bin Laden and Ayeri draw attention to a theological subtext of liberal democracy that Americans and Europeans usually overlook. John Locke (d. 1704), the progenitor of what became the American brand of liberal democracy, was a secularist but he was not anti-religious. In fact, he based his theory of democracy partly on Protestant theological principles. Locke believed that God delegated the freedom of moral and political choice to human beings, who exercise this freedom through what legal historian Jeremy Waldron has called the "Democratic Intellect."[9] This notion is precisely what Shari'a fundamentalists such as Bin Laden and Ayeri fear. For Locke, the will of the people was a better guide to God's will than the efforts of religious scholars. This was because in general theological terms, what the people think best for themselves reflects God's view of what is best for the people: *vox populi vox dei*. For the political theorists who followed Locke, his ideas provided a justification for democracy that could satisfy both Deists and mainstream Protestants. However, a premodern Muslim political theorist such as Ghazali or Ibn Taymiyya would have rejected Locke's concept of the Democratic Intellect as heresy. They also would have viewed his theory of democratic populism as an incitement to anarchy. If Locke's theology of the Democratic Intellect could be construed as heresy in medieval Islam, then one must grant some validity to the Al Qaeda critique of democracy, at least according to certain strands of Islamic thought.

The Cultural Fallacy

However, the choice between democracy and Islam does not have to be all or nothing. Muslims who live in the democratic societies of America and Europe do not have to choose, as Tariq Ramadan puts it, "between the ghetto and dissolution."[10] Although many political Islamists believe that Islamic principles have little or nothing in common with the West, this mistaken view creates a false dichotomy. In fact, there is much in common between Islam and the West, in terms of both religious values and legal philosophy. Ironically, the dualistic worldview of political Islam does little to liberate Muslims from Western cultural hegemony. Instead, as Ramadan has observed, it causes Muslims to "isolate themselves, marginalize themselves, and sometimes, by their excessive emotional, intellectual and social isolation, even strengthen the logic of the dominant system whose power lies in always appearing open, pluralistic and rational."[11]

Advocates of Islamic identity politics, who seem committed to proving Samuel Huntington correct while decrying his theories, have yet to learn that the notion of a "clash of civilizations" is better suited for the hegemonic power than for the subaltern. Often, the "emotional, intellectual, and social isolation" that they create leads them into a rhetorical blind alley. For example, Sayyid Qutb (d. 1966) asserted that similarities between the "Islamic System" and other political or moral systems only "arise from chance in merely particular matters and not from any general philosophy or underlying theory.[12] Nevertheless, he devotes a significant part of his book *Social Justice in Islam* to the subject of freedom of conscience, which is a central concept of liberal-democratic political theory. However, his "clash of civilizations" approach prevented him from acknowledging that Muslims and Westerners share the same political values. For Qutb, "freedom of conscience" did not mean the right to follow one's "inner voice." Instead, in his view, "freedom of conscience" meant a change from a worldly and materialistic *consciousness* to a spiritual and ideological *consciousness*: "freedom from servitude to false objects of sanctity and from a subservience to a fear for its life or its livelihood, or its station, only to fall prey to social values."[13] In other words, freedom of conscience was not a political concept for Qutb; rather, it was a theological and moral concept and was restricted in practice to the rejection of Western materialism and anti-Islamic social pressures. This view, which is still widely accepted among Muslims in North America and Western Europe, reinforces the impression, conveyed by Samuel Huntington and others, that Islamic values and civilization are fundamentally different from Western values and civilization.[14]

For advocates of Islamic identity such as Sayyid Qutb and Osama Bin Laden, the clash of civilizations between Islam and the West is conceived as a conflict of values that plays itself out in the domains of law and culture. In such a view, religion and culture are conflated, much as they are by Huntington. Islam is seen not only as a religious alternative to other faiths but it is also cast as the cultural antithesis of the West. Similarly, Christianity, Judaism and secularism (no meaningful distinction is made between these categories) are cast as Western cultural villains. This rhetorical strategy, in which Huntington's dichotomy of "the West and the rest" is turned against itself, has been called *Occidentalism*.[15] Occidentalism is a critique of Western civilization that utilizes the bipolar model of Orientalism but reverses the polarity so that an idealized spiritual East is valued above a stereotyped materialistic West.[16] According to the Egyptian philosopher and Islamic modernist Hassan Hanafi (who claims to have been the first to use the term "Occidentalism" in print), Occidentalism was meant to be a liberation epistemology, an "ideology for the ruled" that acts as a liberating device for the subaltern, much as Liberation Theology did for Latin Americans in the 1970s. Unlike Liberation Theology, however, Occidentalism relies on the Romantic notions of national character and national culture rather than on the Marxist concept of superstructure.[17]

Because of their roots in European Romanticism, both Islamic Occidentalism and Huntington's Clash of Civilizations theory perpetuate a cultural fallacy that essentializes the idea of difference between Islam and the West and obscures the theological issues that lie behind the specific differences that actually exist. Anthropologist Kevin Avruch has identified six theoretically "inadequate" notions of culture in contemporary political discourse that contribute to ethnic and religious conflicts by essentializing the concept of difference.[18] Each of these notions can be traced to nineteenth-century concepts of culture that remain current today.[19] In the summary that follows, I have linked these fallacious views of culture to the Islamic Identity thesis that is common to the perspective of Salafism, which underlies the political doctrines of Islamist parties such as the Muslim Brotherhood and the Jamaat-i Islam of Pakistan. However, it should be kept in mind that they also apply to a wide variety of Western pundits, from Samuel Huntington to the French National Front leader Jean-Marie Le Pen and to the American Protestant evangelist Pat Robertson.

1   Culture is homogeneous. When applied to Islam, this notion presumes that Islam is free of internal paradoxes and contradictions, such that it provides clear and unambiguous behavioral instructions, a system for how to act as individuals and as a polity.

2   Culture is a thing. This epistemology views Islam as a reified "thing" that can act, believe, assert and take on an identity independent of human actors (such as in the phrase, "Islam supports human rights"). It can even construct a definition of itself. This type of reification is a hallmark of essentialist discourses from the secular Huntington to religious fundamentalists.

3   *Culture is uniformly distributed among members of a group.* In Islamic identity discourses, this notion confers cognitive, behavioral and affective uniformity to all members of the Muslim *Umma*. In other words, all "true" Muslims are alike. An authentically "Islamic" consciousness is the same for all Muslims, as Qutb asserts in *Social Justice in Islam* and other works. Variation within the group is deviance. This leads to the persecution of religious minorities and dissidents within Islam. When applied to the Shari'a, this concept also leads to the notion that Islamic law is a universal natural law, the norms of which can be applied to all nations and all peoples.

4   *An individual possesses but a single culture.* For the advocates of Islamic Identity, a Muslim is only a Muslim. One is neither Sunni nor Shiite, neither Sufi nor Wahhabi. Islamic Identity thus becomes synonymous with a unitary group identity. For Kevin Avruch, this notion results from the privileging of "tribal culture" over cultures that are connected to different groups, structures and institutions.[20] Thus, tribal culture is coterminous with national identity. In Islamic Identity discourses, however, national or ethnic identity is trumped by an Islamic identity that is defined in ideological terms. The "tribe" is thus not the nation but the worldwide Muslim *Umma*.

5   *Culture is custom.* According to this notion, the content of culture is structurally undifferentiated. In the context of Islamism, this is the same as saying that Islam equals Tradition. This point helps explain the common recourse to Hadith over Qur'an by Muslim fundamentalists. It is in the Hadith where one can find normative interpretations of cultural attitudes and behaviors that have been handed down from the early centuries of Islamic history. The prominence of Hadith in Islamic epistemology has contributed greatly to the notion that Islam is a monoculture, despite Qur'anic verses that imply the contrary.

Culture is timeless. Islam, as Tradition, is primordial. It is changeless, and every attempt to change the interpretation of Islam is a threat to the integrity of Islam's divine origin.

In Islamic Identity discourse, the word "Islam" is used nearly everywhere the word "culture" is used in the above examples. In Shari'a fundamentalism, the word "Shari'a" may also be used nearly everywhere the word "Islam" is used.[21] Among Islamic Identity advocates in Western countries, Islam is often conceived as a *milla* (Ottoman millet): a self-contained religious community that is legally distinct from the rest of society.[22] According to many partisans of this view, traditions that come from outside the Islamic *milla* lack authenticity because they are not Shari'a-based and depend instead on the whims of human judgment rather than on the wisdom of God. Osama Bin Laden was thinking along these lines when he stated that Americans "choose to invent their own laws as they will and desire."

If Muslims are to make a comfortable home for themselves in the West, it is necessary to reject the cultural fallacy. Muslims should recognize that post-colonial identity politics is counterproductive outside of the formerly colonized world, except in cases where state religions cause legal problems of recognition for Muslim immigrants. Likewise, majoritarian citizens of Western countries also need to free themselves from the cultural fallacy and stop regarding Muslim immigrants as an alien invading army or a fifth column that will undermine majoritarian values. It behooves both groups to recognize that political movements based on identity differences are nearly always right wing and frequently lead to intolerance, if not extremism. An important step towards wisdom for both sides is to understand that any ideology based on irreducible cultural differences is a conceit. When Muslims and Westerners finally recognize that they are not so special after all, they may see that they actually have much in common. When it comes to concepts of rights and obligations, the commonalities between Islamic and Western values start with the Qur'an.

A Qur'anic Theology of Rights

According to the political philosopher John Rawls, a concept of right is "a set of principles, general in form and universal in application, that is to be publicly recognized as a final court of appeal for organizing the conflicting claims of moral persons."[23] Although the second part of this concept of right has not been fully developed in Islamic jurisprudence, a general and universally applicable concept of rights does appear in the Qur'an. One place where it can be found is in the following verse: "Oh humankind! Keep your duty to your Lord, who created you from a single soul, and created its mate from it and from which issued forth many men and women. And revere the God by whose leave you demand rights from one another and revere the rights of kinship (literally, 'the wombs')" (Qur'an, 4:1). This verse, which in Rawls' terminology establishes the Qur'anic "original position" on rights, bases the concept of right on two universal principles: the universal kinship of humanity and the universal sovereignty of God. It thus places humanity in an "initial contractual situation," in which people are born into society in a matrix of reciprocal rights and obligations that are part of their nature as human beings.[24]

In the Qur'an, the concept of right is most often designated by the Arabic term *haqq*. An example of this usage can be seen in the following verse, which affirms the fundamental right to life: "Do not take a human life, which God has made sacred, except as a right (*illa bi-l-haqq*); this [God] has enjoined upon you so that you might think rationally" (Qur'an, 6:151). The term *haqq*, which can also mean "truth," is used in another verse of the Qur'an to establish the right to freedom of choice. In the Qur'an, freedom of choice is primarily a theological concept, and might best be expressed as "the right to be wrong." "The truth (*al-haqq*) is from your Lord. So whosoever wishes shall believe, and whosoever wishes shall disbelieve" (Qur'an, 18:29).

Many comparative philosophers and legal theorists believe that a concept of right cannot stand alone but requires the related notions of duty and obligation. All three of these notions – right, duty and obligation – can be found in the theological treatment of rights in the Qur'an. The Arabic term for right (*haqq*) can mean "right," "truth," or "justice" depending on the context in which it is used. The notion that all people possess God-given rights as part of their birthright is fundamental to the Qur'anic conception of justice. As one would expect, these rights also require specific obligations as corollaries to their status as rights. Thus, the semantic range of the Arabic term *haqq* in the Qur'an involves both a *right to* a particular good and a *right against* someone in pursuit of that good. Similar notions are also implicit in the concept of *'adl*, another Arabic term that is commonly used for "justice" in the Qur'an.[25] The Qur'anic meaning of *'adl* is comparable to the Aristotelian notion of justice, which connotes "fairness" or "equity."[26] In a previously published article, I summarized the fundamental rights in the Qur'an as the *right to life*, the *right of dignity*, and the *right of freedom of choice*. These rights are accompanied by the *duty of mercy* and *obligation of justice*.[27] In other words, the right to life requires the Muslim to perform the duty of mercy and the rights of dignity and freedom of choice create the obligation for the Muslim to treat other human beings, including non-Muslims, with justice and respect.[28]

However, the mere fact that God has bestowed rights on human beings does not necessarily mean that we respect them in practice. As mentioned above, the Islamic legal schools have never reached a consensus on the application of rights. Because he did not believe in natural or God-given rights, the Utilitarian political philosopher Jeremy Bentham (d. 1832) stated, "Right is with me the child of the law . . . A natural right is a son that never had a father."[29] No practicing Muslim could ever agree that the natural rights mentioned in the Qur'an are "fatherless." However, a Muslim might agree with Bentham about the necessity of the law and say, "A right without a law to support it is an orphan." Rights in practice do not exist in a vacuum; each right that is enjoyed by a person requires a specific obligation from another. The granting of a right to a person implies restrictions on the rights of another – at least to the extent that one is prevented from violating the rights of another. Some formal means must exist to enforce the rights and obligations of individuals and groups within society. This is where theology and philosophy meet the law as far as rights are concerned. In order to be enforced, natural or human rights need laws to support them. However, such laws are not "Shari'a-laws." Shari'a is a concept that is just as abstract and idealistic as the concept of rights. The laws that are needed to enforce the rights and obligations of individuals in society do not come from Shari'a but from *fiqh* – the day-to-day practice of legal reasoning as historically defined by the Hanafi, Maliki, Shafi'i and Hanbali schools of Sunni Islam and the Ja'fari school of Imami Shi'ism.

Muslims who call for the wholesale application of the Shari'a either forget or neglect to mention that one cannot apply the Shari'a in any meaningful way without *fiqh*. Unfortunately, the systematic application of *fiqh* is virtually impossible in Sunni Islam today, where in nearly every country the traditional institutions of *fiqh* have been eliminated by the state or transformed ideologically by the advocates of Islamism.[30] In Sunni countries where Islamism has taken political power, such as in contemporary Sudan, "Shari'a" courts have been set up but the practice of *fiqh* is either attenuated or moribund.[31] At present, there is no new school of legal reasoning in Islam to replace the traditional but largely discredited schools of the past. Sloganeering about utopian ideals does not solve the practical problem of enforcing rights in actual societies.

Without a coherent alternative to the traditional schools of Islamic law, the Muslim Brotherhood slogan, "The Qur'an is our constitution" is practically meaningless with respect to the enforcement of rights. Most Western and many Muslim political theorists would say that neither the Qur'an nor the Shari'a are true constitutions because they do not outline a coherent system of government. Thus, one might ask of the Muslim Brotherhood, as Thomas Paine did of Edmund Burke about the British "constitution" in *Rights of Man* (1791): "Can such people produce the "[Islamic] Constitution?" If they cannot, we may fairly conclude, that though it has been so much talked about, no such thing as an "[Islamic] Constitution" exists, or ever did exist and consequently that the people have yet a constitution to form."[32]

Clearly, the mere fact that a concept of right exists in the Qur'an is no guarantee that it has been enforced adequately in practice. Nor does this necessarily mean that the concept of right in Islam means exactly the same thing as in Western discussions of this subject. Because the exact relationship between duties and obligations has yet to be determined in Islamic moral philosophy, there is a tendency to fall into a confusion of priorities in the attempt to apply one or the other. This problem is particularly acute with respect to rights. To make a valid comparison between the Islamic notions of right and those that are advocated in today's global civil society, one must first study the concept of legal rights in the West, where most of the pioneering philosophical work on this subject has been done. As seen below, a deeper understanding of legal rights in Western legal philosophy can shed light on apparent contradictions and inconsistencies in the Muslim treatment of rights. Since the concept of individual rights in Islam is most often expressed in terms of religious difference, the application of legal rights to religious dissenters and minorities will be used as examples in the discussion that follows.

Hohfeldian Categories of Rights

In the Anglo-American legal tradition, one of the most influential treatments of rights can be found in Wesley N. Hohfeld, *Fundamental Legal Conceptions as Applied in Judicial Reasoning* (1919).[33] According to Hohfeld, the statement, "X has a right to Y," has four possible meanings. These meanings are logical possibilities. Thus, they are not dependent on culture and theoretically can be applied in any legal context, including the Islamic. In contemporary legal theory, these four possibilities are known as "Hohfeldian Categories." Below, I summarize Hohfeld's categories of rights as they might apply to questions of religious belief and practice in a self-styled "Islamic" state. In addition, I have expanded Hohfeld's categories to include duties that are logical corollaries to the Hohfeldian categories, referring to them as "expectations" of certain kinds of behavior from the state. These "expectations" are *rights against* the state that can be demanded by members of a religious minority in return for the *rights to* a particular good that they have been granted. As corollary expectations, they follow logically from the reciprocal model of rights, duties and obligations outlined above.

1 A right may be a *privilege* or a *bare liberty*. In the context of the right of religious freedom, this means, for example, that a Christian subject of a Muslim state has *no duty not to* go to church on Sunday, or that a Shiite subject of a Sunni state has *no duty not to* include the phrase, "Ali is the Friend of God" in his call to prayer. A right as a privilege or bare liberty is the minimal category of rights. The duty that follows from this right may be termed the *duty of non-prevention*. The only right against the state that can be held by a member of a religious minority group as a corollary to a bare liberty or privilege is the *expectation of non-coercion*.

2 A right may be a *claim-right*. In the context of the right of religious freedom, this means most generally that officials of a Muslim state have the duty to allow religious minorities to practice their religion as they see fit. This may be called the *duty of non-interference*.[34]

a Hohfeld also made a distinction between two types of claim-rights: *claim-rights in personam* and *claim-rights in rem*. Claim-rights *in personam* call forth duties that are assignable to particular persons or groups because of a *stipulated right*, such as the duties incumbent on a signatory to a contract or specific rights spelled out in a constitution or code of laws. Formally allowing Christian subjects of a Muslim state to build churches or sell pork in butcher shops are examples of *claim-rights in personam*. The right against the state held by a member of a minority group as a corollary to a claim-right of this type is the *expectation of lawful support*.

b Claim-rights *in rem* call forth duties that are incumbent in principle on everyone. Religious freedom as a *claim-right in rem* would mean that a Muslim state would have the duty to actively assist religious minorities in the maintenance of their religion. This might include providing state funds for the construction of churches or synagogues or the prosecution of Muslim citizens for desecrating Christian or Jewish places of worship. The right against the state held by a member of a minority group as a corollary to a claim-right *in rem* may be called the *expectation of assistance*.

3   A right may involve the ability or *power* of an individual to alter existing legal arrangements. *Rights-as-powers* are often powers of office, such as the U.S. President's right to cast a veto, or rights of trusteeship, in which a trustee has the right to act contractually in the interest of another person. The duties called forth by this right are often contractual in nature and thus are similar to duties that are applicable to claim-rights *in personam*. In the context of a self-styled "Islamic" state, this right may include the power of the ruler to renegotiate the terms of an agreement between the state and its Jewish or Christian communities. Within a particular community, this right might also include the power of religious leaders designated by the state to act as spokespersons for their communities. In modern liberal-democratic societies, *rights-as-powers* granted to community leaders or councils might potentially come into conflict with individual rights of personal autonomy. In general terms, the right held against the state by a member of a minority group as a corollary to the conferral of a right-as-power is the *expectation of self-determination*.

4   A right may constitute a type of *immunity* from legal change. In the context of religious freedoms in premodern Islam, the *right-as-immunity* was most often applied with regard to Qur'anic provisions that allowed the freedom of belief and religious practice of the People of the Book (*Ahl al-Kitab*). It was applied less often with respect to religious dissidents within Islam. The right against the state held by the member of a minority group as a corollary to a right-as-immunity is the *expectation of security*.

Hohfeldian Rights in Premodern Islamic Practice

The *claim-right* is the Hohfeldian Category that is closest to the notion of an individual right in political philosophy. One difficulty with Hohfeld's schema, however, is that it is narrow in scope and does not specify the place of duties within the concept of legal rights. This is why it was necessary to suggest duties as expectations to the four categories listed above. For example, a well-known verse of the Qur'an states with regard to the freedom of religious belief: "There is no compulsion in religion; true guidance is distinct from error; he who rejects false deities and believes in God has grasped a firm handhold that will never break. God is All-Hearing and All-Knowing" (2:256). Muslim apologists frequently overlook how ambiguous this verse really is. There is no compulsion in religion; however, since true guidance is distinct from error, the believer in an "incorrect" religion might reasonably be expected to find Islam eventually. What is the responsibility of Muslims if the errant believer does not do so?

In most contemporary interfaith discussions, the phrase, "there is no compulsion in religion," is seen as something like a *claim-right in rem* because in principle it is incumbent on everyone. However, is this really a claim-right? There is no stipulation as such in the text of the Qur'an. Furthermore, the remainder of the verse strongly implies that God expects non-Muslims to see the light and become Muslims. Therefore, it is just as logical to conclude that this verse implies a mere *privilege* or a *bare liberty* – a right of tolerance only – and not a claim-right. Unlike a claim-right, which obliges Muslims to prevent interference with religious minorities in the practice of their beliefs, a bare liberty requires nothing but non-coercion. If the practice of a minority religion is conceived as a mere privilege, this means that religious minorities would be free to practice their religion but that Muslims have no obligation to make it easy for them. Even more, worship might be construed as the only practice they are entitled to perform. A bare liberty confers no obligation on the state to promote the building of

213

places of worship or to accommodate religious minorities in specific ways.

The effects of such scriptural ambiguities can be examined historically in the different approaches towards religious minorities in premodern Islam. The use of Hohfeldian categories in the analysis of such cases can help explain the wide discrepancies in rights granted to the *ahl al-dhimma* (protected or exempted religious minorities) by Muslim jurists. For example, the Hanafi jurist Abu Yusuf (d. 808), who was legal advisor to the Abbasid Caliph Harun al-Rashid (d. 809), clearly viewed the rights of protected religious minorities as *claim-rights*. For this reason, he was unequivocal in requiring that Jewish and Christian subjects of the Abbasid state be treated with respect and that the state accommodate their reasonable needs. However, the later Mu'tazilite Qur'an commentator Zamakhshari (d. 1144) saw the right of Jews and Christians to practice their religion as only a *bare liberty*. Therefore, not only did he counsel against the use of state resources in constructing and maintaining churches and synagogues but he also considered it permissible to treat *dhimmis* with contempt when they paid their taxes, hoping thereby that "they will come to believe in God and His Messenger and thus be delivered from this shameful yoke."[35] A similar view was held by the Maliki Mufti of Granada Ibn Lubb (d. 1381). For Ibn Lubb, the right of Jews to practice their religion in Granada was also a bare liberty but not a claim-right. He differed from Zamakhshari only in being less concerned with the eventual conversion of religious minorities. Seeing the infidelity of Jews as unlikely to change, he fell back on the formula of *Surat al-Kafirin* (The Unbelievers): "To you your religion and to me mine" (Qur'an, 109:6).[36]

A different interpretation is provided by the Hanbali jurist Ibn Taymiyya (d. 1328), who focuses on contractual relations between the Muslim state and non-Muslim minorities. In his fatwas on the rights of religious minorities, Ibn Taymiyya takes as a precedent the 7th-century CE "Covenant of the Caliph Umar" with the Christians of Syria. According to the terms of this covenant, the

Christians of Syria were granted full security of their persons, their families and their possessions, although they did not enjoy all of the rights of Muslims. This stress on the contractual nature of the relations between the state and its religious minorities suggests that for Ibn Taymiyya, the primary right of the Christians and Jews of Syria was the right of *immunity from legal change*. This corresponds to the fourth of Hohfeld's categories of rights, a *right as a power*. In other words, because the Muslim rulers of Syria were contractually bound by the Covenant of Umar, the Christian and Jews of Syria had the power to demand that the state not change any of the provisions of the covenant.

This was not all, however. The provisions of the Covenant of Umar also included two specific *claim-rights in personam* for non-Muslim minorities. The first was the right to demand from the state the ransom of Christian and Jewish prisoners taken by external enemies of the state along with the ransom of Muslims. Ibn Taymiyya considered this duty a "most serious obligation" (*a'zam al-wajibat*) and negotiated with the Tatars to ransom Christian and Jewish captives. The second *claim-right in personam* was the right of religious minorities to free themselves from the Covenant of Umar and claim equal status with the Muslims if they enlisted in the Muslim army and fought alongside the Muslims in battle. This last right was highly unusual for Ibn Taymiyya's time and illustrates the close attention that Hanbali jurists such as Ibn Taymiyya paid to the letter of the law with regard to contractual obligations. [37] In Hohfeldian terms, the value of contracts is that they can reinforce claim-rights by transforming practices into powers.

However, Ibn Taymiyya was no liberal pluralist. He was very worried about the effect of non-Muslim religious practices on the Muslim public and the theological influence of Christianity on Islam. Viktor Makari has summarized Ibn Taymiyya's personal views of religious minorities in the following way: "[The Christians] managed to abscond from dutiful taxation; they intermingled with the rest of the population; they blazed about in an insolent light. They succeeded in occupying positions of power within the high places of government, of financial administration and of national security. They put their experienced skills for profit, and their crafty amiability to work for their self-enrichment to the detriment of the Muslims . . . The Jews, too, sell wine to the Muslims in Cairo. In the public ceremonies of their cult, they jostle one another ostentatiously where the banners of Islam are unfurled. Their religious practices, and even their edifices which were becoming increasingly numerous, were dangerously encroaching.[38]

Because he was both a conservative theologian and a strict constructionist in matters of jurisprudence, Ibn Taymiyya was caught between his fear of the influence of heretical ideas and his respect as a jurist for the claim-rights of the Christians and Jews of Syria. Personally, he agreed with the Caliph Umar, who reportedly said of the *dhimmis*, "Humiliate them, but do no injustice to them" (*adhilluhum wa la tazlimuhum*).[39] If Umar had indeed made such a statement, this would imply a *bare liberty* with respect to the rights of minorities in practicing their religions. However, Ibn Taymiyya could not overlook the formal agreement drawn up between Umar and the Christians of Syria. The Prophet Muhammad backed such agreements with divine sanction: "As for one who oppresses a covenanter, diminishes his right, charges him with a burden he cannot fulfill, or takes something from him without his consent, I will be the proof against him on the Day of Judgment."[40] According to the principles of Islamic jurisprudence followed by Ibn Taymiyya, the opinion of the Prophet always trumps the opinion of a Caliph. However, the opinion of the Prophet did not trump the opinion of the Caliph Umar to the extent that Ibn Taymiyya advocated the more broadly based claim-rights of religious minorities *in rem*. Relations with such people, he said, were to be held strictly to the limits of their contract, and no further.

Democracy and Religious Rights between Islam and the West

What lessons can we learn from the preceding discussion? First, when assessing the so-called "Islamic" approach to important political subjects such as democracy or rights, one does not have to fall back on essentialist arguments about the "culture of Islam" or the "culture of the West." As demonstrated above, the Hohfeldian categories of rights, which are logically derived and not culture-based, are just as useful as heuristic tools in Islamic legal contexts as they are in Western legal contexts. Using such tools to reveal the logic that lies behind important *fatwas* will help educate both Western observers and the Muslim public that not only is the Shari'a not arbitrary but it also demands the application of a systematic legal methodology. Without such a methodology, it is impossible to apply the Shari'a justly. To put the matter in Islamic terms: without *fiqh*, there is no real Shari'a.

Second, theology still matters in Islam, even in the arguments of would-be jurists such as Osama Bin Laden. Islamist critics of democracy do not reject democracy simply because "they don't like our freedoms," as U.S. President George W. Bush has maintained. It is true that Bin Laden and his Al Qaeda supporters "don't like our freedom," but the reason they do not like our freedom is theological. For Al Qaeda, our freedom to choose our political destiny implies a lessening of God's own power to choose our destiny. This rejection of democracy rests on two fallacies that can be disproved theologically. The first fallacy is a category mistake that conceives of God's power as a finite quantity: an increase in human power means a decrease in God's power. This is easily countered by recourse to the mathematical notion of infinity. If God's power is truly infinite (as all Muslims are supposed to believe) and subtracting any number from infinity still leaves infinity, then subtracting any amount of human power from God's power still leaves God's power infinite. Thus, if God grants some of his freedom to us, this still cannot lessen the amount of God's freedom. The second fallacy is the slippery-slope argument that granting any amount of license will lead to total license and a complete breakdown of morality. This can be countered by pointing out that every slippery-slope argument is a fallacy by definition and that the liberal-democratic concept of freedom of choice does not preclude the choice to be virtuous. Although these arguments may not convince every Muslim Salafist or Islamist, the very fact that we *can* argue such issues puts us in a better position to resolve our differences than by falling back on spurious culturalist assumptions about the "essence of Islam" or the "essence of the West." A wise old saying in philosophy states: "People quarrel because they do not know how to argue."

The third lesson to be learned from this discussion is that Muslims need to devote much more time than they have to the study of moral philosophy and ethics in Western countries. I have tried to show how useful this can be by focusing on just one example of how we might sharpen our understanding of the concept of rights. Muslims need to know what rights are and how the notion of rights has changed over time before we can discuss them meaningfully. If we do not study Western concepts in a systematic way, we will remain susceptible to ideologues like Sayyid Qutb, who arbitrarily defined "freedom of conscience" as "freedom of consciousness" or the "right" to be conscious of Islam as he saw it. In fact, I would go so far as to say that at present, the study of Western legal and moral philosophy is more important for Muslims than the study of classical Islamic philosophy. In practical terms, Jeffrey Stout's *Ethics after Babel*[41] or Kwame Anthony Appiah's *The Ethics of Identity*[42] are more relevant to the place of Islam in a pluralistic world than any classical work of Islamic political theory.

Finally, I remain a strong believer in the virtues of Islamic tradition when it comes to issues of worship and spirituality. I am more pessimistic, however, with regard to the chances of finding traditional Islamic solutions to the social and political problems of our times. Muslims should be concerned about authenticity and should do their best to find resources in the traditions of the past to help them solve the problems of the present. However, when such resources are not available, Muslims should feel themselves empowered to find new resources outside of Islamic tradition or to create such resources themselves. If the Shari'a is to have continued relevance today, Muslims have no choice but to drastically reform the traditional schools of Islamic legal methodology

218

or create new methodologies in their place. Likewise, for Islam to have a coherent theological identity Muslims must balance their current anxiety for the Shari'a with a constructive theology that takes Islamic thought beyond the ideas of the classical Islamic *mutakallimun*. Only in such ways can the Islamic discourse with the West move from mere emotivism to rational arguments.

Notes

1   Osama Bin Laden, "To the Americans" (October 6, 2002), in Bruce Lawrence Editor and James Howarth Translator, *Messages to the World: the Statements of Osama Bin Laden* (London and New York: Verso, 2005), 167.

2   According to Ramadan, "It is meaningless, and in actual fact wrong, to compare the often peripheral discussions that took place among Muslim scholars . . . with the radical reflections that gave birth to Christian theology." The works of Islamic "theologians," unlike their Christian counterparts, "have never gone as far as to open to question three fundamental principles: *the absolute oneness of the Creator, the impossibility of there being a representation of Him, and the truth of His word revealed in the Qur'an*" (italics in the original). I do not see how defending the fundamental principles of Islam would disqualify medieval Muslim *mutakallimun* from being called "theologians," merely because they did not question them radically. By the same logic, medieval Christian theologians would have to be disqualified from being called "theologians" because they did not radically question the concept of the Trinity. See Tariq Ramadan, *Western Muslims and the Future of Islam* (Oxford, U.K. and New York: Oxford University Press, 2004), 11-12.

3   Although he is now most famous as a theologian, Ghazali's appointment as a professor at the Nizamiyya Madrasa was in jurisprudence, not in theology. See Omid Safi, *The Politics of Knowledge in Premodern Islam: Negotiating Ideology and Religious Inquiry* (Chapel Hill, North Carolina: University of North Carolina Press, 2006), 1-19.

4   See Sherman A. Jackson, *On the Boundaries of Theological Tolerance in Islam: Abu Hamid al-Ghazali's Faysal al-Tafriqa bayna al-Islam wa al-Zandaqa* (Oxford U.K. and Karachi, Pakistan: Oxford University Press, 2002). Prominent Sufis in Egypt aided and abetted the prosecution of the anti-Sufi Ibn Taymiyya. This historical detail should serve as a reminder to contemporary liberals that mysticism is not necessarily the answer to religious extremism.

5   Alexis de Tocqueville, *Democracy in America* (New York: Doubleday Anchor Books, 1969), 60.

6   Frank Cunningham, *Theories of Democracy: A Critical Introduction* (London and New York: Routledge, 2002), 9-12.

7   Letter to William Charles Jarvis, 28 September 1820, in P.L. Ford (ed.) *Writings of Thomas Jefferson* vol. 10 (1899), 161.

8   Amir Taheri, "Al-Qaeda's Agenda for Iraq," *New York Post Online Edition*, September 4, 2003. In: *The One Percent Doctrine* (New York: Simon and Schuster, 2006), Ron Suskind claims that Ayeri was behind a plot, eventually called off by Al Qaeda, to attack the New York City subway system with hydrogen cyanide poison gas. He was identified by the CIA as the most important Al Qaeda operative in Saudi Arabia. See "The Untold Story of Al-Qaeda's Plot to Attack the Subways," *Time Magazine*, June 26, 2006, 27-35.

9   Jeremy Waldron, *God, Locke, and Equality: Christian Foundations of Locke's Political Thought* (Cambridge: Cambridge University Press, 2002), 84-85.

10   Ramadan, *Western Muslims*, 63.

11   Ibid, 5.

12   Sayyid Qutb, *Social Justice in Islam*. Translated by John B. Hardie with revised translation by Hamid Algar (Oneonta, New York: Islamic Publications International, 2000), 114-115; this work was originally published in 1940, early in Qutb's career.

13   Ibid, 60.

14   According to Huntington, a fundamental value conflict ("two different versions of what is right and what is wrong") lies at the heart of the difference between Islam and the West. "So long as Islam remains Islam (which it will) and the West remains the West (which is more dubious), this fundamental conflict between two great civilizations and ways of life will continue to define their relations in the future even as it has defined them for the past fourteen centuries." See Samuel P. Huntington, *The Clash of Civilizations and the Remaking of World Order* (New York: Touchstone/Simon and Schuster, 1997), 212. There is a striking similarity between Huntington's view of civilizational conflict and Rudyard Kipling's famous lines from *The Ballad of East and West* (1895): "East is East and West is West and never the twain shall meet, till Earth and Sky stand presently at God's great Judgment Seat."

15   Huntington, *The Clash of Civilizations*, 183.

16   "To be equipped with the mind of the West is like being an idiot savant, mentally defective but with a special gift for making arithmetic calculations. It is a mind without a soul, efficient, like a calculator, but hopeless at doing what is humanly important. The mind of the West is capable of great economic success, to be sure, and of developing and promoting advanced technology, but cannot grasp the higher things in life, for it lacks spirituality and understanding of human suffering." Ian Buruma and Avishai Margalit, *Occidentalism: the West in the Eyes of Its Enemies* (New York: The Penguin Press, 2004), 75.

17   Hassan Hanafi, "From Orientalism to Occidentalism" (1993) in idem, *Islam in the Modern World Volume II, Tradition, Revolution, and Culture* (Heliopolis, Egypt: Dar Kebaa Bookshop, 2000), 400.

18   Kevin Avruch, *Culture and Conflict Resolution* (Washington, D.C.: United States Institute of Peace Press, 1998), 14-16.

19   See, for example, Edward Tylor's famous 1871 definition of culture, which is still regarded as a foundational principle of Cultural Anthropology: "Culture is that complex whole which includes, knowledge, belief, art

man as a member of society." Edward Burnett Tylor, *Primitive Culture: Researches into the Development of Mythology, Philosophy, Religion, Art and Custom* (London, John Murray: 1871), vol. 1, 1.

20 Although this view is superficially similar to that of Benjamin R. Barber, *Jihad vs. McWorld: Terrorism's Challenge to Democracy* (New York: Ballantine Books, 1995), it is more comparable to the theses of Karl Popper in *The Open Society and Its Enemies Volume I: the Spell of Plato* (London and New York, Routledge, 1995 reprint of 1945 original).

21 For an analysis of the concept of "Shari'a fundamentalism," see Vincent J. Cornell, "Reasons Public and Divine: Liberal Democracy, Shari'a Fundamentalism, and the Epistemological Crisis of Islam". In: Richard C. Martin and Carl W. Ernst, eds., *Islam in Theory: Essays in Comparative Religious Studies* (Chapel Hill, North Carolina: University of North Carolina Press), forthcoming.

22 Those who conceive of Islam as a *milla* find justification for their views in a passage of the Qur'an where the Prophet Joseph says: "I have forsaken the *milla* of a people who do not believe in Allah and reject the Hereafter. Instead, I follow the *milla* of my fathers Abraham, Isaac, and Jacob. Never was it our practice to associate partners with God" (Qur'an, 12:37-38). In this verse, the term *milla* refers specifically to the Children of Israel (*Banu Isra'il*), to whom the Qur'an consistently refers in tribal and hence in cultural terms.

23 John Rawls, *A Theory of Justice* (Cambridge, Massachusetts: The Belknap Press of Harvard University Press, 1999 revised edition), 117.

24 See also, "[God] created the heavens and the earth with truth and right (*bi-l-haqq*) and fashioned [Adam] in the best of forms" (Qur'an, 64:3). For the terms "original position" and "initial contractual situation," which are part of Rawls' theory of social contract, see idem, *A Theory of Justice*, 10-19. In the present discussion, I have added a dimension of religiosity to these terms that is not part of Rawls' secular social contract theory.

25 See, for example, "Verily, Allah commands justice (*al-'adl*) and the practice of goodness (*al-ihsan*)" (Qur'an, 16:90). Although the term *ihsan* is commonly translated as "virtue," it is clear from the context of this verse – where *ihsan* appears immediately before the command to fulfill the needs of near kin (*dhi al-qurba*) – that the actual practice of goodness, and not the abstract concept of virtue, is the more accurate interpretation of this term.

26 See Alasdair MacIntyre, *Whose Justice, Which Rationality* (Notre Dame, Indiana: Notre Dame University Press, 1988), "Aristotle on Justice," 103-123. For Aristotle, justice was based on ratios, not on equivalences. These ratios govern the principle of fairness in both distributive justice and retributive justice (or "justice as rectification"). See Aristotle, *Nicomachean Ethics*. Translated by Martin Oswald (Indianapolis, 1981 reprint of 1962 first edition), Book V, 111-130.

27 See, for example, (Qur'an, 49:9), "Make peace between them with justice and act equitably."

28 For the full text of this discussion, see Vincent J. Cornell, "Practical Sufism: An Akbarian Foundation for a Liberal Theology of Difference," *Journal of the Muhyiddin Ibn 'Arabi Society* Volume XXXVI, 2004, 59-84.

29 Jeremy Waldron, "Introduction," to Jeremy Waldron, ed., *Theories of Rights* (Oxford, U.K. and New York: Oxford University Press, 1984), 4.

30 This is not the case in Imami Shi'ism, however, where the traditional juridical institution known as *al-Hawza* remains vital.

31 Despite the negative press it has received about the implementation of Shari'a provisions, northern Nigeria is one of the few places in the Islamic world where new approaches to fiqh are being worked out in practice.

32 Thomas Paine, *Rights of Man*. In: Thomas Paine, *Collected Writings* (New York: The Library of America, 1995), 468.

33 See Wesley N. Hohfeld, *Fundamental Legal Conceptions as Applied in Judicial Reasoning*, Edited by David Campbell and Philip A. Thomas (Dartmouth, New Hampshire: Dartmouth Publishing Company, 2002). The Hohfeldian categories are also summarized in Waldron's *Theories of Rights*, 5-8.

34 However, states often interfere in the religious practices of a community for reasons of public interest. The classic philosophical example given for the necessity of state interference is the prohibition of human sacrifice. One of the most important examples of state interference in religion in the last 50 years was the abrogation of untouchability and other morally objectionable Hindu religious practices by the government of India shortly after independence in 1947. These changes are detailed in the classic study by D.E. Smith, *India as a Secular State* (Princeton, New Jersey: Princeton University Press, 1963).

35 Bernard Lewis, *The Jews of Islam* (Princeton: Princeton University Press, 1984), 14-15.

36 Ibn Lubb's opinions are to be found in Arabic manuscript number 1810, Biblioteca de El Escorial, Spain, ff. 147-155v. I am indebted to Professor Hayat Kara of Université Mohammed V, Rabat, Morocco, for sharing this portion of the manuscript with me.

37 Victor E. Makari, *Ibn Taymiyyah's Ethics: The Social Factor* (Chico, California: Scholars Press, 1983), 127-131; for a summary of the Hanbali attitude to contractual law, see Mohammad Hashim Kamali, "The *Shari'a*: Law as the Way of God". In: *Voices of Islam Volume 1: Voices of Tradition*, edited by Vincent J. Cornell (Westport, Connecticut and London: Praeger Publishers, 2007), 161-162.

38 Makari, *Ibn Taymiyya's Ethics*, 128.

39 Ibid, 130.

40 Ibid, 218 n. 63; this hadith is reproduced inaccurately on 129-130, where *mu'ahid* (covenanter) is replaced by *dhimmi* (religious minority).

41 Jeffrey Stout, *Ethics after Babel: the Languages of Morals and Their Discontents* (Princeton, New Jersey and Oxford, U.K.: Princeton University Press, 1988)

42 Kwame Anthony Appiah, *The Ethics of Identity* (Princeton, New Jersey: Princeton University Press, 2005).

Part V

The role of the state, civil society and international organisations

International Organisations, Democracy and Good Governance: do they practise what they preach?

Nico Schrijver

Increasingly, qualitative criteria in the fields of respect for human rights, democracy and good governance are being formulated and applied in the context of international organisations *vis-à-vis* states, especially Central and Eastern European states and developing states. At the domestic level, these criteria relate to the holding of regular, free and fair elections, a multi-party democratic system, respect for fundamental human rights and effective government policy, including transparency, accountability and effectiveness of public institutions, as well as combating corruption. This contribution assesses the state of the art with respect to democracy and good governance in international organisations themselves. Do they practise what they preach?

The evolution of the international organisation

The international organisation developed rapidly in the course of the 20th century. Next to international institutions of a political character, such as the League of Nations (1919) and its successor organisation the United Nations (1945), a large number of specialised agencies and inter-regional and regional organisations were created.[1] Specialised agencies include the International Labour Organisation, the International Monetary Fund and the International Bank for Reconstruction and Development (commonly known as the World Bank), the Food and Agriculture Organisation of the United Nations, the UN Educational, Scientific and Cultural Organisation (UNESCO) and the International Civil

Aviation Organisation (ICAO). Interregional organisations include the North Atlantic Treaty Organisation and the Organisation of Economic Co-operation and Development, while the Council of Europe, the African Union and the Association of South-East Asian states are examples of important regional organisations.

In most international organisations the principle of sovereign equality among states applies, at least formally.[2] This is most notably exemplified by the principle of "one State, one vote". Decision making takes place by majority, albeit in most international organisations a two-thirds majority or otherwise qualified majority for voting on non-procedural matters is required. By way of example, we will first review decision making within the United Nations.

United Nations Decision Making

Quite soon after the establishment of the United Nations in 1945, developing countries gained a two-thirds majority in the General Assembly of the United Nations. This had a significant impact on the decision making of the Organisation. For example, self-determination of peoples was proclaimed fervently and prominently as an inalienable right, in various declarations.[3] Continuation of colonial rule was identified as being in contravention of the UN Charter. Most western countries finally accepted these fundamental changes in international politics. Next to political self-determination, economic self-determination was soon to be advocated as well. This movement resulted in the recognition of the principle of permanent sovereignty over natural resources, including the right to nationalise foreign property, should the public interest or national security require this.[4] In 1964, developing countries succeeded in establishing the United Nations Conference on Trade and Development (UNCTAD) as a new permanent organ of the General Assembly of the United Nations,[5] while in 1974 the General Assembly adopted a Declaration and Action Programme on the Establishment of a New International Economic Order.[6] Furthermore, in 1976 the General Assembly adopted a controversial 'Zionism is Racism'-resolution, which was revoked only in the 1990s. Western countries often felt considerably uneasy about this "democratic" decision making of the Assembly, which they viewed as "steamrollering" by the Third World and as a "tyranny" of the majority. Yet, quite often they succeeded in halting the steamrollering by withholding their support to certain sectors or certain activities of the United Nations or otherwise pressurising Third World states. However, it would be a mistake to view the General Assembly merely as a "talking shop".[7] Much has been accomplished, especially in re-orientating the United Nations from a primarily peace and security organisation to one which also actively pursues respect for human rights, decolonisation, development and environmental conservation.[8] In all these fields an extensive normative framework has been formatted, especially through series of non-binding resolutions of the General Assembly, which quite often served as forerunners of treaty provisions. Next to this, a large number of new organs, funds and programmes has been established to cater for the functions of the world organisation in these new fields.

The Maintenance of Peace and Security

In 1945, for the first time in world history, the principle of majority rule was introduced to the field of management of international peace and security. Thus the founding fathers deviated substantially from the principle of unanimity which had prevailed in the League of Nations and previously in the arrangements based on the 1815 Congress of Vienna. In 1945, an 11-member Security Council was established, which included five permanent powers (US, USSR, UK, France and China) and six non-permanent members, elected on a mainly geographical basis for two-year terms. In 1965, the membership of the Council was extended from 11 to 15, to reflect the expanded world as a result of decolonisation. For this purpose, the number of non-permanent seats was increased from 6 to 10, obviously in an effort to increase the representativeness of the Council and herewith the democratic legitimacy of its decision making.[9] The Council's decision-making procedure is laid out in

Article 27 of the UN Charter. Each member of the Security Council has one vote. Decisions on procedural matters are to be taken by a majority of nine out of the fifteen votes. Decisions on non-procedural matters also require a majority of at least nine members, but among them should be all the permanent members ('with the concurring votes of the permanent members'). If not, decision making is in principle blocked, due to what has become known as a "veto" by one or more of the five permanent members. During the period of the Cold War there was a real danger of the Council being constantly paralysed as a result of a lack of agreement among its permanent members. Since this might sometimes not be the intention or in the interest of the permanent members, a practice emerged that an abstention of voting by a permanent member would not constitute a bar to legally valid decision making by the Council, as long as at least nine members voted in favour and none of the permanent powers voted against. In this way, various resolutions establishing peace-keeping operations could be adopted, with an abstention by the Soviet Union. In a similar vein, several resolutions could be adopted on the situation in the Israeli-occupied territories, which the United States did not want to support explicitly but did not want to veto either. During the Kuwait-Iraq crisis (1990–91) China abstained on several key resolutions on the UN management of this Gulf crisis, including on Security Council Resolution 678 (1990), authorising the use of force against Iraq after 15 January 1991 should Iraq not have withdrawn its forces from Kuwait by that date. And the unique Security Council Resolution 1593 (2005) on referral of the situation in Darfur to the prosecutor of the newly-established International Criminal Court could be adopted with China and the US abstaining. This procedure to diminish some effects of the right of veto has been generally acknowledged as a new rule of customary international law, *de facto* amending the treaty rule of Article 27 of the UN Charter.[10] Nevertheless, the composition of the Council and the undemocratic nature of its decision making have often remained under attack. In the 1990s a near-consensus emerged that the Council should be expanded with five or six permanent members and additionally, some non-permanent members[11] Yet, which countries exactly should become the five new permanent members proved to be the Gordian knot, which so far nobody has been able to cut: Japan, Germany, a large African country (but which one: Egypt, Ethiopia, Nigeria, South Africa?), an additional Asian country (India or Pakistan?) and a Latin-American country (Brazil or Mexico?). Similarly, it proved to be controversial whether or not such new permanent members should be vested with a right of veto as well. On the one hand one wanted to avoid the impression that the new permanent members would only serve as "second class" permanent members. But, on the other, many view the right of veto as an inherently undemocratic and anachronistic instrument, which should gradually be wiped out rather than reinvigorated by granting it to even more states. Hence, proposals were submitted on stipulating the casting of more than one veto before decision making in the Council can be blocked. However, total abolishment of the right of veto could at first glance look more democratic than it in reality may prove to be. It may well lead to (even more frequent) bypassing of the Council and increased resorting to unilateral action by permanent powers such as the United States, Russia or the United Kingdom. Thus, if one could succeed in making the composition of the Council more democratic without touching on the right of veto, much would have already been gained.[12]

Democracy in international economic institutions

Decision making in the IMF and the World Bank, the so-called Bretton Woods institutions, is still highly undemocratic.[13] The number of votes allotted to each member country as well as the allocation of seats on the governing bodies are determined by the subscription to the capital (the 'quotum') of each country, which in its turn depends to a large extent on the economic and financial power of a country. This "weighted" voting system applies equally to the IMF and the World Bank, as well as to the international institutions associated with the World Bank, such as the International Finance Corporation (IFC) and the International Development

Association (IDA). The result is that in the IMF a high-income country such as the Netherlands, with 16.5 million people, has even more votes (in total 51,874) than a developing country such as India, with a population of nearly 1.1 billion people (41,832 votes). In a similar vein, whereas the size of their populations is approximately equal, Germany has 36.8 times more votes in the IMF than Vietnam (130,332 versus 3,541). This is not to suggest that the size of the population should serve as the sole or the main criterion; it is only logical to weigh economic and financial criteria as well in international economic and financial organisations. Yet, it is obvious that there is something inherently undemocratic in the current decision-making structures in these international institutions. The very fact that some mixed voting groups of Western, Eastern European and developing countries do exist, does not really change this finding. Nevertheless, it may be noted that a certain shift of power has taken place over the years, reflected in the fact that the US share of the votes was drastically reduced from an initial 33% in 1945 to 17% nowadays. Especially Germany and Japan benefited from this, next to other countries such as Saudi Arabia. The Western world as a whole still has a comfortable majority, but in view of the fact that certain substantive decisions require a 70% or even 85% majority, the developing world could *de facto* exercise a right of veto if the developing countries would really operate as a group. However, in practise this seldom occurs.

At first glance, decision making within the newly-established World Trade Organisation is much more democratic. Formally, the principle of one state, one vote applies. However, in practise the old GATT tradition survived of pre-cooking all important decisions in so-called Green-Room consultations, in which only a self-selected group of countries can participate. Subsequently, the compromise as arrived at in the Green Room is then normally adopted by the WTO's official organs, normally by consensus (sic!). Recently, the group of countries participating in such Green Room consultations has become much larger than in the past. During the 1970s, the period of the GATT, a maximum of eight delegations was around. Currently, approximately 25 to 30 countries participate.

They include the so-called Quad (US, EU, Canada, Japan), Australia, New Zealand, Switzerland, Norway, a few Central and Eastern European states and an increasing number of large and medium-sized developing countries, including Argentina, Brazil, Chile, Colombia, Egypt, India, Mexico, Pakistan, South Africa and at least one South-East Asian country. Hence, nearly all small developing countries are excluded, while sub-Saharan Africa is represented solely by South Africa. Despite the formal equal vote for each member in the WTO constitution, in reality this system comes closer to oligarchy rather than democracy. The system is subject to revision. It would be more logical and in tune with modern times to replace it by, for example, a more representative, elected body of, for example, 20 countries, vested with the duty to develop consensus as regards international trade policy.[14] This could be helpful in preventing failures such as most of the recent WTO Ministerial Conferences from 1999 ('The Battle of Seattle') onwards. In essence, the industrial countries of the Green-Room consultations had underestimated, if not neglected, both the various wishes of many developing countries with respect to a new Development/Millennium Round and the interests of civil society groups in issues such as the impact of international trade on labour standards, human rights, the environment and development.

Expanding circle of actors in international relations

Apart from their decision-making procedures, other examples of the democratic deficit in international organisations have also become apparent. Nearly all international institutions are very much state-oriented and maintain relatively few relationships with non-state entities. An exception is the tripartite International Labour Organisation, which includes representatives from trade unions and employers' organisations. Furthermore, a large number of non-governmental organisations have been registered as having observer status with the United Nations. However, they do not really have a voice in consultations, let alone in decision making. Nevertheless, a trend can be noted that civil society, international business and other interest groups organise themselves increasingly at an international level. Not seldom they seek to exert influence on international policy making. Led by a number of well-organised, effective NGOs and supported by countries such as Canada, Norway, Belgium, the Netherlands and Austria, the so-called "Ottawa process" resulted in the adoption and signing of an Anti-Landmines Convention in 1997, launching a total ban on landmines. Most states signed it, albeit China, India, Pakistan, Russia and the US did not join.[15] Similarly, the NGOs were instrumental in pushing for the drafting and conclusion of the Rome Statute (1998) on the establishment of a permanent International Criminal Court. Sometimes, NGOs can also be instrumental in delegitimising efforts of States. An example in case is the Draft Multilateral Agreement on Investment (MAI). The MAI relates to an OECD project to draft a comprehensive international investment treaty. Both the forum and the contents of the draft MAI led to considerable turmoil. Negotiating within the context of the OECD implies that nearly the entire developing world (with the exception of Mexico and South Korea) is being excluded from such consultations, while multilateral regulation of foreign investment affects many non-OECD countries as well. It was the intention that developing countries would be invited to accede to the MAI *after* the conclusion of the treaty; an example of the traditional policy of "for them, but without them". Moreover, the draft focused on property protection rather than on effects of foreign investment on development, employment, the environment and human rights.[16] Many NGOs protested against what they perceived as an one-sided orientation and they labelled it, in a somewhat exaggerated fashion, as "an ecological and social race to the bottom". Much to the disappointment of various governments (including the Dutch government) the negotiations came to a stalemate in the autumn of 1998, especially since countries such as Canada and France decided no longer to support this MAI effort. It proved to be effectively killed by civil society groups.

Concluding observations

Obviously, the way in which the international community has institutionalised its international co-operation is a far cry from principles of democracy and good governance. The decolonisation process has led in certain ways to a democratisation of international relations, in terms of abolishing former structures of dominance.[17] It also led to an enormous increase in the membership of international organisations. For example, the United Nations started with 51 original member states in 1945 and currently has 193 members. The newly-independent states could exert a profound new influence in the political organs of the United Nations, most notably the General Assembly. They could use the latter as a vehicle for change in many fields of international relations and international law, albeit its decisions are in principle non-binding. Yet, these resolutions were often instrumental in capturing and consolidating new concepts and trends. Occasionally, they could even serve as the forerunners of treaties, for example in the fields of human rights, development, arms control, and law of the sea and ocean affairs.[18] Meanwhile, democratisation of the Security Council could hardly materialise; whilst it could be noted that in practise, seven out of the ten non-permanent members are developing countries, China is still the only developing country among the five permanent powers. Basic concepts inherent to good governance, such as the avoidance of double standards, legitimacy, representativeness, effectiveness, transparency and accountability became part of the parlance surrounding the Council only recently and hesitantly. Similarly, international economic decision making is far from democratic, transparent or effective. Oligarchic structures prevail in international organisations, such as the Group of Seven/Eight, the weighted voting system in the IMF and World Bank and the composition of the permanent membership of the UN Security Council. Hence, a considerable tension, if not contradiction, can be noted between what Western states advocate for and often demand from developing countries, and their reluctance to re-shape international consultation in accordance with similar principles of democracy and good governance in international organisations. In the long run, such a policy is bound to undermine the credibility of Western efforts for democracy and good governance within developing countries.

Notes

1   See on this N.M. Blokker and H.G. Schermers (eds.), *Proliferation of International Organizations. Legal Issues*. The Hague, 2001.

2   See Article 2, para. 1 of the UN Charter: 'The Organization is based on the principle of the sovereign equality of all of its Members.'

3   See especially the Declaration on the Granting of Independence to all Colonial Countries and Territories in Accordance with the Charter of the United Nations, GA Res. 1514 (XV), 14 December 1960, adopted by 89 votes in favour, none against, with nine abstentions. For an analysis see A. Cassese, *Self-determination of Peoples. A Legal Appraisal*, Cambridge, 1995.

4   See the Declaration on Permanent Sovereignty over Natural Resources, GA Res. 1803 (XVII), 14 December 1962, adopted by 87 to 2 votes, with 12 abstentions. See also GA Res. 2158 (XXI), 1966 and 3281 (XXIX), 1974. For an analysis see N.J. Schrijver, *Sovereignty over Natural Resources: Balancing Rights and Duties*. Cambridge, 1997.

5   GA Res. 1995 (XIX), 1964.

6   GA Res. 3201 and 3202 (S-VI), 1 May 1974.

7   For assessments of the General Assembly, see M.J. Peterson, *The General Assembly in World Politics*, Boston, 1986 and S. Bailey, *The General Assembly of the United Nations*, London, 1964.

8   See for an account, W. van Genugten, K. Homan, N. Schrijver and P. de Waart, *The United Nations of the Future. Globalisation with a Human Face*, Amsterdam: KIT Publishers, 2006, 304 pp.; T. Weiss, D.P. Forsythe and R. Coate, *The United Nations and Changing World Politics*, Boulder, 3 rd. ed., 1999 and P.R. Baehr and L. Gordenker, *The United Nations: Reality and Ideal*, Basingstoke, 4th ed., 2005.

9   A comprehensive book on the UN Security Council is that by S. Bailey and S. Daws, *The Procedure of the UN Security Council*, Oxford, 3rd edn, 1998.

10 This practice was endorsed by the International Court of Justice in its Advisory Opinion on *Namibia*, ICJ Rep. 1971, p. 16 at p. 22.

11 For a review of all proposals, B. Fassbender, *UN Security Council Reform and the Right of Veto: A Constitutional Perspective*, The Hague, 1998.

12 For a recent update and assessment of the reform debate see N.J. Schrijver, 'Reforming the UN Security Council in Pursuance of Collective Security'. *Journal of Conflict & Security Law* vol. 12 (2007), no. 1, pp. 127-138.

13 Data on current quotas and voting power of member states can be found on the web sites of these institutions: http//www.imf.org and www.worldbank.org.

14   Cf. F. Weiss, 'WTO decision making: is it reformable?'. In: Kennedy and Southwick (eds.), The Political Economy of International Trade Law, Cambridge, 2002, pp. 68-80.

15   Convention on the Prohibition of the Use, Stockpiling, Production and Transfer of Anti-Personnel Mines and their Destruction, 1997, entry into force 1999. For an assessment see J. Goldblatt, 'Anti-personnel Mines: From Mere Restrictions to a Total Ban'. *Security Dialogue* vol. 30 (1999), no. 1, pp. 9-23.

16   See N.J. Schrijver, 'A Multilateral Investment Agreement from a North-South and International Law Perspective'. In: E.C. Niewenhuys and M.M.T.A. Brus (eds), *Multilateral Regulation of Foreign Investment*, The Hague, pp. 17-33.

17   See on this the pioneering book by B.V.A. Röling, *International Law in an Expanded World*, Amsterdam, 1960.

18   See on this, B. Sloan, *United Nations General Assembly Resolutions in Our Changing World*, New York, 1991; N.J. Schrijver, 'The Role of the United Nations in the Development of International Law', in J. Harrod and N.J. Schrijver (eds.), *The UN Under Attack*, Aldershot, 1988, pp. 33–56.

Civil Society – Revolutionary Idea or Political Slogan?

Michael Edwards

It is impossible to have a conversation about politics or democracy these days without someone mentioning the magic words "civil society", so one might think that people are clear what they mean when they use this term and why it is so important. Unfortunately, clarity and rigor are conspicuous by their absence in the civil society debate, a lack of precision that threatens to submerge this concept completely under a rising tide of criticism and confusion.

According to the Cato Institute (2001) in Washington DC, civil society means "fundamentally reducing the role of politics in society by expanding free markets and individual liberty." The organizing committee of the World Social Forum (cited in Boggs 2000, 259) says that civil society is "the single most viable alternative to the authoritarian state and the tyrannical market", while those who are more comfortable in the middle ground of politics see civil society as the missing link in the success of social democracy, central to "Third Way" thinking and supposedly "compassionate conservatism" (Giddens 2001). In academia, civil society has been branded as the "chicken soup of the social sciences" (Stephen White, cited in Post and Rosenblum 2002), the scholarly equivalent of the bestselling self-help books that provide much-needed comfort without that much substance. Adam Seligman (1992), tongue firmly in cheek, calls civil society the "new analytic key that will unlock the mysteries of the social order"; Jeremy Rifkin (1995, 280) calls it "our last, best hope"; the United Nations and the World Bank see it as the key to "good governance" and poverty-reducing growth, and kick-starting civil society in the Middle East has even been used as a motive for the war against Iraq.

As a report from the Washington-based Institute for Foreign Policy Analysis put it in 2004 (2004, 12), "the US should emphasize civil society development in order to ensure regional stability in central Asia" – forgetting that citizens groups have been a prime cause of destabilization in every society since Ancient Egypt.

Some claim that civil society is a specific product of the nation state and capitalism, while others see it as a universal expression of the collective life of individuals, at work in all countries and stages of development but expressed in different ways according to history and context. Some see it as one of three separate sectors of society (state, market and voluntary organizations), others as intimately interconnected and even inter-penetrated by states and markets. Is civil society the preserve of groups predefined as democratic, modern, and "civil" in some universal normative sense, or is it home to all sorts of associations, including "uncivil" society like militant Islam and American militias, or to traditional associations based on inherited characteristics like religion and ethnicity that are so common in Africa and Asia?

Are families "in" or "out" of civil society, and what about the business sector? Is civil society a bulwark against the abuse of state power, an indispensable support for government reformers or dependent on public intervention for its very existence? Is it the key to individual freedom through the guaranteed experience of pluralism or a threat to democracy through special interest politics? Is it a noun – a part of society, an adjective – a kind of society, an arena for societal deliberation or a mixture of all three? Can you build a civil society through foreign aid and intervention, or is this just another imperial fantasy? Overall, what is to be done with a concept that seems so unsure of itself that definitions are akin to nailing jelly to the wall? And in any case, do these questions really matter, except to a small band of academics who study civil society for a living?

When an idea can mean so many things it probably means nothing, so I think the time has come to be rid of the term completely or, now that it has acquired a life of its own, to at least be clearer with each other about the different interpretations in play. Consensus is impossible given the range of views on offer, but clarity is not, and greater clarity can be the springboard for a better conversation about the promise and potential of civil society as a basis of hope and action for the future, *and* about the pitfalls of using this term as a political slogan or a shelter for dogma and ideology. Recognizing that civil society does indeed mean different things to different people is one of the keys to moving forward, because it moves us beyond false universals and entrenched thinking. And for those who want to discard the term completely, my plea would be, not yet – "don't throw the baby out with the bathwater." Ideas about civil society and democracy can survive and prosper in a more rigorous critique.

Three schools of civil society thinking

In part, the fog that has enveloped this term is the result of an obsession with one particular interpretation of civil society as the world of voluntary associations, forgetting that there are earlier and later traditions that have just as much to offer. It was Alexis de Tocqueville that started this craze on his visits across the Atlantic in the 1830s, seeing America's rich tapestry of associational life as the key to its emerging democracy. Americans of all dispositions have an incurable tendency to form voluntary associations, as he famously declared (de Tocqueville 1861/2003). Originally however, civil society, at least from Aristotle to Thomas Hobbes, represented a *kind* of society that was identified with certain ideals. And in modern societies, realizing these ideals – like political equality or peaceful coexistence – requires action across many different institutions, not just by or among voluntary associations. In this sense, civil society is often used as shorthand to describe the "good society", the society of our dreams, the society we want to live in, to create and leave to those we love. Most recently, philosophers have developed a new set of theories about civil society as the "public sphere" – the places where citizens argue with one-another about the great questions of the day and negotiate a constantly-evolving sense of the "common" or "public" interest – the social consensus that is the backbone of any functioning democracy.

If we are to have a sensible conversation about civil society and democracy, then we need to deconstruct these three different schools of thought and then see how they are related to each other in different contexts. The first school believes that voluntary associations act as "gene carriers" of the good society – microclimates, if you will, for developing values like tolerance and cooperation, and the skills required for living a democratic life. The trouble is that real associational life is home to all sorts of different and competing values and beliefs (think pro- and anti-abortion groups for example, or peace movements and the National Rifle Association in the USA). There is another problem with this thesis too, because the values and beliefs we want to see developed in democracies are fostered in all the places where we learn and grow, and where political dispositions are shaped, and that means in families, schools, workplaces, colleges, universities, and political institutions large and small. We actually spend a lot more time in these places than we do in voluntary associations, so these experiences should be especially important. For the same reason, by themselves, voluntary associations can rarely secure the level of political consensus that is required to secure and enforce broad-based social reforms – there is just too much difference and diversity of opinion. That is why civil society, to quote John Keane (2003) "is riddled with danger, since it gives freedom to despots and democrats alike."

Therefore, my second school of thought – civil society as the "good society" – is very important, because it sets the contributions of voluntary associations in the wider context and guards against the tendency to privilege one part of society over the others on ideological grounds – voluntary associations over government for example, or business over both. Good neighbors cannot replace good government, and nonprofits should not be asked to substitute for well-functioning markets. Historically (think of the US in the 20th century and East Asia after World War II), success in achieving good society goals has always been based on social contracts negotiated between government, business and citizens.

However, if the good society requires coordinated action between different institutions all pulling in the same direction, how do societies decide in which direction they want to go, and whether it is the right one, as conditions and circumstances continue to change over time? How are collective choices made, trade-offs negotiated and ends reconciled with means in ways that are just and effective? For answers to these questions, we have to turn to my third school of thought and consider civil society in its role as the public sphere.

The concept of a "public" – a whole polity that cares about the common good and has the capacity to deliberate about it democratically – is central to civil society thinking. The development of shared interests, a willingness to cede some territory to others, the ability to see something of oneself in those who are different and work together more effectively as a result – all these are crucial attributes for effective governance, practical problem-solving and the peaceful resolution of our differences. In its role as the "public sphere", civil society becomes the arena for argument and deliberation as well as for association and institutional collaboration, and the extent to which such spaces thrive is crucial to democracy, since if only certain truths are represented, if alternative viewpoints are silenced by exclusion or suppression, or if one set of voices is heard more loudly than those of others, the "public" interest inevitably suffers. When all politics are polarized, public policy problems become embedded, even frozen, in polities that cannot solve them – think of health care and welfare reform in the US, for example. Breaking the resulting gridlock requires the creation of new publics in support of broad-based reform – exactly what is missing in the US right now.

Synthesis: a richer picture of civil society

Each of these three schools of civil society thinking has something to offer the debate about democracy, but each by itself is incomplete and unconvincing. The logical thing to do is to connect them together, so that the weaknesses of one set of theories are balanced by the strengths and contributions of the others. What does that mean in practice?

Civil society as the good society keeps our "eyes on the prize" – the prize being the goals of poverty-reduction and deep democracy that require coordinated action across different sets of institutions. However, the vision of the good society says little about how such goals are going to be achieved, and associational life does seem to be an important – if incomplete – explanatory factor in most contemporary settings. Structural definitions of civil society – the first approach I described – are useful in emphasizing the gaps and weaknesses of associational life that need to be fixed if they are to be effective vehicles for change. However, the differences and particularities of associational life generate competing views about the ends and means of the good society, anchored in religion, politics, ideology, race, gender and culture. Without our third set of theories – civil society as the public sphere – there would be no just and democratic way to reconcile these views and secure a political consensus about the best way forward. In turn, a healthy associational ecosystem is vital to the public sphere, since it is usually through voluntary organizations and the media that citizens carry on their conversations. Finally, the achievements of the good society are what make possible the independence and level playing field that underpin a democratic associational life – by reducing inequality, for example, and guaranteeing freedom of association, anchored in the law.

Hence, it is not difficult to see how each approach builds on the others in order to offer a more compelling explanation of civil society's significance. One can construct a similar tripartite relationship at the global level too by examining "global civil society" as an additional layer of transnational associational activity, a new kind of global society (or international relations) marked out by respect for human rights and the peaceful resolution of differences, and as an emerging global public sphere exemplified by events like the World Social Forum, Internet sites like open Democracy (www.opendemocracy.net) and innovations such as open-source technology.

Thinking about the issues in this way helps us to pose an actionable set of questions instead of arguing in the abstract over which theory is correct. And for me, the most important question is as follows: how do shifting patterns of associational life help or hinder the realization of good society goals (including deeper democracy), and what can we do to revive the public sphere if we believe it is an important transmission mechanism between the two? In other words, what is the link between civil society as a means to an end and civil society as an end in itself, and what can we do in concrete terms to promote these links so that they are more successful?

Civil society – from theory to action

These questions generate a rich agenda for public policy discussions, though a complicated one since there is no obvious consensus on the answers and the empirical evidence is both ambiguous and contested. I would cite three schools of thought, all relying on North American research, so perhaps less relevant elsewhere. The first is the "social capital" school exemplified by the work of Robert Putnam (2000), who sees associational life in general as the driving force behind the positive social norms on which the good society is built – norms such as cooperation, trust and reciprocity. If this is correct, the logical policy option is to encourage as much volunteering and voluntary action as possible, even if some of it is used for nefarious purposes. Somewhat magically in my view, these differences will, Putnam argues, work themselves out in the general scheme of things, perhaps in ways that are socially and politically analogous to Adam Smith's "hidden hand" of the market.

The second school of thought – which I call the "comparative associational" school for want of a better description – is perhaps best exemplified by the work of Theda Skocpol (2003), who sees particular configurations of associational life as the key to securing the public policy reforms that the good society requires. In the USA, these configurations include nationally-federated, mass-membership, cross-class groups like Parent-Teachers Associations, labor unions, and the Orders of the Moose, Elks and others, which have all declined so much over the last fifty years. It is these associations, Skocpol argues, that used to build social and political consensus across American society and to provide strong bridges between citizens and government that led to reforms like the GI Bill of 1944, which had a hugely positive impact on welfare. In this case, the logical task for policy-makers is to identify and support those configurations of associational life that constitute the most important transmission mechanisms between citizen action and democratic functioning – a more difficult task than it seems, as we shall see .

My third school of thought – the "school of skeptics" (perhaps best exemplified by the work of Nancy Rosenblum: 1998) – does not see any reliable or predictable link between the structure of associational life and the achievements of the good society and so offers little by way of conclusions for policy and practice save the mantra, "do no harm."

For me, none of these positions are completely convincing, especially in contexts other than the USA, and the appropriate policy options obviously depend on which position one subscribes to. Nevertheless, there are some interventions that would be useful across the board. The first thing we need to do is to strengthen the pre-conditions for a healthy civil society in all three senses by attacking inequality and discrimination, giving people the means to be active citizens, reforming politics to encourage more participation, guaranteeing the independence of associations and the structures of public communication, and building a strong foundation for institutional partnerships, alliances and coalitions. Inequality is the poison of civil society because it endows citizens with different levels of resources and opportunities to participate in associational life and the public sphere, and therefore in fashioning the goals of the good society, so things like support for education, childcare and a living wage – which are not usually seen as civil-society building interventions – may be among the most important areas of all. Maintaining an explicit linkage between the promotion of social and economic equity and the deepening of democracy is the key to avoiding an, often unimpressive, shopping list of policy interventions such as NGO capacity-building and increased community service.

Second, we need to support innovations in associational life that encourage citizen action to operate in service to the good society, rather than as a substitute for politics, market reform and the demands of democratic state-building. That does not mean turning the clock back to the 1950s and forcing teenagers to join traditional associations, but reinventing associational life to suit the realities of a very different era, in which time and energy are more limited, worn down by the demands of work and unsupported family obligations.

Such measures are highly context-specific, but if I was to construct an agenda for action from my Ford Foundation experience in the USA for example, I would focus on building stronger links between policy and advocacy NGOs, community organizations at the grass-roots, service deliverers and the media; connecting associations across different interests and agendas so that they can form stronger coalitions in favor of political reform; and encouraging a more democratic relationship between grassroots constituencies and those in the NGO sector who claim to speak on their behalf. We need to reduce the costs and risks of citizen participation (for example, by making it easier to organize at the workplace) and connect different forms of participation so that volunteering does not become a substitute for political engagement, as is happening among many younger people in America today.

It is also important to make room for surprises – like the potential political effects of self-help groups like Alcoholics Anonymous and

Weightwatchers (two of the largest voluntary associations in America today, with over 25 million members) or the Boy Scouts and mosque associations in Lebanon (which turn out to be among the most progressive organizations socially and politically), or burial societies in South Africa (which played a major role in the fight against apartheid), or labor unions in France and Brazil (which have given an important stimulus to new and less hierarchical forms of transnational organizing: Edwards 2004).

Conclusion

To conclude, civil society is simultaneously a goal to aim for, a means to achieve it and a framework for engaging with each other about ends and means. When these three "faces" turn towards each other and integrate their different perspectives into a mutually-supportive framework, the idea of civil society begins to explain a great deal about the course of politics and social change and of course, will continue to serve as a practical framework for organizing both resistance and alternative solutions to social, economic and political problems. Many of the difficulties of the civil society debate disappear when we lower our expectations of what each school of thought has to offer in isolation from the others, and abandon all attempts to enforce a single model, consensus or explanation. This may not deter the ideologues from using civil society as a cover for their own agendas, but it should make it easier to expose their claims and challenge the assumptions they often make.

This is one reason why, to answer the question I raised at the outset, becoming clearer about civil society *does* matter in more than the academic sense. When President Vladimir Putin boasts of developing a new NGO infrastructure to help regain Russian influence in Ukraine, Georgia and elsewhere, or when politicians on both sides of the Atlantic continue to be engaged in a forced march to civil society in the Middle East, it is clear that the ways in which these ideas are interpreted *does* have a real impact on the lives of real people in the here and the now. "Moscow's policy places civil society at the heart of its comeback strategy" says Ivan Krastev (2005), neatly demonstrating the dangerous elasticity of this concept when used for political ends. As John Maynard Keynes's famous dictum reminds us (cited in Edwards 2003), "practical men in authority who think themselves immune from theoretical influences are usually the slaves of some defunct economist", just as present-day civil society builders are motivated by ideas deeply rooted in different schools of thought, but often unacknowledged, untested and insufficiently interrogated. That is hardly a satisfactory foundation for understanding and strengthening the role of civil society in democracy and development.

References

Boggs, C (2000) *The End of Politics: Corporate Power and the Decline of the Public Sphere*. New York: Guilford Press.

Cato Institute (2001) Undated fundraising letter signed by Cato Institute President, Edward Crane.

De Tocqueville, A. (1861/2003) *Democracy in America*. London: Penguin Classics.

Edwards, M. (2003) *Future Positive*. London: Earthscan/James and James.

Edwards, M. (2004) *Civil Society*. Cambridge: Polity Press/Blackwell Publishing.

Giddens, A. (ed.) (2001) *The Global Third Way Debate*. Cambridge: Polity Press.

Institute for Foreign Policy Analysis (2004) *Central Asia in US Operational Strategy and Planning: Where do we go from here?* Washington DC: Institute for Foreign Policy Analysis.

Keane, J. (2003) *Global Civil Society*. Cambridge: Cambridge University Press.

Krastev, I. (2005) *Russia's Post-Orange Empire*. London: openDemocracy.net (http://www.opendemocracy.net/people-ukraine/postorange_2947.jsp).

Post, R and N. Rosenblum, "Introduction". In: R. Post and N. Rosenblum (eds.) *Civil Society and Government*. Princeton. Princeton University Press.

Putnam, R. (2000) *Bowling Alone: The Collapse and Revival of American Community*. New York: Simon and Schuster.

Rifkin, J. (1995) *The End of Work*. New York: Putnam.

Rosenblum, N. (1998) *Membership and Morals: the Personal Uses of Pluralism in America*. Princeton: Princeton University Press.

Skocpol, T. (2003) *Diminished Democracy: from Membership to Management in American Civic Life*. Oklahoma City: University of Oklahoma Press.

Seligman, A. (1992) *The Idea of Civil Society*. Princeton: Princeton University Press.

Civil Society, Governance and Globalisation[1]

Kumi Naidoo

O ver the last decade the size and importance of civil society has increased significantly. The recent proliferation of NGOs and the growing strength of global civil society networks have been evident in the streets, the policy conferences, the board rooms, the classrooms and even at the World Economic Forum. However, this movement is not without internal and external challenges, not the least of which is civil society engagement with an ever increasingly globalised world.

Problematizing Globalisation

CIVICUS, along with several other civil society organisations, is often in the somewhat unusual position of attending both the World Social Forum and the World Economic Forum. I say unusual, because the two events are often presented as completely antithetical to one another. Indeed, on the surface at least, they are strikingly different types of gatherings and many question how it is possible to engage with both processes. Yet at a basic level, both of these annual global meetings are grappling with three of the key issues of our day – namely globalisation and its manifold effects, the meaning and role of civil society and citizen participation and challenges to effective governance at local, national and global levels.

In many ways, the World Social Forum can be understood as both a product of globalisation – and as its very embodiment. It is the much-discussed phenomenon of globalisation that provides the impetus for the WSF – and for the hundreds of similar events at the regional and national level that have been convened over the past several years. What has erroneously been called the "anti-globalisation" movement is ironically one of the most globalised movements of our time. Globalisation has drawn the people of the world into closer proximity with one another; it has intensified contact between them; lowered many – but by far not all – types of barriers to the movement of goods, ideas, technology and cultural products; and accelerated the pace at which information is shared.

It is the more benign aspects of globalisation that have made possible gatherings like the WSF, where tens of thousands of people from scores of countries organise themselves to descend upon a chosen destination at a given time, using email and the Internet to coordinate everything from the programme schedule and travel arrangements, to the advance exchange of discussion papers.

Yet there are *other* aspects of globalisation, which motivate these meetings to be called in the first place – it is the harsh contradictions of globalisation, its unevenness, its sheer cruelness that is driving people to join forces in collective efforts to discuss and debate ways to harness the forces of globalisation for the common good. These critiques of globalisation are now well known:

- Globalisation is exacerbating global inequality and its "rules" – to the extent we can call them that – appear to be driven by the rich at the expense of the poor. The relentless lauding of so-called "free trade" in fact masks a set of double standards that protect certain markets in wealthy countries and deny poor and developing countries the chance to benefit from the most promising segments of their own economies.
- Globalisation and the forces driving it, is throwing up a set of intractable challenges that brazenly cross national borders and which, by their very definition, defy national-level solutions. The spread of environmental degradation, HIV/AIDS, human trafficking, the drug trade and terrorism are all enabled by globalisation.
- At the same time, the momentum toward economic, political and cultural integration weakens the ability of national govern-

ments to take actions in the national interest. Globalisation is having an impact upon the role of elected representative institutions at the national level and is elevating powerful new actors, such as supranational governing institutions and transnational corporations. Local control over decision making is rapidly shifting upwards to structures and processes that are not accountable to ordinary citizens.

Another contradiction of globalisation can be seen in the curtailment, particularly in the years following the tragic events of 2001, of what we might call "international civic mobility". As an African, travelling on an African passport and working at the global level, I often muse that if I were to write a book about my tenure at my current job, it would be called *Visas, Bloody Visas*. While cheaper travel has increased the movement of many, there has never before been the level of legal restriction on the movements of people from poor countries to rich countries, unless they have distinctive skills that the developed economies need.

Arguments about globalisation tend to occur in extreme terms – globalisation is often presented as either "all good" and full of promise for a better future on the one hand, or as irreparably flawed and diabolical on the other. John Clark, in his book *Worlds Apart: Civil Society and the Battle for Ethical Globalisation*, refers to these two camps as the "agony school" and the "ecstasy school". Yet globalisation is too complex and multi-faceted to be boiled down to a caricature. Independent surveys[2] conducted in northern and southern countries over the last few years reveal that citizens are ambivalent about globalisation: they hold generally favourable opinions about globalisation and global integration, yet they are highly anxious about growing inequality and the loss of local control. They are concerned about non-economic dimensions of globalisation as well, such as threats to local culture and the disappearance of indigenous languages.

The grassroots action we have been witnessing on the streets, in cyberspace, outside the headquarters of the World Bank and IMF and on the roads and railways to G8 meetings is emerging in direct response to a perception that, increasingly, important decisions affecting people's lives and well-being are being made in non-transparent ways in supranational institutions that are not accountable to citizens and not accessible to citizen engagement. Decisions about trade rules, intellectual property rights, macro-economic restructuring policies, privatisation of vital public services and debt relief are made behind closed doors in ways that are largely perceived to be undemocratic.

It is against this backdrop that the notion of "civil society" has re-entered mainstream discourse. Civil society is, of course, not a new concept but it is one that has been re-discovered over the past two decades with this rise in citizen activism. Unfortunately, in the media and in the minds of some people, views about civil society as a whole are often framed by the actions of its "un-civil" elements – groups who espouse violence and destruction or who pursue racist or exclusionary goals. Activists are often portrayed as "radicals" who are not interested in dialogue.

I want to dispel this image. What the World Social Forum and recent global civil society gatherings have come to represent for many people around the world are spaces where the voices of average citizens "count" in discussions around social, political and economic justice. They are venues where people and groups who feel increasingly alienated from the prevailing global system can join together to explore alternative visions for a more ethical form of globalisation that works for the benefit of average people, rather than simply for the benefit of powerful interests.

Civil Society in the Context of Globalisation

Attempts to define civil society are often contested but one way to think of it is in terms of activities that are undertaken for the public good by groups or individuals in the space between the family, the state and the market. This means that we must look today not only at non-governmental organisations (NGOs) – often taken as synonymous with civil society – but also at a rich array of heterogeneous civic elements that includes trade unions, foundations, faith-based and religious groups, community-based organisations, social movements and networks and ordinary citizens who are active in the public sphere.

It is often said that civil society burst onto the public stage at the Earth Summit in 1992. When thousands of citizens who attended the Earth Summit left Rio, they did so with much optimism and a belief that an historical watershed had been achieved. In a way they were right: Rio was the first major conference where "civil society" became a prominent player at the global level. Since the Earth Summit, civil society has come into its own as an important political, social and economic actor. The last decade has witnessed a dramatic growth in the number of citizen groups, as well as in their capacity, scope, reach, public profile and influence. This "global associational revolution," as it has been called, is being driven by the same forces that are producing globalisation – democratisation, the spread of new technologies and global integration of various forms – but it is also reacting to many of the effects of globalisation that I mentioned above.

Historically, much of the work of civil society organisations or CSOs, has occurred at a micro level, where they are involved in providing important services to vulnerable communities in areas as diverse as health care, education and professional training, legal advice, humanitarian relief, women's empowerment, technical assistance in agriculture and environmental protection and so on. Civil society groups have often stepped into the uneasy vacuum of post-conflict situations and have compensated for the state – not uncontroversially – in the growing number of instances where vital public services have been rolled back due to macro-economic reforms.

Increasingly, however, civil society groups have recognised the need to rethink the well-known slogan "think globally, act locally". Experience has shown that in and of itself, acting locally will not get to the root causes of many social and economic problems – if the real locus of power is global, then there is a need to "think locally and act globally" as well. A growing number of CSOs have become actively engaged in advocacy work, campaigning and policy-making. Public campaigns on issues such as landmines, debt relief and for the establishment of the international criminal court have had a definable impact.

As civil society has matured, its credibility with outside audiences has grown. Many governments seek to harness the expertise and local knowledge of civil society groups in policy-making. High-profile civil society groups, particularly those working around environmental issues, have developed a certain 'brand recognition'; their endorsements or criticisms of business practices, for example, carry weight with the public and have become an important force with which the private sector must reckon. Perhaps most importantly, civil society groups generally enjoy a high level of public trust – in fact, a recent survey revealed that among 17 institutions, ranging from national governments to educational systems to media and the legal system, NGOs are the institution most trusted by average citizens after their country's armed forces[3].

The Challenges Facing Civil Society

Accordingly, civil society is attracting a new level of scrutiny in its role as a major public actor. It is being forced to grapple with both external and internal challenges, from those who are seeking to make civil society stronger and more credible, as well as from those who question its right to play certain roles. I would like to touch briefly upon five of these challenges.

The first is a challenge of power and power imbalances within civil society. The sector is vibrant and extremely diverse. It encompasses both major transnational NGOs with multi-million dollar operating budgets and tiny citizen-based organisations with highly constrained resources, access to information and capacity. It embraces highly structured groups such as trade unions alongside loose issue-based social movements. While this diversity adds to the sector's richness, it also throws up fundamental questions about whose voices are heard and at which venues, how resources are accessed and distributed and who is speaking for whom.

The second challenge internal to civil society is about bridging narrow interests and broader goals. Many civil society actors are committed to advancing a specific issue, whether this involves protecting rainforests, promoting fair labour practices or advancing women's rights. While recent civil society activity has been noteworthy for the alliances that have been formed among groups with different areas of interest, there remains a type of "silo mentality", which prevents CSOs from working across areas of speciality, toward common goals.

For example, dialogue between human rights organisations and development organisations has historically been weak and many potentially productive synergies have evaded us. With many human rights organisations now embracing social and economic rights and with many development organisations adopting a rights-based approach to their work, it is an opportune time to bridge this divide. The dichotomy between the world of volunteering (defined as the provision of direct services to communities in need) and the world of social activism (defined as those that are more concerned with structural and policy changes) remains a challenge. We also need to create an environment where, for example, NGOs rise to defend workers' rights of association in cases where trade union rights are threatened and where trade unions vocally defend the rights of NGOs.

A third internal challenge for civil society is to articulate a coherent vision for a more just and equitable global system. One of the frequent criticisms of the so-called "anti-globalisation" movement, is that it is *against* everything imaginable but not *for* anything discernible. Although many within the movement are working proactively for social and economic justice, civil society is challenged to move beyond debate and *ad hoc* mobilisations and to formulate a strategy for achieving its vision. The core issue, however, may not be an absence of alternative visions but rather the fact that the world's powerful governments appear unwilling to engage with these alternatives. As an example, the 2001 study produced by Third World Network for the UNDP, entitled *The Multilateral Trading System: A Development Perspective*, provides a detailed set of recommendations for transforming the international trade system into an instrument for balanced and equitable human development. Yet because they seek to redress power imbalances, such visions are often rejected out of hand.

The fourth challenge is one that emanates from outside civil society. The allegation is made that citizen activism threatens to undermine democratic systems by "short-circuiting" established procedures for decision-making. This is a critique that we in civil society vehemently reject. An active, engaged citizenry is essential for a healthy democratic society. We must resist the notion that democracy equals elections and that a victory at the ballot box is a blank cheque to rule without any interface and dialogue with citizens in between election periods. To reduce democracy to the singular act of voting once every four or five years is clearly an error. Civic activism complements representative democratic practices and makes them more effective by drawing citizens more fully into public life and providing a constant check on official accountability.

Clearly, it does not make sense for political leaders to deprive themselves of the policy knowledge that civil society actors acquire from working directly with vulnerable communities. Who better to inform the drafting of a domestic violence law than women who work with survivors of such violence? Who better to inform the drafting of an adult literacy strategy than those that work day in and day out with adult learners in our communities? Who better to help craft a rural or urban development strategy than those working on the ground addressing these issues? Engagement with citizen voices leads to more effective policies that better address the concerns of primary and secondary stakeholders, which integrate innovative ideas and knowledge from the local level and result in greater impact and ownership within communities.

The fifth challenge is perhaps the most complex of all and is heard both inside and outside civil society. Here, I am referring to the challenge of legitimacy and the related issues of transparency and accountability.

Challenges to civil society's legitimacy come from many quarters. They are often voiced by national political leaders and occasionally, by prominent voices at global institutions. It is frequently said that civil society groups do not represent the views of anyone but themselves and that if they are accountable at all, it is usually "upward" to their sponsors, rather than "downward" to those they purportedly serve. Those that offer this critique sometimes evoke a range of derogatory acronyms to describe certain kinds of wannabes NGOs: BONGOs (business-organised NGOs), PONGOs (politically-organised NGOs), BRINGOs (Briefcase NGOS), DONGOs (donor-organised NGOs), GONGOs (government-organised NGOs) MONGOs (My own NGO), and RONGOs (royally-organised NGOs).

At the 2002 World Economic Forum, the then-Director General of the WTO Mike Moore, said in a session that the WTO was only willing to engage with those civil society groups that operated in a transparent fashion, demonstrated accountability and which were elected on the basis of a defined constituency. These are commendable criteria and if the WTO applied this criteria rigorously to its member governments, WTO membership would be significantly smaller. Issues of legitimacy run both ways. When tens of thousands of citizens demonstrate against international institutions such as the WTO, the IMF and the World Bank in Seattle, Prague, Washington, Buenos Aires, Barcelona or Johannesburg, one has to wonder where the legitimacy of official institutions ends and civil society's begins.

Legitimacy cannot be taken for granted and must continuously be earned. And civil society groups are taking up this challenge head-on. Self-regulation mechanisms such as codes of ethics and standards of excellence have been adopted at the national level by civil society in several countries; a culture of transparency in governance structures is also gaining strength across the sector. For example, in June of 2006 the International NGO Accountability Charter was launched with more than 55 NGO signatories to date (see www.civicus.org).

There is also a powerful accountability factor at play with the functioning of CSOs, which I call the principle of "perform or perish." Not a single cent secured to undertake CSO activities is secured on the basis of obligation. Whether funding is derived from a government department, individual, foundation, business organisation or multi-lateral institution, resources will not continue to be available if civic organisations are not performing on the basis of their vision, mission and objectives. Most governments and inter-governmental organisations, to a lesser extent, are guaranteed a revenue flow from taxation or from countries' annual member contributions, even if performance is mediocre or substandard.

I would like to underscore, therefore, that the issue of civil society legitimacy is a valid one – particularly when it is voiced with an eye to building up the long-term credibility and effectiveness of civil society as an actor. All too frequently, however, the critique is lodged by those who would dismiss the right of civil society groups to give voice to citizen concerns and to engage in decision-making processes.

Civil Society, the Crisis of Governance and the "Democracy Deficit"

The view that government has a monopoly on truth and wisdom, I am afraid, reflects an outdated notion of governance – one that sees it as the exclusive domain of governments. In the case of electoral systems, governance occurred through a system of representative democracy, where citizens delegated votes to individuals who would represent them and leaders who would take decisions on their behalf.

It is rapidly becoming a truism that this old notion of governance is breaking down in an era of globalisation and with the emergence of a devastating "democracy deficit" in several local and national contexts and certainly at the global level. Surveys reveal declining levels of citizen trust in political institutions. In many democratic systems "form" has largely overtaken the "substance" of democracy: elections may be held but fewer and fewer people are choosing to vote and the meaningful interface between citizens and the elected is minimal between election periods. Affiliation with traditional political parties is on the decline as the parties themselves are characterised by a lack of internal democracy or fail to address issues that citizens believe are important. The influence of monied interests in many political systems is also turning citizens away from traditional engagement in favour of new forms of participation.

Although faith in traditional political institutions is waning, this should not be taken as a sign of citizen apathy. On the contrary, people are finding new and more direct ways to become involved in public life and decision-making – marking a shift from representative democracy to what is often called participatory democracy. Citizens are arguing for a new notion of governance that requires political leadership to engage with citizenry in ways that allow for ongoing input into decision-making and policy formation.

These new models take many forms, ranging from concerted attempts to build public-private partnerships to the establishment of transparency and oversight mechanisms, which allow civil society groups to play quasi-regulatory or watchdog functions. The Social Watch network, based in Uruguay, is an excellent example of how civil society groups have taken the initiative to monitor progress on international commitments and to report publicly on findings. This type of public accountability mechanism is now widely regarded as an essential part of good governance.

Finally, civil society groups are slowly carving out a more active role in actual decision-making processes, as witnessed in their direct participation over the last decade in UN conferences with some national governments including civil society participants in their delegations. Certain innovative international commissions involve civil society groups as equal stakeholders in policy-making, rather than in an after-the-fact consultative role.

While the space for civic participation in the global policy-making environment is growing, however, the overall picture overwhelmingly remains one where citizen voices are marginalised or are belatedly solicited after key decisions have been taken. Some key examples:

If we were to ask ourselves to name the single most important act that a national government engages in annually, we would most probably agree that it is drawing up the national budget. In analysing budgets, we can see the extent to which a government values children, gender equality, older people, education and so forth. However, when we look at the level of influence that parliamentarians have in the budgeting process, let alone that of civil society, it is frighteningly minimal in many systems of governance. What does this say therefore about the quality of governance and the strength of democracy?

If we reflect on the current position taken by certain governments with regard to the situation in Iraq, we find clear instances where governments are blatantly disregarding the views of their backbench MPs, ignoring the views of their citizenry and, in some cases, crassly manipulating arguments and supposed "evidence" to continue a military presence that has provoked a devastating humanitarian and refugee crisis.

To understand the voicelessness that so many citizens feel, we perhaps need to look more deeply at the discourse around social exclusion. In the coming decades humanity should judge itself not on the basis of the progress made by the most privileged sections but on the basis of the progress made by those that have been historically marginalised. This includes not only uncontested minority communities, such as people living with HIV/AIDS, people with disabilities, racial, ethnic, religious and cultural minorities, indigenous peoples, people with alternative sexual orientations, people who are not literate and so on. It also should include constituencies not often thought of as minorities *per se*.

Young people are becoming increasingly alienated from public life. On my continent, Africa, given the decimation being caused by HIV/AIDS and the fundamental impact it is having on our demography, in very real ways young people are not simply the leaders of tomorrow but are the leaders of today as well. We must also consider older people and take note of the levels of alienation they feel and the fact that we deprive ourselves of their experiential wisdom. We must acknowledge the scandalous fact that, after decades of activism for full gender equality, women still occupy on average less than 10% of leadership positions in government and business. What does it say about the quality of our democracy when women are so heavily under-represented even in long-standing democratic countries, let alone in those that are fledgling democracies? When we add this all up, it becomes increasingly difficult to deny that the democratic voice does not prevail in public life and that we are facing a serious "democracy deficit" on multiple levels.

We do not suggest that civil society is intrinsically good and that governments are intrinsically bad. That is far too simplistic a position to take. However, we need to recognise that effective democracy needs a vibrant civil society as well as an effective and accountable government. Both face struggles of accountability but they bring a vital diversity to governance and provide complementarity and mutual accountability systems. We can anticipate that this arena will always be contested – but this should strengthen democratic practice, rather than weaken it.

Democratising Global Institutions and Governance

Given the shift of power from national to global levels, it has become a critical priority for civil society to be engaging at a global level, yet it is here that the "democracy deficit" is felt most strongly. Many of the global institutions that have become increasingly powerful in our current age were constructed at a particular moment in world history that is a far cry from the context in which we currently find ourselves. The geopolitics of 1945 continue to dominate the governance structures of key institutions, even at this point well into the post-colonial era. We need to concede that many of these public institutions appear to be operating under rules and logic that are not in keeping with the realities that citizens confront around the world today.

The challenge of finding meaningful forms of engagement between civil society and intergovernmental organizations cannot be overemphasised. Creating channels of access should not be confused with establishing truly participatory procedures. The Poverty Reduction Strategy Papers (PRSPs) are a good case in point. The decision to link donor support to PRSPs is in part a response to the global changes discussed earlier, the evolving role of civil society and the recognition of the need for greater local ownership with citizen involvement. PRSPs, however imperfect, are providing new opportunities for citizens to engage in policymaking. However, in order to realise the promise of the PRSPs, the World Bank, its member governments and the donor community will have to do much more to realign their processes and support and give citizen participation the weight it deserves – it should not be optional or *ad hoc*, or simply an add-on late in the process. It needs to be supported by capacity building for citizen groups to engage with governments and for governments to engage with civil society, through transparency, communications, supportive laws and regulations for freedom of association and fundraising.

This is critically urgent since many civil society voices are beginning to lose faith in the PRSP processes. The director of one European development agency has noted that the PRSPs are supposed to be locally owned concepts and processes but in our view, this hardly ever happens effectively. Particularly, civil society is sometimes not consulted, sometimes as a last minute afterthought. In some countries, such as Bolivia, the more policy-oriented national CSOs with know how have been passed up for "grass-roots" consultations, which has actually divided civil society and left the national NGOs being told they do not sufficiently represent "the people". This also meant that the more operationally focused local NGOs were an easier and less critical "consultation partner" for the government. We believe the PRSP process in principle is excellent – but the reality is very slow and not giving us much hope at the moment, especially if we factor issues like gender and diversity into the formula.

We cannot trivialise the complexity of meaningful participatory processes. Naturally, these processes generate thorny issues, such as the availability of financial and time resources, choices about participants and the overall transparency of the processes themselves. However, as James Wolfensohn, the ninth President of the World Bank remarked: "If we fail to allow the time to genuinely open the process to different development actors and to the poor themselves, in the design, implementation and monitoring of poverty reduction strategies we might win some immediate battles, but we'd lose the long-run war to develop the accountable institutions that are essential to poverty reduction. Drafting strategy papers in Washington that are subsequently signed off by governments in the name of the people should be a thing of the past"[4].

This high-level public commitment to participatory processes is laudable and also needs to be mainstreamed into the many programmes in which the World Bank and other International Financial Institutions (IFIs) are involved. It is encouraging to see the Bank supporting viable and innovative examples of participatory decision-making processes, such as the well-known municipal budgeting process in Porto Alegre. Yet these kinds of principles do not seem to have been internalised into decision-making processes within the Bank itself. Where are the alternatives voices, let alone the voices of the poor? In order for IFIs to become accountable institutions, they must be willing to bring their own decision-making processes into line with those it is encouraging its clients to use.

Democratising individual global governance institutions, such as the United Nations, World Bank, IMF and WTO, is a challenge that requires serious and urgent attention. The Bank and IMF are now less dependent upon contributions from rich countries than they once were and it is essential that their governance structures be changed radically to reflect these shifts. Admittedly, the ball here rests in the court of the rich countries, which exercise a disproportionate level of influence and there are serious questions about the political will that exists to make Bank governance more equitable.

Thomas Jefferson, the architect of the US Constitution, once said, "I am certainly not an advocate for frequent changes in laws and constitutions. But laws and constitutions must go hand in hand with the progress of the human mind. As that becomes more developed, more enlightened, as new discoveries are made, new truths disclosed, and manners and opinions change with the change of circumstances, institutions must advance also, and keep pace with the times".

It is naïve to expect that institutions constructed more than sixty years ago, in a different global context, can be made more appropriate and relevant to our age with only minor changes. We can agree with Jefferson that we do not want to take the changing of institutions too lightly but clearly, the time has come for a revamping of global governance institutions within a more visionary framework that puts the interests of people at the centre of our deliberations, aimed at substantive institutional change.

262

Final Thoughts

Few would contest that we are in the midst of one of the most volatile and dangerous periods of world history. New threats to our security – both natural and man-made – challenge us as never before to find common ground in pursuit of social justice and sustainable development. I would argue that if this is to be successful in the long run, we are facing a double challenge of reinventing democracy, along the lines discussed above and reinventing a viable, equitable and just economic system that is premised less on the imperative of crude economic growth and more on a model of economic development that marries environmental sustainability, poverty eradication and broad-based development. Failure to insert notions of justice, equity and fairness into this process will be fatal indeed.

One of the challenges that we face in this process is not to allow current institutional limitations to constrain our ability to envision a different kind of global governance framework. We have to pose some bold questions about the fundamental changes that are needed to create a framework that is more fair and equitable than the one we are currently working within. We must question the prevailing logic of a system that energetically enables the movement of capital, but not of people, across boundaries; a financial system that essentially rewards unemployment and consolidates a notion of jobless growth; a system that rewards rampant overconsumption rather than grappling with the more complex challenge of sustainable development.

Our vision should be of a world where citizens and the groups they choose to organise are regarded as legitimate stakeholders, not only by the public, among whom they already enjoy high levels of trust, but by governance institutions that value engagement and recognise the many benefits it brings.

Our vision should be of a world where those of us that are serious about the long-term future of this planet address these questions –

difficult and as admittedly intractable as they are – honestly, courageously and with a commitment to ensuring that the views of not only government and business are considered, but also those of citizen groups working at the local, national and global levels.

Failure to do this will leave us charged by future generations with tinkering with incremental adjustments here and there, when what was required and needed was a fundamental rethinking of an international governance architecture that is rooted in notions of democracy, social and economic justice and sustainability.

In conclusion, let me urge you to recognise that we all face the challenge of doing our work in our different institutional environments in ways that respect and value the integrity, wisdom and contributions that the poor themselves can bring to the development process. The poor should be considered as full citizens and not simply victims, as full citizens and not simply recipients, as full citizens and not merely beneficiaries or charity cases. If there is one message you take with you today, it should be that every single human being that walks this planet has the potential to make a positive contribution to public life. The challenge for all of us as citizens is to ensure that we create just, meaningful and relevant ways in which this contribution can be harnessed for the public good. Unless we put people, and particularly those that have been historically excluded, at the centre of public life, our development goals will continue to evade us.

Note

1 This contribution deviates to some extent from the SID lecture given on February 19th, 2007 at the Vrije Universiteit Amsterdam.
2 Environic Survey, 2001 and 2002.
3 Study completed by the Canadian firm Environics and launched at the World Economic and Social Forums in January 2003.
4 James Wolfensohn, in: *Voices and Chaos at a Macro Level: Participation in Country-Owned Poverty Reduction Stategies*, edited by Pamesh Shah and Deborah Youssef, February 2002, World Bank, p. 1.

Summary of Lectures

Bernard Berendsen and Frans Bieckmann

Democracy and Development, the title of the lecture series organised by the Netherlands Chapter of the Society of International Development in the season 2006/2007 in itself suggests there is a positive relationship between the two: more democracy implies more openness and checks and balances, more accountability and less corruption, and all this would be conducive to sustainable development.

Also, more democracy would mean more competition among politicians and political parties vying for political power to introduce and implement better policies. More checks and balances would keep the political elite under control, reducing the risk that such power would be used for private interests instead of the public good.

Still, as is made clear in the background paper to the series, "Democracy, Nation Building and Development", it is questioned whether democracy is to be considered as the form of government that is best able to facilitate decision making and resolve internal conflicts in a peaceful way *as well as* to provide conditions for social and economic development *and* the reduction of poverty. An ambitious agenda indeed!

Experts in the field have during the series of nine lectures from October 2006 through June 2007 given their views on the matter. They addressed questions like: what comes first, democracy or development; is there a choice between democracy and stability; can democracy be promoted from outside; should we focus on the introduction of democratic institutions or on the promotion of democratic culture and are different cultures equally compatible with democratic systems of government? Finally, should the

265

promotion of democracy be seen as part of regular development cooperation and what are the respective roles of national governments, international organisations and civil society?

The series was concluded by a closing conference in September 2007 with contributions from a.o. the newly appointed Minister for Development Cooperation of the Netherlands, Mr Bert Koenders, Prof William Easterly of New York University and Vidar Helgesen of the International Institute for Democracy and Electoral Assistance. Their contributions are included in this volume as well.

Agnes van Ardenne-van der Hoeven, the Netherlands Minister for Development Cooperation in the first lecture, *Development starts at the ballot box*, focussed on the relationship between democracy, good governance and development. She emphasised the right of poor people to vote for their own future and voiced her strong conviction that not only the rich but also the poor can afford or cope with democracy. In fact, she said, democracy is their best hope for peace and prosperity.

While on the one hand experts like Robert Barro and Fareed Zakaria maintain that development should come first and democracy will follow, Van Ardenne pointed out that recent research by Daniel Kaufmann had demonstrated that the causal link runs from better governance, including political and civil liberties, to economic development, and not the other way around.

Van Ardenne took a "rights approach" to democracy and depicted democracy as a moral value that does not depend on the place: the roots of democracy can be found everywhere.

Arguing that democracy is good for development, Van Ardenne focussed on how democracy can be promoted: from encouraging the emergence of a strong and independent press to promoting a culture of tolerance. As she said: "A true democracy understands that uniformity is weakness and diversity is power".

She saw an important role for civil society organisations: "Strengthening civil society is crucial since it represents the demand side of the political equation". At the same time as a representative of the Dutch Government she also works on the supply side, engaging in honest and open dialogue with poor country governments on the state of their democracies and working with them to make sure that the state can live up to the expectations and demands of the governed.

Paul Collier in his lecture on *Democracy and Fragile States* addressed two questions: does democracy resolve the problem of violent conflict in Africa and does it help to resolve the problem of economic stagnation? Not surprisingly, as a scientist, Collier was much less optimistic than Van Ardenne on the power of democracy to resolve conflicts. He concluded on the basis of statistical experience that the propensity to conflict is much more likely in low income countries with stagnation or worse, economic decline, and that are dependent on primary commodities. Whether democracy contributes to stability depends on the level of *per capita* income in a country: in rich societies democracy makes things much safer, in poor societies it has the opposite effect. Whether in Africa or Asia, at levels far below $ 2500,- *per capita*, democracy appears to increase the risk of civil war.

However, half of all civil wars occurred in post conflict situations gone wrong. On the basis of statistical experience the risks of going back into conflict are lower in severely autocratic countries. Overall, the risk of countries going back into conflict is on average 40%, but if you rule out the range of severe autocracy, the risks are more like 70%. So, Collier concluded, we have to accept that we are actually building extremely fragile situations by insisting on democracy.

Collier then questioned the role of elections in post-conflict situations: they shift the risk of going back into civil war from the year before the election to the year after the election. Peace keeping operations tend to aggravate the situation as long as peace keepers tend to use this post-conflict election as the milestone to withdraw.

Collier concluded that if we are going to have democracy and we have to have elections, then we need our international peace keeping forces there for a long time. In fact, they have to be kept for a sufficiently long time for economic growth to settle in and bring post-conflict risks down. So, according to Collier, external peace keeping and economic development are complementary, which also justifies big aid packages in post-conflict situations over a longer period then is usually the case.

Collier further questioned whether democracy, if not conducive to conflict resolution in poor societies, at least may help to reform the economy. He stated that elections during incipient processes of reform actually chill the reform process: they slow it down. Elections tend to be overtaken by populist agendas especially in poor countries that lack a critical mass of well educated people.

Finally Collier turned to the case of resource rich countries as a result of new discoveries of natural resources and high prices. On the basis of experience again countries with big resource rents may be better off for the first five years but will be worse off in the longer term. Democracy will make matters worse as, contrary to mature democratic societies, the resource rich poor countries typically lack checks and balances. Still, Collier maintained that especially in Africa with its ethnically diverse societies, there is no alternative to democracy.

To conclude, according to Collier, democracy has been oversold, missold and undersold.

It has been oversold by using that image of the East European revolutions as a model for what would happen everywhere. It has been missold because of the image that we have pushed down the throats of developing countries elections instead on focussing first on the introduction of checks and balances in society. It has been undersold by not pointing out strongly enough that there is no alternative to democracy, especially in ethnically diverse Africa, while at the same time avoiding the twin deformities into which democracy in these low income countries often turn into: populism and patronage. Both can be very costly.

David Beetham in his lecture on structural and cultural preconditions for democracy took a more analytical approach to democracy. First of all he defined what he meant by an effective electoral democracy and formulated two basic preconditions for such an electoral democracy. The first is a functioning state, the second a minimum level of agreement on nationhood within a country's border. He took Iraq as an example of a country clearly lacking these two preconditions, explaining the failure of the project to impose electoral democracy on it.Beetham then turned to the question whether there is a further precondition for democracy, something called *a democratic culture*, which he doubts. He is sceptical of any attempt to categorise whole belief systems as either supportive of, or antithetical to democracy *tout court*.

Beetham argued on the other hand that low levels of popular trust in democratic institutions are a response to their performance, not the product of some pre-political cultural pattern. The problem lies not so much with the citizens and their supposedly endemic cultures, but with the characteristics and behaviour of their governing elites. Ideally the electoral sanctions would solve the problem: the prospect of the politician losing office if he did not serve the wider public interest and was only interested in his own well-being. In practise, there was more needed than that.

What is required in addition, according to Beetham, is that the electoral sanction is supplemented by a robust apparatus of "lateral accountability", comprising published codes of conduct, registers of financial interests, legal limits on election spending, and so on, together with independent institutions with powers of investigation and enforcement.

Where the institutional approach seeks to strengthen the mechanisms of public accountability, the economic approach aims to limit the opportunity for self-serving politicians by reducing the resources directly controlled by the state, and the amount of economic activity that is subject to political as opposed to market determination or decision.

The third, political, route to a government which serves the public interest involves a radical change in the political elite and implies a social-democratic mobilization from below.

After the politician, the economist and the political scientist, **Thomas Carothers** as a practitioner of democracy promotion, turned his attention to *the history of democracy promotion*, focussing on contemporary democracy promotion as a response to the third wave of democracy, starting in 1989.

Carothers saw the 1980's as an essential start-up period where democracy promotion was deeply and in some sense fatally entangled with Cold War politics. The 1990's, starting with the fall of the Berlin Wall, saw the beginning of a New Consensus: suddenly the expansion of democracy was a dominant theme in the world and democracy promotion was the response.

With the end of the Cold War, democracy promotion was no longer seen in that context. Instead, democracy promotion was attached to the development agenda. Partly this was a response to the growing recognition of governance problems as a key obstacle to development. The "good governance agenda", including accountability, transparency, participation and governmental responsiveness, had many pro-democratic features. Democracy promotion became fashionable with a growing number of organisations working in the field and with growing interest from the side of bilateral aid agencies and international organisations. Democracy promotion gained legitimacy and was universally adopted as a common strategy with however two severe limitations. Both the US and Europe were still maintaining warm, sometimes cosy relationships with non-democratic governments. Secondly, the external support, the outside work in those years were rarely very decisive.

By the end of the 1990's, a turnaround took place. During the '90's the global democratic trend had gradually slowed down and in many places stagnated. It had become more difficult for democracies to deliver the goods to their people and at the same time, rivals to democracy were growing. The success of Russia's and China's economic development over the last five or six years, in China's case even much longer, had greatly strengthened the idea of the strong hand model once again.

In addition, the massive flow of oil and gas revenues had been a tremendous benefit to many non-democratic governments and concerns over energy supplies weakened Western willingness to put pressure on any of these governments regarding their non-democratic practices.

After 9/11, according to Carothers, the War on Terrorism instantly led to the reattachment of democracy promotion to the geostrategic agenda and had a major impact on it. He believed the association of democracy promotion with the war in Iraq has been devastating to the legitimacy of the concept of democracy promotion. For many people in the world, democracy promotion has become a way of describing efforts to get rid of governments that the US does not like and a cover for ouster efforts. What people perceive is that the war on terrorism involves closer relationships between Western governments and non-democratic governments for the sake of security cooperation. American legal abuses abroad have badly hurt the statue of the US as a model of democracy or as a legitimate democracy promoter.

As a consequence, Carothers concluded, we are no longer in a world in which there is a growing international consensus on political values. It has become harder to establish trust with partners and with governments on the ideas and ideals of democracy promotion.

There are some lessons for the US from this experience, e.g. dissociate democracy promotion from the use of unauthorised military force against another country, but also for Europe. Now is the time for Europe to come forward and show the world what really are the distinctive principles of a European approach. Until now, according to Carothers, the response of the European Commission to the challenges of democracy promotion in the last ten years has at times been surprisingly weak.

After the practitioner of democracy promotion, **Kumi Naidoo** of the World Alliance for Citizen Participation added his voice on the subject of democracy and development, focussing on *civil society, governance and globalisation*. As suggested in the title of his lecture, he took the debate on globalisation as a starting point and defined the role of civil society in that context as organisations representing people engaged in discussions around social, political and economic justice, and explore alternative visions for a more ethical form of globalisation that works for the benefit of average people rather than simply for the benefit of powerful interests.

As a consequence of globalisation, CSO's have shifted their attention from the local to the global level. Experience has shown that acting locally will not get to the root causes of many social and economic problems.

Naidoo addressed the question whether civil society groups represented the views of anyone but themselves. It is said that, if they are accountable at all, it is usually "upward" to their funders rather than "downward" to those they purportedly serve. He agreed that legitimacy cannot be taken for granted. Self-regulation mechanisms such as codes of ethics and standards of excellence have been adopted at the national level and a culture of transparency in governance structures is also gaining strength. Civil society groups work to derive mandates and legitimacy for their activities through extensive consultation processes.

Naidoo was of the opinion that the system of representative democracy is to a certain extend outdated in an era of globalisation and with the emergence of a "devastating democratic deficit" in several local and national contexts. In his view people are looking for and finding new and more direct ways to get involved in public life and decision making, marking a shift from representative democracy to what is often called participatory democracy.

These new models take many forms like public-private partnerships and the establishment of transparency and oversight mechanisms. In other words, we need to recognise that effective democracy needs a vibrant civil society as well as an effective and accountable government.

Turning to the global level, it is here that the democratic deficit is most clearly visible. Democratising individual global governance institutions such as the United Nations, the World Bank, IMF and WTO, is a challenge that requires serious and urgent attention.

He finally cites a former Dutch Minister for Development Coöperation, Mrs Eveline Herfkens, who according to Naidoo correctly contends that four key deficits must be addressed if globalisation is ever to work for the world's poor: deficits of regulation of the global economy, deficits of economy, deficits of coherence among the global institutions and deficits of financing. In other words, if development is to serve the interests of the poor, democracy should be part of the picture.

Taking one step back from Naidoo's view that effective democracy needs a vibrant civil society, **Michael Edwards** of the Ford Foundation took in his lecture on *Civil Society, Revolutionary Idea or Political Slogan*, a closer look at the empirical evidence on the civil society-democracy links which he considered as both complex and context-specific. Civil society is, according to Edwards, seen by many people in many different ways, but he states that recognising that civil society does indeed mean different things to different people is one of the keys to move forward.

Edwards identified three different schools of thought on what constitutes civil society. The first sees civil society as "the world of voluntary organisations". The second school sees civil society as a kind of society that was identified with certain ideals requiring action by many different institutions, not just civil society organisations. The third, more recent school of thought sees civil society as the "public sphere", the social consensus that is the backbone of any functioning democracy.

These three concepts or schools of thought are related but different in different ways: not all voluntary associations respond equally to certain ideals that are associated with the "good society" and, between different associations there is often too much difference of opinion to secure the level of political consensus that is required to secure and enforce broad-based social reforms.

Edwards attaches particular importance to the concept of civil society as the "good society" because it sets the contribution of voluntary associations in a wider context and guards against the tendency to privilege one part of society over the others on ideological grounds. Historically, Edwards claims, success in achieving good society goals has always been based on social contracts negotiated between government, business and citizens. At the same time, the third school of thought is particularly important for answering the question how societies decide the direction in which they want to go and whether it is the right one as conditions and circumstances continue to change over time.

So the three schools of civil society thinking need to be connected. Civil society as the good society keeps our "eyes on the prize". Civil society as the world of associational life is important to fulfil the need for coordinated action across different sets of institutions while structural definitions are useful in emphasising the gaps and weaknesses of associational life that need to be fixed if they are to be effective vehicles for change.

Civil society as public sphere finally is required to secure a political consensus about the best way forward. In other words, civil society is simultaneously a goal to aim for, a means to achieve it, and a framework for engaging with each-other about ends and means.

Nico Schrijver, as an expert on the multilateral system of governance, pointed at the democratic deficit that was also earlier raised by Kumi Naidoo. In his lecture on *International Organisations, Democracy and Good Governance, do they practise what they preach?* Schrijver emphasised that the democratic deficit of international organisations undermined their credibility in their efforts to promote good governance and respect for human rights.

The application of the one-country, one-vote system in the United Nations General Assembly after the Second World War brought some fundamental changes in international politics. Third World countries were for the first time in a position to outvote Western countries and introduce new concepts and reorient the United Nations Organisation from a primarily peace and security organisation to one which also actively pursued respect for human rights, decolonisation, development and environmental conservation.

In the field of the management of international peace and security an 11 member Security Council was established with 5 permanent members and 6 non-permanent members. In 1965 the membership was extended from 11 to 15 to reflect the expanded world and in an effort to increase the representativety of the Council and the democratic legitimacy of its decision making. However, the permanent members effectively possessed veto power in the Council. This still allowed the Council to take decisions on peace keeping operations and other political sensitive issues as permanent members who might have objected on such occasions abstained from voting. Discussions are still ongoing on ways to increase the democratic character of the Security Council.

In the international economic institutions, i.c. the IMF and the World Bank, decision making is still highly undemocratic as the number of votes are determined by the subscription to the capital of each country, which in turn depends to a large extent on the economic and financial power of a country.

At first glance decision making within the newly established WTO is much more democratic. Formally, the principle of one State, one vote applies. Most important decision however are taken in so-called Green Room consultations in which only a self-selected group of countries can participate.

Schrijver illustrated the democratic deficit also in other international organisations, including the ILO, and pointed at the active role of NGOs having acquired observer status with the United Nations Organisation. Civil society, international business and other interest groups organise themselves increasingly at an international level.

NGOs were some years ago effectively able to successfully lobby against the introduction of a Multilateral Investment Agreement in the context of the OECD which they considered as being focussed on property protection rather than on effects of foreign investment on development, employment, environment and human rights.

Schrijver concluded that a considerable tension if not contradiction can be noted between what Western states advocate and often demand from developing countries, and their reluctance to re-shape international consultation in accordance with similar principles of democracy and good governance in international organisations.

Kim Campbell, former Prime Minister of Canada, combined her background as a Soviet specialist with that of an academician with teaching experience in gender and power and *democratic transitions and consolidation*. But first of all, as a former Prime Minister she claimed to be a practitioner of democracy: "Those who have held public office, even when you leave, you still have a sense of responsibility for the world".

As a co-founder of the Club de Madrid, she has been actively engaged in bringing together the experience of politicians who have led democratic transitions in their own countries and using the Club de Madrid's resources, knowledge, experience and convening capacity to promote democratic transition and consolidation around the world.

Like Tom Carothers, that other practitioner of democracy promotion, Campbell in her lecture on *Alternatives for Liberal Democracy*, realised that the optimism felt by supporters of democracy at the turn of the 21st Century, had been dimmed by certain realities: a recentralisation of power was taking place in Latin America ("caudillismo") and Russia.

Most devastating however was the unravelling of the efforts to create democracies in Afghanistan and Iraq. Like she said: "So discouraging has been the result of "regime change" in these two countries that I am finding an increasing number of people who are disillusioned with, or even outright hostile to, the whole idea of democracy promotion". She went on to ask the question whether it was naïve to think that democracy can take root in non-Western, economically underdeveloped countries.

Against those who claim that democracy is a Western value, she maintained that democracy can be expressed in a myriad of institutional designs and policy outcomes that could fit any culture. Nevertheless, according to Campbell, there are four non-negotiable features of democracy: rule of law, independent civil society, free and fair elections and accountability.

Turning on the question of what consists of liberal democracy or who is a liberal democrat, more and more people tend to associate liberal democracy with "small government, free trade and a market economy". That is because with the fall of communism many began to equate market economies with democracy, and the fall of the Berlin Wall was seen as the final proof of the superiority of capitalism as an economic model.

So the "Washington Consensus" became the model of capitalism that was to be recommended and supported for the newly emerging post-communist societies, notwithstanding that they lacked any of the preconditions that had enabled the older industrial democracies to reduce the size of their state owned sectors.

As a former Soviet specialist Campbell was horrified to watch the privatisation of the Soviet economy to a public where there was negligible business acumen and no legal framework to provide regulation and protection. Unfortunately, she said, neither the "black market" entrepreneurs of the Soviet era nor members of the Communist party or the KGB were imbued with the understanding of how to create legal systems that constrain the excesses of the market.

Campbell maintained that economic liberalism in a democracy is a function of philosophy, choice and interest. Economic liberalism is not a pre-condition for democracy. For example, in France people discuss the role of public regulation in determining maximum working hours. The argument is at the heart of the kinds of policy competitions that characterise politics in a democracy.

Campbell questioned the role freedom of religion plays in a democracy. In early days as our countries were growing there was discrimination based on religion. In a country like Canada people are nowadays not even aware of the religion of the Prime Minister.

The question of religion in politics is coming up again as we have a growing presence of Islam that is complicated by the implications of "political Islam"or "Islamism". Democrats from the Islamic world however maintain that there is no conflict between the values of Islam and the values of democracy.

Campbell said she is worried by the growth of ethnic identity as a basis for political identity in mature democracies. She considered it to be a move in the direction of illiberal democracy, because it suggested that ethnicity or national identity is more fundamental than the way you think.

As a representative of an institution that engaged in democracy promotion, Campbell had to admit that "democracy cannot be imported or exported, but should be supported". People who are familiar with the functioning of democracy can share their experience but that does not mean that you can create the institutions or the love of those institutions externally.

She questioned whether the Eastern European transitions will last. Much depends on what was there before. Totalitarianism is the worst basis on which to found a democracy.

In a training session with representatives of one of Putin's political parties they used the expression "sovereign democracy", meaning they wanted to have democracy their own way. Campbell insisted that a few things are non-negotiable: the rule of law, open civil society, accountability and free elections.

She concluded by saying that liberal democracy is alive and well. There are different degrees of economic liberalism that are compatible with democracy and we need to understand the importance of building on local values and traditions but the key democratic values are non-negotiable.

Daniel Kaufmann, renowned for his work on corruption and governance with the World Bank, referred to the governance crisis, still ongoing in June 2007, in the Bank itself by saying that "first and foremost one has to start with a good example at home". The starting point for his lecture on *Governance, Corruption, Democracy and Development in Latin America: Empirics in International Comparative Perspective* was that governance, including anti-corruption policies, democratic processes, and so on, are fundamental to growth and development. He was of the opinion that the Washington Consensus neglected or underestimated the importance of governance issues from the start. As a consequence, in Latin America economic policies focused too much on the short term at the expense of medium to long term issues, resulting in an uneven growth performance or what he termed as "elevator economics". Kaufmann distinguished three clusters of governance:

1   the political dimension, referring to the process in which governments are selected, monitored and replaced;
2   the economic dimension which refers to the capacity of governments to implement policies and provide public services to its citizens; and

3   the institutional dimension referring to the way the state through its institutions manages social and economic interaction.

In order to measure governance, Kaufmann introduced two measurable indices for each of the three dimensions: *voice and accountability* and *political stability* in the political area, *effectiveness of the government* and *the quality of the regulatory framework* in the economic area, and, thirdly, *the rule of law* and *control of corruption* in the institutional field.

In this way according to Kaufmann, corruption is put in the broader context of governance which is important because, in order to fight corruption, one has to look at the whole system of governance: "At the end of the day, corruption is a symptom of poor institutional quality and governance".

Kaufmann rated countries according to each of the six indicators. Notwithstanding margins of error, they are not so large as not to be able to make sensible comparisons. To this end he introduced 4 or 5 meaningful categories. Looking at the results, they begin to challenge some conventional or popular notions. E.g. not all industrialised countries are in the good governancy category and also there is a enormous variation within each continent. So do the data challenge pessimism? There is a group of countries in Africa that show a significant improvement in governance even in the short term. Some countries have significantly improved on voice and democratic accountability. On the other hand, for every country that has improved there has been one that has deteriorated. So, on average, there has been no significant improvement on governance around the world over the past 15 years. Also judiciary independence is stagnating for different regions leaving an enormous challenge. In Latin America there had even been a slight deterioration over the past 10 years.

Looking at the growth performance of Latin America some countries had grown quite fast over the last couple of years, but the performance had been very unstable and by comparison with other continents (not only Asia but also Southern Africa) had not been very impressive. Moreover there was no evidence which suggested that there had been any improvement in equality. As a consequence, the region remained extremely unequal in terms of income distribution.

In the institutional area Latin America scores badly on average, also in comparison to the new countries in Eastern Europe and even with the East Asian tigers. Looking at more disaggregated data, the picture emerges of wide spread political corruption and capture of state institutions by the elite.

In countries where state institutions are captured by the elite, the dynamic small to medium size enterprises in the private sector tend to grow only at half the rate as in more competitive environments. Kaufmann emphasised the importance of freedom of press for mitigating state capture and the control of corruption. Looking at micro level he found a very clear link between the extend of corruption and the performance of institutions in terms of provision of social services.

On corruption, Kaufmann pointed out, "it takes two to tango". If a multinational company is operating in a rich OECD country, the extent to which they pay bribes is quite low, but if they go outside the OECD area, they begin to adapt very quickly to the environment in the receiving country, despite the fact that it is totally illegal according to the OECD convention on international bribery which was adopted already more than five years ago. The tigers in East Asia, in terms of corporate bribery, come out far better than countries of Southern Europe.

After all, Kaufmann sees there is a two way street between improving civil liberties and political competition on the one hand and improving corruption control on the other and both contributing to economic development. Similarly economic growth has some impact on furthering democratic consolidation. Economic growth tends to be more robust if there is less inequality and where there is less corruption there is increased satisfaction with the role of market forces. In Latin America the popularity of democratic systems does not depend so much any more on favourable economic development. However, persistent corruption impacts negatively on the citizens satisfaction with democracy. Kaufmann finally points at the importance of financial reform as political finance is a major source of misgovernance and financial reform is crucial for macro-economic stability.

Kaufmann ended with citing two examples of the importance of transparency and of collaboration between the industrialised world and the emerging economies:

- in Uganda people were beginning to hold their local authorities accountable for the mismanagement of the education system after they found out that only 15 % of the budgeted funds were actually spent on education;
- countries in Eastern Europe and the former Soviet Union being given a perspective on membership of the EU were making tremendous efforts to open up and improve their governance in economic and political terms.

The final speaker in the lecture series, **Anwar Ibrahim**, former Prime Minister of Malaysia, addressed the issue of the (in)compatibility of *Democracy and Islam*. He wondered why Islam was singled out in this context and not Christianity, Hinduism, Buddhism or Confucianism.

He started with saying that the fundamental principle of freedom of conscience, of expression, sanctity of life, property and honour and dignity of men and women, was sacrosanct in Islam and could not be compromised. The question is therefore: why is it not universally applied?

Anwar Ibrahim then presented some historical evidence, illustrating that nothing prevents Muslim societies to accept the principle of democratic rule. Already in 1955 Indonesia, the largest Muslim society in the world, organised its first free and fair elections. Later, democracy was hijacked, not by the Islamists but by the secularist, nationalist President Sukarno. As a consequence Indonesia for the next thirty years had to grapple with authoritarian dictatorship until the end of the Suharto era.

More recently Indonesia has seen a peaceful transition into a vibrant democracy: the media are free, the leaders are openly criticised, issues of corruption have surfaced, judicial decisions have been questioned and elections have been conducted in a very free and fair manner.

Anwar Ibrahim then pointed at another large country, with the second largest Muslim population in the world: India. According to a recent report on the position of Muslims in India, the Muslim community appeared to be the least developed, the poorest and most marginalized, worse then the untouchables and the lowest caste. Manmohan Singh, the President of India, responded by announcing the protection of minority rights, including the rights of the Muslim people.

Anwar Ibrahim concluded that, according to the Confucian principle of reciprocity, it would be the duty of all Muslim rulers, all over the world, to ensure that the rights of the minority non-Muslims will be protected in their societies.

The third example cited by Anwar Ibrahim was Turkey, predominantly Muslim and economically quite successful. Turkey has to choose not so much between Islamists and secularists but between being free and democratic or subject to military rule. Anwar Ibrahim expressed the hope that "friends here, including Europe, would make their position clear that they are in favour of freedom and democracy".

As Indonesia, India and Turkey are non-Arab countries, what about Arab countries? Anwar Ibrahim took Iran as an example. Already in 1951, Mohamed Mossadeq was elected prime minister a democratic way. He was later toppled "by the CIA and the British". Fortunately the Dutch did not belong to the "coalition of the willing" of that time! So it is not surprising that any Iranian, when you speak to them and say you want them to be democratic, they would answer: "You want to preach on behalf of the Americans?"

In the end, all leaders, in Indonesia, India, Turkey or Iran, were promising freedom and democracy and used the free press to disseminate their message. So there is no question that these countries would at present "not be ready for democracy". Also, the question of incompatibility of democracy and Islam is not a question for debate in Muslim societies: nobody there says they are incompatible. It is just the dictators, the ruling autocracies, that do not want democracy.

On the other hand one should realise that autocratic rulers everywhere, including the Middle East and Asia, are encouraged by measures to suspend civil liberties in the US to curb civil liberties in their own societies as well. Likewise, the Iraq war, because of its faulty and fraudulent plan and implementation, had led to chaos in Iraq and a complete disillusionment and distrust of Muslims against the US.

Anwar Ibrahim finally questioned whether Islam and Democracy would be incompatible because, according to Islamic scholars, the ultimate authority lies in Allah. In the view of these scholars human beings would continue to err and transgress against God in everything including the promotion of gender equality. According to Anwar Ibrahim, these views have not convinced Muslims on the whole to reject democracy. But if Muslims accept democracy, would they stick to its principles and accept the outcome under all circumstances?

There are telling examples of politicians in the West having difficulty to accept the outcomes of democratic elections in Muslim countries as was the case in Algeria with the FIS and in Palestine with Hamas. Not accepting outcomes of democratic elections is a recipe for disaster.

Anwar Ibrahim pleaded for a culture of tolerance, of giving some room for maneuver, some right to navigate, without compromising on matters of principle. Once countries accept and adopt constitutional guarantees Western countries must be prepared to work with them, even of they do not fully conform to this theoretical, philosophical construct accepted by the West. In other words, "The Europeans and the Americans can not and must not dictate the language of discourse in other societies".

Taking himself as an example, Anwar approved of the admonishment by economist and Nobel laureate Amartya Sen not to compartmentalise people. As Muslim, Malaysian and Asian, Anwar Ibrahim says he still he likes to read and appreciate Shakespeare and Ahmatova, he associates himself with the Bill of Rights and the Jeffersonian ideals and considers himself an admirer of Tocqueville's book on "Democracy in America".

If you encourage people through education and development, half the problems of the world would be solved and "democracy and Islam" would no longer be an issue!

In response to Anwar Ibrahim's lecture, *Vincent Cornell* of Emory University in Atlanta, Georgia, gave an elaborate and comprehensive view on how democracy and rights could be reconsidered in Islamic societies: *Between Theology and Law: Reconsidering the Islamic View of Democracy and Rights.* He draws three lessons.

First, when assessing the Islamic approach to important political subjects such as democracy or rights, one does not have to fall back on essentialist arguments about the "culture" of Islam, or the "culture" of the West. In both societies, rights are logically derived and not culture-based.

Second, the rejection of democracy by Osama Bin Laden as representative of Al Quaeda and by other Islamic scholars rests on two fallacies that can be disproved theologically.

Third, Muslims need to devote much more time than they have done so far to the study of moral philosophy and ethics in Western countries.

To help them solve the problems of the present, Muslims should feel themselves free to find new resources outside the Islamic traditions of the past or to create such resources themselves.

On Thursday 13 September 2007 the SID lecture series on "Democracy and Development" concluded with a closing conference in The Hague, hosted by the Dutch Ministry of Foreign Affairs. First keynote speaker was the Minister for Development Cooperation, **Bert Koenders**. In his speech, *Democracy meets Development*, the minister reflected upon the lectures in the SID series and stated that the theme of the day is "at the core of my policy". Democracy, he said, is a vital element of the process of political change and emancipation in developing countries. There is overall progress in developing countries towards more democracy, but unfortunately also the violence in the world has "democratized". There is always this ambiguity, Koenders said: "Democracy can exacerbate conflict, but it can also bring about enormous progress." We must be aware that imposing western models of democracy can be "extremely counterproductive". "We must discard illusions about creating democracy by force, as we have seen in the cruel reality of Iraq."

Koenders described the diverse and long roads that Europe walked to reach a state of democracy. And still we have to be cautious, because democracy is not something we can take for granted, as the continuous attacks of populism in the Netherlands show.

Democracy is more than establishing a political system, the minister went on. "It is part of a larger project for the rule of law and broad participation."

Reacting on the book "A white man's burden" by William Easterly, Koenders underlined the call for "searchers" and said that "the economic and political complexity of societies is a given. You can't plan a market; you can't plan a democracy".... "The dynamism of the poor at the bottom has much more potential than the plans of those at the top". However, this dynamism must be translated into plans at the top to provide service delivery, to foster pro-poor growth, to improve the educational system, to plan for energy systems and infrastructure to reach the poor.

After reflecting on the unclear relationship between democracy and economic growth, Koenders stated that conflicts in many developing countries in the last decade are not caused by democratisation itself, but by "the failure to deepen democracy". Democratisation therefore should not be halted until a more stable society has been reached, but, on the contrary, more emphasis is needed on "power-sharing mechanisms and strong civil society organisations and state institutions".

Koenders took a verbal trip around the world, commenting on the state of democracy in several regions. In the Arab world "the supposedly non-Islamic character of democracy has been used too often by autocratic rulers in Arab countries to ward off democracy, and by the west as an excuse for maintaining a double standard", Koenders said, and "the diversity of Islamic activism offers scope for cooperation with Islamic organisations as democratic actors".

For Africa the main question in this respect is whether "democracy is an alternative to patronage". Formal democracy is on the rise in Africa since the Cold War is over – more chosen political leaders and less violent coups. But political institutions do not yet function optimally, and, although important, they are not enough. Thus, said Koenders, he will focus on improving the quality of democracy in Africa, through encouraging peer pressure, civic education, and a stronger role for the media and other "watchdogs" to ensure greater accountability.

In Latin America the ongoing democratisation is challenged by the rising inequality and by institutionalised crime, which have to be addressed in order for democracy to survive. Because citizens don't see change in their fate, they turn to new nationalist movements. "The role of political parties cannot be emphasis enough", Koenders continued. Confidence in political parties worldwide is lower than ever, and therefore the ministry keeps on supporting the Netherlands Institute for Multiparty Democracy (NIMD), in order to strengthen political parties in, for example, Guatemala.

In the remainder of his speech the minister outlined four central policy points with regard to democratisation. The first one was "a more political conception of good governance and deepening democracy". The second policy issue is "a democracy and development agenda". Development cooperation should not weaken the national democratic institutions and local politicians should be accountable to their own peoples in the first place, not to donors.

The third policy item has to do with fragile states, the main focus in the overall strategy of this minister. In post-conflict countries the issue of "legitimacy" is essential, Koenders said. "We have to avoid creating parallel responsibilities and parallel mechanisms of accountability" by taking over the provision of essential services to the victims of the conflict.

Koenders fourth and last point concerns "women's rights". In a functioning democracy all citizens have equal rights. Women often fall behind. Empowering them does also foster economic growth, deepen (local) democracy, and make health care systems function better.

The ministers last remarks were dedicated to the international context. The international political climate 'is far from perfectly democratic. There are unequal relations of power at intergovernmental as well as local level.... Geopolitical interests count for more in the world than development.... Therefore efforts to deepen democracy at national level must be accompanied by efforts to democratise international organisations, strengthen the international legal order and ensure more coherence between the words and the actions of non-state actors, countries and organisations.'

Second keynote speaker of the day was **William Easterly** who started by stating that there is a new consensus among development economists: "that we don't know how to achieve development". During the past decades so many theories, blueprints, trends and success countries have been put forward, and later have proven not to be effective at all. The answer, according to Easterly, lies in the topic of the day: *Freedom and Democracy*. "Let individuals be free to figure it out for themselves." He cites Friedrich Hayek, who has stated that only the free interaction of individuals produces innovation. And "development is always innovation", says Easterly. "It is freedom and democracy that makes possible this process of inventing new answers."

This process can, by definition, not be planned. Which is what succeeding bureaucracies, both multilateral and bilateral, have been doing for years. IMF and World Bank, through the Structural Adjustment Programs, but also the Millennium Development Goals, have failed or will fail in Easterly's opinion for this reason.

He distinguishes several forms of freedom: freedom to trade, invest and innovate; freedom of speech, press, assembly and religion; and freedom of foreign control, including imperialism, invasion, colonialism and structural adjustment. And, not to forget, freedom from foreign aid, which is another way of imposing external conditions and wishes on a process that can only be endogenous. All of these freedoms, Easterly underlines, are "one and indivisible".

Development economist Easterly then criticized some econometric models – like those used in Paul Colliers new book The Bottom Billion – because development, growth, democracy or civil war can never be measured as they entail complex social processes and it is not possible to determine what causes what. But there are some relationships that can be measured, he goes on, namely the correlations between democracy and per capita income. He shows some figures and says that extensive research has showed that democracy has a strong and positive impact on per capita income. "The same goes for economic freedom", he goes on. "What I am trying to argue is that free markets and democracy go together." Using another figure, Easterly says that democracy is also highly correlated with the quality of government service delivery.

So it is democracy and freedom that we have to strive for. But we can never impose democracy. Nor will another form of foreign control be of any help: foreign aid. The most successful countries, according to Easterly, are those that 'followed their own unique paths of development like China, India, Vietnam, Turkey, Chile, Singapore, Taiwan, South Korea, Mauritius, Botswana.... Societies that move towards more individual freedom have shown rapid economic growth.... The opposite of this is when the donors are in charge and are telling you what to do.'

In his concluding remarks Easterly once more emphasized the need for freedom: 'When the experts are in doubt and they can't agree, then just let the ordinary people, the free market entrepreneurs, the democratic activists, the intellectual dissenters, the political activists, let them figure it out for themselves.'

Third keynote speaker of the day was **Vidar Helgesen** with his lecture on *Democracy Building Globally: How can Europe Contribute?* He started by analysing the global situation of democracy building, which is "less rosy than only a few years back", because of: "the so-called Freedom Agenda in U.S. foreign policy ... with Iraq epitomizing the problems"; the western response to the election victory of Hamas which has "led to a serious legitimacy challenge when demands are put forward for democratic elections elsewhere"; and a broader polarisation between North and South in both the UN and the WTO, strengthened by the rise of regional powers, "often rich in energy resources but poor on democratic practice".

On the positive side, Helgesen mentioned the adoption by the African Union of a Charter on Democracy, Elections and Governance, and the discussion on a similar discussion in ASEAN.

Democracy building is more than stimulating elections. It is also the building of the national democratic capacity and political party assistance. The development community should engage much more in democratisation issues, because these are crucial to make development cooperation work.

Like Koenders did earlier, Helgesen elaborated on the inconclusive academic literature about the linkages between democracy and development. This relationship is complex, partly because of the evolving concepts of both democracy and development during the past decades. However, Helgesen concluded, "there is evolution towards a more common ground for democracy and development". Firstly, both are considered as desirable, as "values to be pursued in themselves". Secondly, development is more than economic growth. And thirdly, democracy is more than the formal institutions; democracy "is also expected to deliver in terms of a better quality of life".

It is widely accepted, Helgesen said, that democracy and good governance are key ingredients of development. The flip side of this, however, is that western concepts and mechanisms, like the PRSPs but also monitoring procedures by aid donors, dominate the discussions. This limits the internal democratic debate, favours executives and civil society organisations, and undermines parliaments and political parties.

There is an urgent need for global leadership in the field of democracy building and development, with Europe as the most obvious but still invisible candidate. According to Helgesen, the EU should take the lead and be much more ambitious. "The European Instrument for Democracy and Human Rights is well and good, but is detached from the much bigger and broader development cooperation programmes". Europe should also build on its being an example for other regions of economic and political integration, Helgesen concluded his speech. 'Because there is no longer an American leadership in democracy building, today is the time for Europe.'

Last speaker of the day was **Lena Hjelm-Wallén**, former Swedish foreign minister, deputy prime minister and defense minister for the social democrat party. Her closing remarks, *Looking Forward*, were critical and somewhat pessimistic. She started by saying that to discuss the link between democracy and development seemed a bit useless, because that link is so obvious. "Since long ago we know that development – in order to be sustainable – needs dedicated people who take the responsibility for projects". For this collective structures are needed, starting from the village level, that maintain the achievements. This body – a council, a shura, a working group or whatever – should be democratic.

The local level of democracy is often forgotten and underestimated, Hjelm-Wallén stated.

'So for development to stay sustainable: participation, ownership, responsibility at all levels, from the village to the state, are needed and necessary qualities, all attributed to democracy. And for sustainability to be long-term, both development and democracy must be homegrown.'

After elaborating a bit on the case of China, the former minister turned to the question about the capacity of a democratic regime to enable their citizens to have a better life. There is ample evidence of a failure to deliver. "For example, in Latin America, also democratic countries show large income distribution disparities." Respect for human rights, especially for women, is still lacking in many cases. 'Unfortunately, I have to add that when governments in the West – the US as well as in the EU – decide not to accept the outcome of democratic elections, strong obstacles are also created to the struggle for democracy worldwide.'

Hjelm-Wallén also underlined the importance of political parties and the limitation of the political space by outside actors such as international donors which impose their conditions. The latter may lead to lesser credibility for national political actors, less national debate about development issues, and less motivation for political parties to pick up economic and social programs.

Just like Vidar Helgesen, Lena Hjelm-Wallén stated that "the EU should and could do much more.... The EU can and must use its 'soft power', not only in its development cooperation, but also use its role as an important political actor on the international stage".

Conclusion

Bernard Berendsen

W hat can we learn from these lectures on democracy and development, what conclusions can be drawn after all?

I

On the question of *what comes first*, several speakers have been quite clear. Politicians like Agnes van Ardenne and Kim Campbell and policy advisors and development practitioners like Daniel Kaufmann believe that there is a causal relationship between democracy and development. So does Easterly who states that it is freedom and democracy that makes possible this process of inventing new answers that is a requisite for development.

Vidar Helgesen admits that academic literature about the linkages between democracy and development is both abundant and inconclusive. This might be because both development and democracy have many definitions and are understood in many different ways. Lena Hjelm-Wallén underscores the importance of collective responsibility which is essential for development and is also part and parcel of a democratic culture at all levels.

Others like Paul Collier are more doubtful and point at examples of non-democratic countries like China and more recently Russia who have been economically quite successful.

Many speakers have pointed out that democracy, in particular electoral democracy, is not enough. Beetham mentions three requirements in addition to electoral democracy to be fulfilled: measures to enhance accountability, a reduction of the resources under state control (i.e. smaller government) and a radical change in the political elite implying a social democratic mobilisation from below.

II

On the question of *democracy versus stability* Paul Collier again drew important lessons from statistical evidence. He pointed out that the propensity to conflict, and therefore the incidence of instability is much more likely in low-income countries then in mature and rich countries and that, on the other hand, the risk of going back into conflict is lower in autocratic countries. He concludes that we are actually building extremely fragile situations by insisting on democracy in poor countries. The situation is even worse in resource rich poor countries who typically lack checks and balances.

Berendsen and van Beuningen agree that what can be observed in reality is that political entrepreneurs compete for electoral support, *not* in order to obtain access to state power and to serve development and the common good, but aiming to obtain access to the *loot* constituted by public resources, in order to administer them as their own patrimony and distribute them among themselves and their clienteles (state capture, patronage and clientelism, corruption).

Paul Collier still insists there is no alternative to democracy, especially in ethnically divers Africa. However one should avoid the twin deformities which democracy in these low income countries often turn into: populism and patronage. Both can be very costly.

Bert Koenders therefore underscores the importance of political stability as a prerequisite for development and makes fragile states the main focus of his policy in support of post-conflict countries while trying to avoid creating parallel responsibilities and parallel mechanisms of accountability.

III

On the question of the *legitimacy of democracy promotion* and whether external promotion of democracy is at all possible many speakers pointed at the disastrous consequences of the US initiated war on terror and the subsequent war in Iraq. Thomas Carothers concluded that the association of democracy promotion with the war in Iraq had been devastating to the legitimacy of democracy promotion and that it had become harder to establish trust with partners and with governments on the ideas and ideals of democracy promotion.

Similarly, Kim Campbell characterised the efforts to create democracies in Afghanistan and Iraq as "most devastating". She said: "So discouraging has been the result of "regime change" in these two countries that an increasing number of people are becoming disillusioned with or even outright hostile to the whole idea of democracy promotion". Vidar Helgesen agrees that the global situation of democracy building is less rosy then only a few years back, because of the so-called Freedom Agenda in US Foreign policy, with Iraq epitomizing the problem.

According to Carothers there are important lessons here for the US but also for Europe: dissociate democracy promotion from the use of unauthorised force against another country, but also for Europe that now is the time to come forward and show the world what really are the distinctive principles of a European approach. His plea for an alternative, European approach to democracy promotion was echoed by van Ardenne, Berendsen and van Beuningen, Vidar Helgesen and Lena Hjelm Wallén.

IV

The question of *culture and democracy* was addressed by David Beetham. His conclusion was, and this was shared by all speakers, that institutional arrangements that typically belong to electoral democracy are not sufficient. As mentioned before, additional requirements are, in short: measures to enhance accountability, small government and a radical cultural change in the political elite. But if culture is that important, what is the role of religion in this?

Beetham is sceptical of any attempt to categorise whole belief systems as either supportive of, or antithetical to democracy.

Anwar Ibrahim dealt with the question in a straightforward way: there is no conflict between the values of Islam and the values of democracy. The fundamental principle of freedom of conscience, of expression, sanctity of life, property and honour and dignity of men and women are sacrosanct in Islam. He illustrated this with historical examples of large, predominantly Muslim countries or countries with large Muslim populations, like Indonesia, India and Turkey whose people had no difficulty in accepting democratic rule in the past.

On the other hand he agreed that Muslim scholars had often voiced opinions that contradict this view. This will however not prevent Muslim people to participate in elections if they get a chance. The question of incompatibility of democracy and Islam is not a question for debate in Muslim societies. "It is just the dictators that don't want it".

He concludes that it is education and development that will help people to stop to compartmentalise each other and put an end to the debate on the so-called incompatibility of Islam and democracy.

Vincent Cornell supported this view, arguing that in both Muslim and non-Muslim societies individual rights are logically derived and not culture based and that Muslims should feel free to look for solutions to present day problems outside the Islamic traditions of the past.

V

Several speakers addressed the issue of *the role of the state, international and non-governmental organisations*. In their background paper to the series Berendsen and van Beuningen argue that recently the state has been losing its quality as the focal point of public decision making and that the principles of human rights, democracy and the rule of law that are defined in relation to national and sovereign states are in danger of losing their traditional centre.

This view was shared by Kumi Naidoo who said that the system of representative democracy was to a certain extent outdated in an era of globalisation and with the emergence of a "devastating democratic deficit" at local, national and international level. People are now looking for and finding new and more direct ways to get involved in public life and decision making, marking a shift from representative democracy to what is often called participatory democracy. Here he saw the need for a vibrant civil society to contribute to an effective and accountable government.

The democratic deficit at international level was most clearly demonstrated by Nico Schrijver who looked at the multilateral system of governance. He emphasised that the democratic deficit of international organisations undermined their credibility in their efforts to promote good governance at national level. He concluded that there is a considerable tension if not contradiction between what Western states advocate and demand from developing countries and their reluctance to reshape international consultation in accordance with similar principles of democracy and good governance in international organisations.

What we consider as "civil society" was scrutinised by Michael Edwards who linked up three schools of thought: civil society organisations as the world of voluntary organisations, civil society as exemplary of the "good society" and civil society as the "public sphere". This third meaning puts CSO's in the public and political domain as it requires them to secure a political consensus on what they consider as the best way forward. This also means that in their governance they will need to be open and transparent. Naidoo agrees: "Legitimacy (of CSO's) cannot be taken for granted". Only if they are open and transparent, will they be legitimised to take part in and effectively contribute to the public debate on the "good society" as the ultimate aim of (good) governance.

Contributors in order of appearance

Agnes van Ardenne-van der Hoeven was a member of the Vlaardingen municipal council, from 1988 to 1994, where she represented the Christian Democratic Alliance (CDA). From 1990 she also served on the municipal executive, as the alderman for economic affairs. She was a member of both the CDA's Foreign Affairs Committee (1986-1996) and the Advisory Council on Peace and Security (1990-1994). From 1994 to 2002, Agnes van Ardenne was a member of the House of Representatives of the States General and of the North Atlantic Assembly and the Council of Europe Parliamentary Assembly. She has also been vice-chair of the development organisation CEBEMO (now part of CORDAID), co-founder of a centre for development cooperation in Vlaardingen, chair of the EPP/EUCD Women's Section and secretary of the Dutch branch of UNICEF. On 22 July 2002, Agnes van Ardenne became Minister for Development Cooperation in the first Balkenende government. She was appointed to the same post in the second Balkenende government on 27 May 2003 and in the third Balkenende government on 7 July 2006. Agnes van Ardenne is currently the Permanent Representative of the Netherlands to FAO, WFP and IFAD.

Daniel Kaufmann is the Senior Manager for Governance, Finance and Regulatory Reform at the World Bank Institute. He is also a researcher and expert advisor in the fields of governance, anti-corruption and institutional reform, and has designed new empirical methodologies in governance with colleagues at the World Bank. With his team, they support countries that request assistance in their efforts to improve governance and the environment for private sector development. He frequently advises state leaders, senior officials and civil society on strategies to improve governance. Previously he held positions as Lead Economist in the Development Economics Group and in the Eastern Europe/FSU region. During the early nineties he was the first Chief of Mission of the Bank in Ukraine. He was a core team member in producing the *World Development Report 1991*, distilling the key lessons from development experience. He was a Visiting Scholar at Harvard University in the mid-nineties, where he conducted research on the climate for investors and enterprise worldwide, and on institutions and corruption, and provided policy advice. He has a Ph.D. in Economics from Harvard University (USA, 1982). He has published in leading economic and public policy journals.

William Easterly, a former World Bank economist, is an expert on international development, long-run economic growth and the effectiveness of foreign aid. He has worked in most areas of the developing world and is also a professor of economics at New York University. He is visiting fellow at the Brookings Institution in Washington. In addition to his academic work, he has written widely in recent years for The Washington Post, Wall Street Journal, Financial Times, Forbes, and Foreign Policy, among others. He is the author of *The White Man's Burden: Why the West's Efforts to Aid the Rest Have Done So Much Ill and So Little Good* (New York: Penguin Press, 2006).

Bernard Berendsen is member of the Advisory Council on Foreign Relations of the Ministry of Foreign Affairs in the Netherlands. He started his international career at the Central Bank in Sudan in 1969. In 1970 he joined the United Nations Economic Commission for Asia and the Far East in Bangkok, Thailand. He completed his PhD thesis at the Erasmus University Rotterdam in 1978 on the subject of regional models of trade and development dealing with issues of international trade, economic development and integration. He joined the Ministry of Foreign Affairs in the Netherlands in 1975. After various assignments in The Hague he became Director for Africa in 1994, was posted in Jakarta from 1997 until

2000 and became Netherlands ambassador in Tanzania before retiring in 2005.

Cor van Beuningen is the Director of SOCIRES, a Dutch based think tank specializing in governance, democracy and civil society organizations in the public domain.

He holds Masters Degrees in regional planning and in public administration. Mr van Beuningen has 20 years of experience in international cooperation, including 10 years of field experience in Latin America, Africa and Asia, being employed by both governmental and non-governmental development agencies. He is advisor to the Netherlands Institute for Multiparty Democracy, and to several other public and private institutions involved in non-commercial public-private partnerships, both in the Netherlands, in Eastern Europe and elsewhere.

Paul Collier is Professor of Economics at Oxford University, Economics Department, het is director of the Centre for the Study of African Economies and Professorial Fellow of St Antony's College. He works on a wide range of macroeconomic, microeconomic and political economy topics concerned with Africa. He is a Professor Associate of CERDI, Université d'Auvergne; Fellow of the CEPR, London; and was Director of the Development Research group at the World Bank (from April 1998 to April 2003). He holds a Distinction Award from Oxford University, and has won the Edgar Graham Prize. His book *The Bottom Billion: Why the Poorest Countries Are Failing and What Can Be Done About It*, published in 2007 caused quite a rouse.

Albert (Bert) G. Koenders was appointed Minister for Development Cooperation on 22 February 2007. Born in Arnhem on 28 May 1958, he studied political science at the VU University, Amsterdam and political and social sciences at the University of Amsterdam. He received an MA from Johns Hopkins University, after studying at the School of Advanced International Studies in Bologna and Washington DC from 1979 to 1981. Since 1997, Mr Koenders has been a member of the House of Representatives of the States

General. From 2000 to 2002 he was also visiting professor of international relations at Johns Hopkins University in Bologna. He has held numerous positions, including president of the NATO Parliamentary Assembly, member of the French-Dutch Cooperation Council and chair of the board of the Parliamentary Network on the World Bank.

Thomas Carothers is Vice President for Studies-International Politics and Governance at the Carnegie Endowment for International Peace in Washington D.C. An expert in democracy promotion and democratization, he also directs the Endowment's Democracy and Rule of Law Project. He is the author or editor of eight books on democracy promotion, including most recently, *Confronting the Weakest Link: Aiding Political Parties in New Democracies* (2006) and *Promoting the Rule of Law: The Search for Knowledge* (2006). He has also published many articles in prominent journals and his works have been translated into many languages. Mr Carothers holds degrees from Harvard Law School, the London School of Economics and Harvard College.

Kim Campbell – first female Prime Minister of Canada, 1993. She also held the cabinet portfolios of Minister of State for Indian Affairs, Minister of Justice and Attorney General and Minister of Defence. Ms Campbell served as Canadian Consul General in Los Angeles and taught at the Kennedy School of Government at Harvard University. She served as Secretary General of the Club of Madrid, an organization of former Presidents and Prime Ministers, and currently sits on its Board of Directors. Ms Campbell is past Chair of the Council of Women World Leaders and past President of the International Women's Forum. She sits on the board of the Crisis Group, the Middle Powers Initiative and the Forum of Federations, among others.

In January 2006 **Vidar Helgesen** was appointed as the Secretary-General of the Stockholm-based intergovernmental organization International Institute for Democracy and Electoral Assistance (International IDEA). Mr Helgesen, a Norwegian national, was appointed Norway's Deputy Minister for Foreign Affairs in October 2001 and remained in this position until October 2005. During this period, Mr Helgesen led Norway's efforts in peace talks between the government of Sri Lanka and the Tamil Tigers. Born in 1968, Mr. Helgesen studied and trained as a lawyer and has long been involved in and active on the Norwegian political scene. From 1998 to 2001, Mr. Helgesen acted as Special Adviser to the President of the International Federation of Red Cross and Red Crescent Societies in Geneva. In 2007 Mr Helgesen was nominated as member of the UN Peacebuilding Fund Advisory Group.

Lena Hjelm-Wallén, former Deputy Prime Minister of Sweden, former Minister for Foreign Affairs and Minister for International Development Cooperation for the Social Democratic Party. During her 20 years in the Swedish Cabinet she also held the position as Minister of Education and Cultural Affairs. Ms Hjelm-Wallén chairs several institutions: International IDEA, Olof Palme International Center, Swedish Committee for Afghanistan and Swedish Foundation for Strategic Research.

David Beetham has written extensively on democracy and human rights, including economic and social rights. He is Associate Director and a major contributor and author for the UK Democratic Audit, which is based in the Human Rights Centre, University of Essex. He has recently directed a comparative programme of democracy and human rights assessment for the International Institute for Democracy and Electoral Assistance, Stockholm, and a programme on parliament and democracy for the Inter-Parliamentary Union, Geneva. He holds the position of Professor Emeritus, University of Leeds.

Anwar Ibrahim is former deputy prime minister and finance minister of Malaysia. Early in his career, he became a protégé of the former prime minister of Malaysia, Mahathir, but subsequently emerged as the most prominent critic of Mahathir's administration, which led to Anwar's dismissal, prosecution – many would say outright persecution – and imprisonment. In 2004, he was released and since that time he has held lecturing positions at St. Anthony's College at Oxford, the School of Advanced International Studies at Johns Hopkins University and at the School of Foreign Service in Georgetown University. He has advised the World Bank on questions of governance and accountability.

Vincent J. Cornell is Asa Griggs Candler Professor of Middle East and Islamic Studies at Emory University in Atlanta, Georgia. He has been a practicing Muslim for more than 35 years. He has taught at Northwestern University and Duke University. He was also the Director of the King Fahd Center for Middle East and Islamic Studies at the University of Arkansas. His pre-modern interests cover the entire spectrum of Islamic thought from Sufism, to philosophy, to Islamic law. He has lived and worked in Morocco for nearly six years, and has spend considerable time both teaching and doing research in Egypt, Tunisia, Malaysia and Indonesia.

Nico J. Schrijver is Professor of International Law at Leiden University and the Academic Director of the Grotius Centre for International Legal Studies. He also serves as a Affiliate Professor at the Institute of Social Studies, The Hague and as Visiting Professor of the European Union and North-South Co-operation at the *Université Libre de Bruxelles*. He is a former Member of the Board of the Dutch chapter of SID and currently President of the Netherlands Society of International Law and member of the UN High-level Task Force on the Rights to Development. He is the author of *Sovereignty over Natural Resources. Balancing Rights and Duties* (Cambridge: CUP, 1997; paperback re-issue 2008), co-author of *The United Nations of the Future. Globalisation with a Human Face* (Amsterdam: KIT, 2006) and co-editor of *The Security Council and the Use of Force: Theory and Reality-A Need for Change?* (Leiden: Nijhoff,

2005), *International Law and Sustainable Development Principles and Practice* (Leiden: Nijhoff, 2004).

Michael Edwards is the Director of the Ford Foundation's Governance and Civil Society Program, based in New York. Prior to joining Ford he was the World Bank's Senior Civil Society Specialist, based in Washington DC. Educated at the Universities of Oxford and London (UK), Michael has published widely on NGOs and civil society, international development and cooperation, and research-practice links. His most recent books are *Future Positive* (Earthscan, revised edition) and *Civil Society* (Polity Press/Blackwell), both released in 2004.

Kumi Naidoo, born in South Africa, became involved in the South African liberation struggle at the age of 15. As a result of his anti-apartheid activities, he was expelled from high school and arrested in 1986. Upon his release he was subject to persistent police harassment and went underground for one year before finally deciding to live in exile in England until 1989. Mr Naidoo is a Rhodes Scholar with a D.Phil in Politics from Magdalen College, Oxford. He also holds a B.A. in Politics and Law from the University of Durban-Westville, South Africa. He has published and spoken widely on issues relating to civil society, education and resistance to apartheid. Mr Naidoo has been Secretary General and Chief Executive Officer of CIVICUS: World Alliance for Civic Participation since 1998.

Frans Bieckmann (1963) is Editor-in-Chief of the bimonthly English science magazine on globalization and development The Broker (www.thebrokeronline.eu) and partner in the research bureau Wereld in Woorden <http://www.wereldinwoorden.nl>, which specializes in international relations, globalization and development cooperation. He studied international relations at the University of Amsterdam, graduating cum laude with a study of regional economic cooperation in the southern cone of Latin America. Since 1994 he has worked as an independent journalist and researcher. In the book *De wereld volgens prins Claus* (2004), he described the involvement of the Dutch Prince Claus with Africa and development cooperation. He is now writing two books. One about 40 years history of the Dutch ngo HIVOS, to be published in June 2008, and another one about the international community and Darfur.